Approaches to Teaching Stendhal's *The Red and the Black*

Approaches to Teaching World Literature

Joseph Gibaldi, series editor

For a complete listing of titles, see the last pages of this book.

Approaches to Teaching Stendhal's *The Red and the Black*

Edited by

Dean de la Motte

and

Stirling Haig

The Modern Language Association of America

New York 1999

Library of Congress Cataloging-in-Publication Data

Approaches to teaching Stendhal's The red and the black / edited by Dean de la Motte and Stirling Haig.
p. cm. — (Approaches to teaching world literature ; 62)
Includes bibliographical references and index.
ISBN 0-87352-747-X (cloth). — ISBN 0-87352-748-8 (pbk.)
1. Stendhal, 1783–1842. Rouge et le noir. 2. Stendhal, 1783–1842—Study and teaching. I. De la Motte, Dean, 1961– . II. Haig, Stirling. III. Series.
PQ2435.R72A66 1998
843'.7—dc21 98-54245

ISSN 1059-1133

Cover illustration for the paperback edition: *Napoléon Bonaparte, First Consul*, 1804, by Jean-Auguste-Dominique Ingres (1780–1867).
Musée des Beaux-Arts, Liège, Belgium.
Transparency for the reproduction provided by Scala/Art Resource, New York.

Set in Caledonia and Bodoni. Printed on recycled paper

Published by The Modern Language Association of America
10 Astor Place, New York, New York 10003-6981

CONTENTS

PREFACE TO THE SERIES

In *The Art of Teaching* Gilbert Highet wrote, "Bad teaching wastes a great deal of effort, and spoils many lives which might have been full of energy and happiness." All too many teachers have failed in their work, Highet argued, simply "because they have not thought about it." We hope that the Approaches to Teaching World Literature series, sponsored by the Modern Language Association's Publications Committee, will not only improve the craft—as well as the art—of teaching but also encourage serious and continuing discussion of the aims and methods of teaching literature.

The principal objective of the series is to collect within each volume different points of view on teaching a specific literary work, a literary tradition, or a writer widely taught at the undergraduate level. The preparation of each volume begins with a wide-ranging survey of instructors, thus enabling us to include in the volume the philosophies and approaches, thoughts and methods of scores of experienced teachers. The result is a sourcebook of material, information, and ideas on teaching the subject of the volume to undergraduates.

The series is intended to serve nonspecialists as well as specialists, inexperienced as well as experienced teachers, graduate students who wish to learn effective ways of teaching as well as senior professors who wish to compare their own approaches with the approaches of colleagues in other schools. Of course, no volume in the series can ever substitute for erudition, intelligence, creativity, and sensitivity in teaching. We hope merely that each book will point readers in useful directions; at most each will offer only a first step in the long journey to successful teaching.

Joseph Gibaldi
Series Editor

PREFACE TO THE VOLUME

One of the greatest nineteenth-century French novels, *The Red and the Black* is widely taught to French majors, but it is also presented in translation in courses on French or world literature, comparative literature, and European intellectual history. It frames questions concerning love and ambition, individual identity and fulfillment, the individual's relation to a society with rapidly changing norms, and the situation of the novel as reflection of reality.

Stendhal consciously set out to anchor his novel in the France of his day, choosing "Chronique de 1830" 'Chronicle of 1830' as the subtitle and "La vérité, l'âpre vérité" 'Truth, harsh truth' as the first among numerous epigraphs in a novel that is studded with idiosyncratic, constantly changing running heads as well as chapter titles. A note from the "publisher" states that the book was about to come out when the revolution of 1830 occurred but that there is reason to believe the book was composed in 1827. (It was actually written in 1829 and 1830.) The reason for this alleged delay remains unexplained and is probably no more than a case of political nerves on Stendhal's part, but his publisher is not done. Indeed, the publisher intervenes in the second part of *The Red and the Black* to engage the author in a discussion of what we now call realism. The author, fearing to bore his readers, voices his apprehension that "[l]a politique au milieu des intérêts d'imagination, c'est un coup de pistolet au milieu d'un concert" 'Politics in the midst of imaginative activity is like a pistol shot in the middle of a concert.' To which the publisher retorts, "Si vos personnages ne parlent pas politique, ce ne sont plus des Français de 1830, et votre livre n'est plus un miroir, comme vous en avez la prétention" 'If your characters don't talk politics, then they are no longer Frenchmen of 1830, and your book is no longer a mirror, as you claim' (419; 304; 2.2). Stendhal had already used the comparison to a pistol shot in a concert in three earlier works, and he was to repeat it in *La chartreuse de Parme* (*The Charterhouse of Parma*). But the mirror comparison mentioned by the publisher remains one of the most famous (and unsatisfying) definitions of realism in the history of the novel. The author-narrator protests:

> Eh, Monsieur! un roman est un miroir qui se promène sur une grande route. Tantôt il reflète à vos yeux l'azur des cieux, tantôt la fange des bourbiers de la route. Et l'homme qui porte le miroir dans sa hotte sera accusé par vous d'être immoral! Son miroir montre la fange, et vous accusez le miroir! Accusez bien plutôt le grand chemin où est le bourbier, et plus encore l'inspecteur des routes qui laisse l'eau croupir et le bourbier se former. (398)
>
> Look here, sir, a novel is a mirror moving along a highway. One minute you see it reflect the azure skies, next minute the mud and puddles of the

> road. And the man who carries the mirror in his pack will be accused by you of immorality! His mirror shows the mud and you accuse the mirror! Rather you should accuse the road in which the puddle lies, or, even better, the inspector of roads who lets the water collect and the puddle form. (289; 2.19)

Two great problems for American students, realism and history, are set forth here, and the way best to frame these questions when teaching *The Red and the Black* is the subject of this volume. The enormous scope of change in French history that shapes this novel is inaugurated by events of which most undergraduates have at least some scratchy knowledge, namely, the French Revolution and the establishment of the Napoleonic foundations of the modern French state. Yet all student readers will benefit from a considerable amount of contextualizing, which one can provide in a variety of ways described in this volume, ranging from assigning secondary reading in historical sources to giving in-class presentations with illustrations from the novel. The history of this most tumultuous period of French history naturally includes the history of class, another social reality of which many students, in their democratic innocence, have little concept. While *The Red and the Black* certainly brings class tensions into sharp focus, it remains necessary to emphasize that the classes were almost hermetically sealed, making breaches in them such as Julien effects all the more remarkable. If Julien appears to be succeeding in his ambition to rise in the world as he enters the Hôtel de La Mole, this is merely the result of a whim of the marquis de La Mole, as the abbé Pirard reminds Julien. As for the marquise, the abbé continues, she considers clergymen to be no more than "household servants necessary for her salvation" (190; 2.1). For her, "having had ancestors who went on the crusades is the only quality that interests her in a person. Money comes far behind that" (189; 2.1). Money and class are simply not synonymous. Wealth, unaccompanied by noble birth, is a mark of crassness: for the upstart Jew, M. de Thaler ("Mr. Dollar" or "Mr. Tallyer"), it warrants only the mockery of the Hôtel de La Mole. Thus in Restoration France it was still only birth, not merit, that guaranteed acceptance, though in the end Julien seems on the verge of successfully applying a slogan adopted from an earlier Napoleonic and revolutionary age: "les carrières ouvertes au talent" 'careers open to talent.' But even Julien Sorel is enraptured by his fleeting metamorphosis into "M. *de* La Vernaye," and he manipulates his identity by adopting hypocrisy as a protective strategy.

The Red and the Black is also a key text in almost every undergraduate course treating the development of realism in the European novel. Its famous image of the novel as mirror neutrally reflecting social reality is dated in an age in which language is no longer conceived as a transparent medium transmitting pure, uncoded reality, yet it can still lead to lively discussions of the nature and limitations of literary mimesis. As many contributors to this project have noted, Auerbach's economical, thirty-five-page chapter "In the Hôtel de la Mole" (in

Mimesis: The Representation of Reality in Western Literature) is still an excellent departure for class discussion; moreover, it covers two other great French realistic novels often paired with *The Red and the Black*, Balzac's *Le Père Goriot* and Flaubert's *Madame Bovary*.

Irony, a general problem in literary aesthetics, is of crucial importance for readers of *The Red and the Black*, who must become attuned to the narrator's relationship to the characters, Julien in particular. The distance the narrator establishes between himself and his protagonist's aspirations and illusions constitutes a good portion of Stendhal's message, but it is a distance that is often missed by novice readers who may be struggling to seize the details of the plot. Thus the narrator does not view Julien's admiration for Napoleon uncritically; indeed, he more often than not presents it as excessive and misplaced. The entire conversation between Falcoz and Saint-Giraud at the beginning of book 2 constitutes a *mise en garde* that Julien, like many readers, cheerfully disregards in favor of a visit to Malmaison, where he weeps with tender memories of the emperor and Josephine and is pickpocketed by a friendly veteran. Although narration is far from transparent in *The Red and the Black*, readers must still be schooled in seeing the characters through the narrator's eye (and I, for his own subjectivity is in play). Narratorial commentary must always be weighed for irony or sarcasm.

A number of questions of gender come into play in *The Red and the Black*. Julien is often characterized as feminine, as when Mme de Rênal, led by her romantic fancy, imagines him at first glance as "une jeune fille déguisée" 'a girl in disguise' (48; 21; 1.6), and the opposition of feminine types embodied in the maternal Mme de Rênal and the masculine Mathilde de La Mole extends well beyond the stereotyping of *blondes* and *brunes*. Mathilde's vigor is such that Julien admiringly exclaims of her patrician hauteur: "Le ciel devait à la gloire de ta race de te faire naître homme" 'For the honor of your family, providence should have formed you a man' (536; 392; 2.42). Constraints on female independence were severe in the France of 1830. Career choices were virtually nil (companion, maid, prostitute). Women were legally considered minors, and divorce was outlawed between 1816 and 1884. Women were denied the vote, so throughout the nineteenth century all talk of "universal suffrage" signified suffrage for men only. (Frenchwomen first voted in 1946.) In such an atmosphere it is credible for the narrator to characterize Mathilde as behaving so outrageously as to be unimaginable. Readers of the period would have perceived both women as scandalous and disgraceful representatives of "the weaker sex." Building on gender, students can use *The Red and the Black* as a springboard for analyzing larger cultural patterns.

The Red and the Black stages most famously the drama of reading; it is a novel where the books count for as much as do symbolic details such as ladders, heavily pruned trees, and a suit of blue cloth. They contribute to the referential grounding of the fiction to the same extent as do the work's historical references and may prove less difficult for students to decipher. Reading and its analogue, misreading, abound in Stendhal's novel, and they are linked to the revelation of happiness in the prison. It is largely thanks to reading that Julien realizes in extremis that love ought to have been an end in itself rather than a means merely to rise in the world. Reading, like the definition of success as it develops throughout the nineteenth century, may at first be framed within an economic model, that of paying off; but ultimately it is seen as a gratuitous, pleasurable experience of purely aesthetic value: it is part of the Stendhalian *chasse au bonheur*, the pursuit of happiness. But does Julien the reader take such a disinterested approach to reading? It would appear not. His commitment to memory of many lengthy texts is a calculation, a scheme to promote his social rise; he makes reading subservient to a practical goal, and a rather crass one at that. But at the same time the depictions of reading in *The Red and the Black* are so many *mises en abyme* of our students' own striving to make their reading practices pay off in a context (the classroom) where reading must close with a grade that sanctions their performance. Reading, dubbed the "unpunished vice" by Valery Larbaud, here allegorizes and problematizes the very process and institution of literature as we practice and promote it today.

The present volume, like others in the Approaches to Teaching World Literature series, is divided into two parts: in "Materials" we discuss practical matters of general pedagogical interest to any instructor preparing to teach *The Red and the Black*; in "Approaches" we present the core of this volume, the essays that offer many ingenious pathways for coming to terms with a great novel and its continuing potential to engage its readers.

We are grateful to the Modern Language Association for sponsoring this volume and for obtaining the useful comments its consultant readers kindly provided. We thank also those persons, listed at the end of this volume, who generously took time to answer the questionnaire we circulated in the early stages of conceiving this project. And we wish to give special thanks to Joseph Gibaldi, the series editor, for providing key assistance in moving this book to its completion.

Part One

MATERIALS

Editions and Translations

French Editions

About half of the survey respondents who teach *The Red and the Black* in French use the Garnier-Flammarion edition, citing the introduction by Michel Crouzet as one of its strong points. A word of caution: university and personal libraries may contain the 1964 edition, which was reprinted in 1996 with the same chronology, introduction, and cover (a still from the Claude Autant-Lara film of the novel starring Gérard Philipe as Julien and Danielle Darrieux as Mme de Rênal) but with quite different pagination. If Garnier-Flammarion continues with this practice, there will doubtless be further changes in pagination. The page references here are to the 1996 edition. The remaining responses are scattered among Folio, Livre de Poche, Classiques Garnier, and Dell (long out of print). Despite the often-cited problem of the novel's length, only one-eighth of the respondents indicated that they use excerpts or abridged versions (Nouveaux Classiques Larousse, Nathan-Littérature, Leggewie, Bordas, Bishop). Reasonable cost for students is the chief consideration in the ordering of the texts.

English Editions

Two-thirds of the respondents teach *The Red and the Black* in French only, while one-eighth teach in both languages; one respondent teaches the novel only in English. (The remainder did not answer the question.) Two English translations are cited, those by Catherine Slater (Oxford World Classics) and Robert M. Adams (Norton Critical Editions). No English translation of *The Red and the Black* is without its critics, and Adams's is no exception. The wry comments on his translation in the contributions by Sandy Petrey and Anthony Purdy offer an idea of what can be at stake in the choices confronting a translator. While Adams's translation dates back to 1969, its sections "Background and Sources" and "Criticism" remain highly useful. The background includes the informative essay "France in 1830: The Facts of Life," from which the reader will learn much regarding measures and money (allow for inflation), the Church, politics, and the law, all briskly presented in American terms. Among the sources are excerpts from the trial of Antoine Berthet as reported in the *Gazette des tribunaux*. The criticism section reprints selections from several of the books and articles recommended by our respondents (e.g., Auerbach, Girard, Hemmings; see "Recommended Readings" below). Now out of print is the translation of C. K. Scott-Moncrieff, once highly regarded as a translator of many other works by Stendhal and Proust.

Courses and Course Designs

Respondents teach *The Red and the Black* for reasons that range from the novel's important place in the canon and literary history to the personal. Thus a third of respondents mention its high place in the canon, while Juliet Flower MacCannell, speaking no doubt for many readers and teachers, candidly confesses to a "love of Stendhal and a desire to share it." At the more general level of interest, a third of respondents cite *The Red and the Black*'s place in the development of realism. Yet a number of respondents favor the novel for its depiction of the Romantic hero and express interest in its pitting of the individual versus society. Bridging this apparent Romantic-realistic opposition, perhaps, Michal Peled Ginsburg writes that *The Red and the Black* "allows one to talk of the passage from a picaresque to full-fledged realist novel," and in a similar vein Allan Pasco writes, "Its picaresque features make a good transition from the eighteenth-century novel [. . .]." He, like other readers, praises *The Red and the Black* as an eminently readable novel that appeals to students. Lisa G. Algazi states, "The story of Julien is one to which students can relate in some ways—an ambitious young man trying to make his way in the world speaks to college students of the nineties who never stop thinking about their job prospects." As might be divined from her contribution to this volume, Algazi thinks of *The Red and the Black* as "a decisive text in the development of maternal subjectivity in French fiction." A third of the respondents admire Stendhal's clear picture of French society in the early part of the nineteenth century but acknowledge that students require much elucidation.

Eighty percent of the respondents work in foreign language departments. The remainder are comparatists. The majority teaches *The Red and the Black* in French to French majors, mostly in upper-division courses. The most common upper-division-course arrangement is the survey of nineteenth-century (or nineteenth- and twentieth-century) French literature. Next come courses on the novel (Romantic or realist; *The Red and the Black* suits both), then Romanticism courses, followed by comparative literature survey or genre courses, where Stendhal is taught in translation. Thus one finds courses entitled Romanticism, The Apprenticeship Novel, French Literature in Translation, and The Development of the French Novel. More unusual titles were Romanticism and the Anxiety of Definition and The Scandal of Realism. Linking topics are the individual and society, the psychology of love, irony, Napoleon, forms of realism, and the evolution of narrative instance and focalization.

By far the difficulty most often cited in teaching *The Red and the Black* is its length: most respondents allot between two and three weeks to teach it in a semester-length course, although some teach it in two weeks, some in four. After length, the most commonly cited problems have to do with history, politics, and religion, including specific episodes such as "The Secret Note" and the conversation between Falcoz and Saint-Giraud at the beginning of book 2.

Stendhal's apparent desire for historical specificity in his "Chronicle of 1830" has ironically led to some textual opacity. This is the famous "pistol shot in the middle of a concert" that the author and his publisher themselves discuss in book 2, chapter 22. All informants felt a strong obligation to help students understand the historical and political contexts through direct explanation, assigned secondary reading, or both. Twenty percent of respondents mentioned Stendhal's complex use of irony as a problem. Respondents also noted that American students have a very hard time understanding social class in general.

Students are drawn to the love of Julien for Mme de Rênal and the amorous dynamics of the text in general. Julien's bold, sometimes "transgressive" behavior appeals to them, as does Mathilde's. "They appreciate the funny love scenes," states Mary Anne O'Neil, and Priscilla Ferguson writes in this vein that "the *comedy* strikes true." Mary Ellen Birkett notes that student interest seems to be shifting to the female characters per se; the volume's section on gender and class should meet that interest. Catherine Nesci reports that students are puzzled when a seemingly "good" ending ("mon roman est fini" 'the novel of my career is over' [491; 359; 2.34]) is followed by a "bad" ending (Julien's shooting of Mme de Rênal), "but Mouillaud's, Brombert's, and Brooks' interpretations help them understand it better." Thus of contemporary interest to today's students are family dynamics, including generational conflict and the family romance (one-eighth); social class (one-eighth); the novel's portrayal of the psychology of love (one-third); questions of the self and identity or independence (one-third); and ambition and students' own hopes for social and economic success, or what might be termed the problems of young people in a competitive society (one-half).

With such a variety of interests, it is unsurprising that respondents often described their classroom approaches to the text as "eclectic" or "pragmatic." The dominant descriptors were "psychological" and "psychoanalytical," the latter sometimes with a feminist twist: thus the family triangle, but with emphasis on women and the maternal rather than on the young protagonist and the filial. Yet all respondents reported some form of combined approach that linked in various permutations the psychological, historical, sociological, formal (narratological), and thematic.

Instructors often present *The Red and the Black* in conjunction with other works, and the instructor's approach often affects the choice of the other works. Respondents whose approach is psychoanalytical and feminist sometimes choose Rousseau's *Julie ou la Nouvelle Héloïse* or Sand's *Indiana*. Balzac's *Le Père Goriot* (one-half) and Flaubert's *Madame Bovary* (one-fourth) or *L'éducation sentimentale* (one-eighth) are most favored, since they lend themselves to the study of the apprenticeship novel and of the development of realism and may also be used further to resolve some of the problems cited above, such as irony, as well as history and politics. Comparative literature courses bring in Austen's *Pride and Prejudice*, Emily Brontë's *Wuthering Heights*, and

James's *Washington Square*. And the novel can be paired with other works by Stendhal, such as "L'abbesse de Castro" (from his *Chroniques italiennes* [*Italian Chronicles*]).

Small-group work is a favorite means of stimulating class discussion for one-half of respondents. It consists of forming groups of three or four students and assigning them short, key passages to report on to the class as a whole. Groups could be asked to argue for or against a proposition, such as the following: "In this passage, Julien is or is not a typical parvenu." The groups could also be asked to study an excerpt along with a set of focus questions concerning a common theme (love, ambition, liberty, money, etc.); the same questions could be related to the secondary reading (if secondary reading has been assigned), and students could look for excerpts illustrating issues analyzed by the critics. Another one-fourth of respondents feel that distributing focus questions in advance of reading assignments helps general class discussion. One respondent favors having one student present a problem for a brief (five-minute) general discussion: Should we admire Julien? What does Stendhal criticize in the Parisian nobility? Why does Julien allow himself to be put to death? Psychological motivation and questions of verisimilitude were recommended topics for discussion, with questions dealing with Julien's character a favorite. *The Red and the Black* depicts social mobility, as Ross Chambers remarks, while "simultaneously forcing a choice between 'interests' (duplicity, complexity) and 'happiness' (spontaneity, simplicity, 'authenticity')." For dealing with the question of closure in the novel, Michal Peled Ginsburg recommends asking the students to try writing another ending to *The Red and the Black*: the assignment "always leads to a good class discussion and shows the impossibility of bringing the novel into a proper closure." In her seminar called Realism from Stendhal to Proust (which uses works in translation), Carol Rifelj has students post responses to discussion questions on an electronic bulletin board before class. In preparing for papers, her students present a thesis statement supported by examples; the ensuing class session, "while seemingly geared to questions of writing, in fact [consists] of an excellent discussion of the novel." Nearly half of our informants screen the videocassette of Autant-Lara's 1954 film version of the novel.

Recommended Readings

Background Materials

Our respondents were asked to recommend background and critical readings for students and for instructors. Although this produced some overlap, it is notable that one-third feel that reading *The Red and the Black* in its entirety is enough to expect of students and thus neither require nor recommend secondary reading.

Those whose students read the novel in English deem the critical selections in Adams sufficient background material. The most frequently required reading is Erich Auerbach's chapter in "In the Hôtel de la Mole" in *Mimesis* (assigned by one-third). The durability of this chapter is certainly noteworthy inasmuch as the original German edition of *Mimesis* was published in 1946 and rapidly translated into English. The reasons for its popularity may be that it remains accessible to the general reader and students and that, despite the title, the essay deals with the development of realism and covers Balzac and Flaubert as well as Stendhal.

General Introductions

Auerbach is followed by Victor Brombert, *Stendhal et la voie oblique* or *Stendhal: Fiction and the Themes of Freedom* (about one-third). Also cited are René Girard, *Deceit, Desire, and the Novel* (praised for the applicability of "triangular desire" to Stendhal's novel), Harry Levin, *The Gates of Horn*; and two works by F. W. J. Hemmings: *Stendhal: A Study of His Novels* and *Culture and Society in France, 1789-1848*. Respondents also mentioned introductory works by Pierre-Georges Castex, Michel Crouzet, Stirling Haig, Christine Klein and Paul Lidsky, and Geneviève Mouillaud. For reserve reading in French history of the period, Carol Rifelj recommends Gordon Wright, *France in Modern Times* (ch. 9, "The Bourbon Experiment," and ch. 14, "Society, Structures, and Trends"); John Lough and Muriel Lough, *An Introduction to Nineteenth-Century France*; and Theodore Zeldin, *France, 1848-1945* (ch. 11, "Marriage and Morals," and ch. 13, "Women"). We also recommend the relevant section in Alfred Cobban's well-known *History of Modern France*, volume 2 (covering 1799–1871), and the lengthier, classic study by Guillaume de Bertier de Sauvigny, *La Restoration* (*The Bourbon Restoration*).

The Instructor's Library

The range of readings suggested by respondents is so great that we can name here only those works mentioned at least twice: Shoshana Felman's studies on "madness" in Stendhal; Carol Mossman's analysis of *The Red and the Black*'s problematic closure, *The Narrative Matrix*; Sandy Petrey's *Realism and Revolution*; and Jean Starobinski's essay on the matter of identity in Stendhal. Several respondents also suggested additional readings in key Stendhal texts, such as *De l'amour*, "L'abbesse de Castro," *La vie de Henry Brulard*, and *Lamiel*. Crouzet, whose introduction to the Garnier-Flammarion edition is often mentioned, published a well-reviewed monograph on *The Red and the Black* (Le rouge). Many other useful books and articles are cited in the essays in part 2.

Visual and Multimedia Aids

As noted, about half of the respondents show the videocassette (sometimes selected scenes) of the Autant-Lara film of *The Red and the Black*. Carol Rifelj suggests Patrice Chereau's *La reine Margot*; she also uses a short segment of Abel Gance's 1927 film *Napoléon*. One-fifth supplement class lectures on French history with slides of nineteenth-century French painting and architecture. One respondent plays a selection from Hector Berlioz's *Symphonie fantastique* and another from Stendhal's beloved *Il matrimonio segreto* by Domenico Cimarosa. We recommend the Kenneth Clark video on Romanticism in his series (pt. 12, "The Fallacies of Hope"). Despite the sometimes ephemeral nature of World Wide Web sites, we venture to list this one on Stendhal: http://www.alpes-net.fr/~reysset/index.html. Rifelj points out that there are already many helpful CD-ROMs, among them *2000 ans d'histoire de France*, *Le Louvre: peintures et palais* (available in English as *The Louvre: The Palace and Its Collections*), and *Napoléon, l'Europe et l'empire*. The CD-ROM *Stendhal: Œuvre romanesque* appeared in 1997.

Part Two

APPROACHES

Introduction

As readers and teachers of Stendhal's novel can attest, its richness means that the present volume of approaches can serve only as a series of signposts to direct students and instructors alike to productive classroom discussion, research, and writing on *The Red and the Black*. The diversity of theoretical and pedagogical concerns elaborated in the essays that follow testifies to the novel's seminal and exemplary place in the history of nineteenth-century—and indeed, European—literature and culture.

The Red and the Black has a particularly meaningful, albeit complex, relation to the specific historical moment of its composition and publication, preceding and following as they do the July Revolution of 1830. Teachers and students will find it instructive—if not imperative—to take into account the sociopolitical context of the novel. Recent scholarship and teaching have attempted to shift the emphasis of literary studies away from strictly formal approaches and toward more broadly contextual considerations that nevertheless incorporate close readings of literary and nonliterary texts. This sea change is evident throughout the present volume, which begins with a series of complementary discussions of the multiple contexts (historical, political, literary) of Stendhal's novel. James Smith Allen discusses the historical context of 1830 and suggests how the novel might even be taught *as* history, while Priscilla Parkhurst Ferguson demonstrates how Stendhal weaves the specter of revolution into the very fabric of his novel. Peter Brooks, whose seminal *Reading for the Plot* was mentioned by several other contributors and survey respondents, provides the historical and biographical context to unravel the central but baffling episode of the secret note. Mary Ellen Birkett situates *The Red and the Black* in the larger cultural context of Romanticism, the dominant aesthetic or school of the first half of the nineteenth century. Instructors planning courses on Romanticism, revolution, or history and literature, will find these four essays, grouped together under the heading "Contextualizing *The Red and the Black*," at once a useful introduction to and a sophisticated exploration of the historical background of the novel.

Coming to grips with a text of the complexity—not to mention sheer length—of Stendhal's novel can be as daunting to instructors as it is to their students, and the essays in "Strategies of Reading" share specific approaches or points of departure that make larger considerations more readily accessible through highly focused critical perspectives. Catharine Savage Brosman, in her discussion of the opening chapters of the novel, and James T. Day, in his analysis of its self-referentiality, both suggest pathways of discussion that provide concrete access to and comprehension of *The Red and the Black*. Juliet Flower MacCannell, in her explanation of the dynamic opposition—both between Julien and Restoration society and within himself—of the "man of power" and the "man of feeling," situates Julien in a context that today's student can understand but that is a complex matrix of politics, imagination, and desire. Mary Anne O'Neil makes plain the importance of understanding Stendhal's earlier theoretical work *De l'amour* (*On Love*) to a fuller comprehension of the amorous relationships at the center of *The Red and the Black*.

We do not wish to suggest that formal approaches are no longer valid or current. On the contrary, one could argue that the techniques of close reading or explication de texte that have been the hallmark of the formalisms (New Criticism, stylistics, structuralism and semiotics, deconstruction) so prevalent in the middle decades of the twentieth century have fused with previously distinct or even antagonistic modes of interpretation (historicism, Marxist or social criticism, narrative literary histories). *The Red and the Black*, which repeatedly refers to its own fictionality while simultaneously making insistent mimetic claims, demands that we think critically about its structure—its "grammar"—and about how such formal considerations reinforce (or conflict with) its dominant themes. It is from such a perspective that Gerald Prince analyzes how the novel functions as narrative and how narrative features illuminate the novel as a whole. Michal Peled Ginsburg links the plot, Stendhal's aesthetics, and the notion of freedom in a way that has, beyond its formal interest, profound social implications; her essay suggests again how difficult it is to separate structural and ideological considerations and provides instructors with a useful link to essays that appear earlier in the volume. Pauline Wahl Willis demonstrates how paying attention to minor characters early on in students' reading of the novel helps create and deepen their interest and comprehension.

The largest section of the volume, "Questions of Gender and Class Identity in *The Red and the Black*," has as its central concern the construction of gendered, social, and even racial identity. Its prominence reflects both current critical preoccupations and, far more important, the overwhelming emphasis Stendhal himself places on these same questions. Doris Y. Kadish, in fact, demonstrates how enlightening—and enlivening—the juxtaposition of canonical and noncanonical, literary and nonliterary texts can be in the classroom, by contextualizing issues that are central both to an understanding of *The Red and the Black* and to the students' ability to make connections between this all-so-canonical work of fiction and contemporary society. Sandy Petrey considers the identity of Stendhal's hero, Julien Sorel, in the light of theories of performativity, while Lisa G. Algazi examines it from the perspective of a Lacanian analysis of maternity and paternity. Cheryl A. Morgan's essay explores the relation between social norms of class and gender and the behavior of Stendhal's characters, particularly Mme de Rênal and Mathilde de La Mole. Maryline Lukacher gives a case study of intertextuality, in which maternity in *The Red and the Black* is "rewritten" in a text by Marguerite Yourcenar. The essays in this section speak eloquently, and often provocatively, to questions of class and gender, and they may be usefully placed in dialogue with one another. Instructors should find the blend of practical pedagogical advice, theory, and case studies especially suggestive.

Finally, it is a commonplace of Stendhal scholarship to point out that he was probably ahead of his time and that he suspected his true audience might well lie in the future. Indeed, he also knew that literary fame was a matter of chance and often compared it to the odds of holding a winning lottery ticket. The simile's most striking formulation comes in his autobiographical *Vie de Henry Brulard*: "Et moi, je mets un billet à une loterie dont le gros lot se réduit à ceci: être lu en 1935" 'As for me, I'm holding a lottery ticket in which the grand prize comes down to this: to be read in 1935' (194 [1955 ed.]; our trans.). In the pair of essays that close this volume, Anthony Purdy and Carol Rifelj take the author of *The Red and the Black* into the twenty-first century: Purdy examines how hypertext can serve as a useful analogy—whether or not hypertexts or other virtual versions of texts (multimedia CD-ROMs or World Wide Web sites, for example) are actually used or created by faculty members or students—of the multilayered, nonlinear act of reading that a text imbedded in history can require, while Rifelj provides a rich array of tools (video, databases, student discussion groups or Web sites, CD-ROMs, etc.) that can be incorporated into student work on Stendhal's novel, as well as practical advice on how best to do so.

NOTE

All parenthetical page references to *The Red and the Black* in this volume appear after the translations; page numbers for the French appear first, then those for the English. In block quotations, the page numbers appear separately after the quotation and the translation. Unless otherwise noted, all quotations from the French text are taken from the Garnier-Flammarion volume, edited by Michel Crouzet (1964, but with pagination of the 1996 printing); quotations from the English text are taken from the Norton Critical Edition, translated and edited by Robert M. Adams (1969). For readers' convenience, book and chapter numbers are also included following page references to the French text and the English translation.

CONTEXTUALIZING *THE RED AND THE BLACK*

History in *The Red and the Black*

James Smith Allen

> Pourvu qu'on ne plaisantât ni de Dieu, ni des prêtres, ni du roi, ni des gens en place, ni des artistes protégés par la cour, ni de tout ce qui est établi; pourvu qu'on ne dît du bien ni de Béranger, ni des journaux de l'opposition, ni de Voltaire, ni de Rousseau, ni de tout ce qui se permet un peu de franc-parler; pourvu surtout qu'on ne parlât jamais politique, on pouvait librement raisonner de tout.
>
> Provided one didn't joke about God, or the priests, or the king, or the men in power, or the artists protected by the court, or about any part of the establishment; provided one said nothing good about Béranger, or the opposition newspapers, or Voltaire, or Rousseau, or of anything which involves the use of free speech; provided, above all, that one never talked politics, one could talk freely about anything whatever.
>
> —Stendhal, *The Red and the Black*

Speaking freely all the same, Henri Beyle's *The Red and the Black* marks a revolutionary moment. Its first edition of only 750 copies belies its historical implications when Alphonse Levavasseur put it on sale with the enticing second subtitle, *Chronicle of 1830*, just five months after the July Revolution (20; 1; 1.1). Even though critics then (and since) had no trouble seeing through the claim to timely historicity—in keeping with the publisher's note, the novel concerns the Restoration more than it does the revolution—*The Red and the Black* owes much to the disruptive forces at work in nineteenth-century France. Politics in the midst of imaginative activity, as Stendhal cleverly remarked here and elsewhere, may have been like "un coup de pistolet au milieu d'un concert" 'a pistol shot in the middle of a concert' (419; 304; 2.22). But no work can entirely escape such an intrusion, much less its history, and Stendhal's novel is certainly no exception.

The year 1830 is a convenient backdrop to the real and perceived changes that assume a literary life of their own. Who can deny the importance of 1789 to the political conflicts of Restoration France portrayed here? The ultraroyalists, who were more royalist than the king and who forgot less than they learned, never succeeded in resuscitating the Old Regime's absolute monarchy. Louis XVIII had issued a conservative "charter" to recognize in principle the rule of law, the separation of powers, certain fundamental human rights, and, indirectly at least, national sovereignty—all products of 1789, France's first violent revolutionary year. The subsequent succession of regimes did not fundamentally alter the enduring legacy of the Declaration of the Rights of Man and Citizen (1789), any more than it did that of the Civil Constitution of the Clergy (1791), confirmed in modified form by Napoleon Bonaparte and Pius VII in the Concordat of 1802. The church in France remained subject to the state right down to their formal separation in 1905, a situation that provided the rationale if not the logic to ultraroyalists' efforts to ally throne and altar during the Restoration.

The 1789 Revolution's reordering of society from corporative and customary estates to social classes of individuals defined by contractual and property rights also appears in Stendhal's novel. Whatever the special privileges enjoyed by the marquis de La Mole, they are mere vestiges of the much more substantial authority enjoyed by the aristocracy under the Old Regime. Equality before the law, presumably for everyone, leveled social distinctions dramatically, just as it democratized tax exemptions and access to political power. A more mobile society of merit became a genuine possibility that Napoleon demonstrated to all would-be elites of talent and great good fortune, first in the military and then in the public institutions susceptible to its example. Following the examples of François Joseph Lefebvre, the imperial marshal, and his wife, Catherine Hubscher, the regimental laundress, Julien Sorel ascended from provincial peasant to future aristocrat, an ascent plausible only in the circumstances created by revolutionary upheaval. Besides church and state, society was more open thanks to the events of 1789.

Comparable economic changes underlie Stendhal's work. A traditional subsistence agrarian economy during the Old Regime was rapidly giving way to a more modern market-oriented agriculture. The growing prosperity of Old Sorel and his tightfisted peasant counterparts is conceivable in a new economic setting, one characterized by the historian Guillaume de Bertier de Sauvigny as "the initial reverberations of a profound revolution" toward industrial capitalism

(*Bourbon Restoration* 220). *The Red and the Black* opens to the cacophonous clatter of nail mills powered by the river Doubs, the harbinger of a new economy driven by entrepreneurs like Julien's hardworking and innovative friend Fouqué. Even Julien is tempted by the new wealth of industrial activity that Napoleon's wartime command economy and the Restoration's institutional resources could not entirely contradict. The power of the state to foster industrialization was widely recognized after 1830.

Revolution redirected creative energies too. Despite the Académie Française and its supporters, the neoclassicism of the Old Regime was moribund. Not only did 1830 see the election of Alphonse de Lamartine to the immortal forty, but like Julien and the outraged academician, it also witnessed the succès de scandale of Victor Hugo's play *Hernani* at the Comédie Française (338; 242; 2.10). Népomucène Lemercier's infamous formulas for the perfect tragedy and the perfect comedy gave way, albeit tempestuously, to the unruly creativity of the Romantic *drame*. The same reaction to the apparent limitations of balance, order, harmony, and tradition affected poetry, painting, sculpture, and architecture, everywhere in fact the Enlightenment's artistic ideals were prescribed, well into the nineteenth century, by the revolutionary and Napoleonic preference for the classical model of the Roman republic. Thanks to the *idéologie* of the comte de Destutt de Tracy and the eclecticism of Victor Cousin, continuity across the revolutionary cultural divide lingered longer in the social sciences and philosophy, while literature and the arts sprung violently, though briefly, free from such constraints, whatever Stendhal's apparent reticence.

The author was himself predisposed to accept historical change. Born in 1783, Henri Beyle, alias Henry Brulard the autobiographical persona, was very nearly a child of the Revolution, though his home in provincial Grenoble was not the Parisian epicenter. Like Napoleon the Corsican in whose service Stendhal traveled across the continent to Moscow, he enjoyed the preferment that the Revolution offered young men of reasonable talent and moderate fortune (of course, his well-placed relative Pierre Daru helped). The empire validated this personal achievement as a functionary in the Ministry of War, and the Restoration channeled it into the literary effort of his dilettante *beylisme* until the more serious composition of *The Red and the Black*. Far from a disaster for the quick-witted, Napoleon's defeat in 1815 gave Stendhal time and energy to read and write. It also provided the budding author the opportunity to observe the enduring effects of historical change in the law, especially in its codification, which regularized judicial procedure in cases like the cabinetmaker Laffargue's murder of his older mistress in Bagnières. In December 1827 the *Gazette des tribunaux* reported on Antoine Berthet, a real-life Louis Jenrel, another apparent model for Julien, who also attempted to kill his lover in church, unlike Hector Berlioz, who wisely changed his mind. The crime was a Restoration modification, not a revocation, of the Napoleonic penal code (1811).

Most germane to Stendhal's literary interests were the activities of his fellow authors whose novelistic practice he adapted to his own. They provided a historicity of a more discursive sort. Like Honoré de Balzac, who might have been the Walter Scott of French literature, Stendhal learned his craft from the example of others anxious to lend more verisimilitude to prose fiction. The melodramatic impulses of the Romantic novel were giving way to more constrained conventions in plot, character, setting, mood, and tone, in part under the influence of contemporary journalism and its focus on *actualité*. The physiologies of various sorts, something of a mania when Stendhal was writing *The Red and the Black*, moved writers to greater precision in social observation and description. Stendhal's earlier efforts in art and music criticism, travel writing, autobiographical reflection, and prose fiction—for example, his *Histoire de la peinture en Italie* (1817), *Vies de Haydn, Mozart et Métastase* (1814), *Promenades dans Rome* (1829), *Journal* (unpublished; written 1801–14), and *Armance* (1827)—all contributed to the spontaneity of style in this novel. Given as critics were to more declamatory rhetorical poses, they noted and deplored Stendhal's discursive immediacy. Romanticism had triumphed in fact long before neoclassicism had conceded its critical claims, forcing Stendhal to anticipate by fifty years a more appreciative reception of his literary achievement. As he noted in correspondence with Virginie Ancelot, this novel was "non conforme aux règles académiques" 'contrary to academic rules,' or any other conventions, for that matter (*Correspondance* 2: 205).

Still, in historical terms, *The Red and the Black* develops what Max Weber terms "ideal types" (323–24). The transformation of the Old Regime's society of orders, for example, clearly influences the novel's treatment of the clergy, the aristocracy, and the third estate. The first order looms larger than life, perhaps because its power in Restoration France was outsized. Rivalries between honest and sincere Jansenists like the abbés Chélan and Pirard on the one hand and calculating and conspiratorial Jesuits like the Congregationists on the other command a disproportionate share of the novel's narrative only in retrospect. At the time, their struggles preoccupied Stendhal's contemporaries every bit as much as both struggles and contemporaries exercised his imagination here. Despite claims to more Gallican liberties than ultramontanists could accept, the church remained a powerful social and political institution before 1830.

The same is true of the second order, the aristocracy. It may have been weakened by internal divisions over Napoleon's creation of new titles, but the aristocracy dominated French secular society with a vengeance after 1815. Habits of deference (and arrogance) died hard in nineteenth-century France, lending plausibility to Julien's resentment of social differences throughout the novel: on learning of his appointment as a tutor to the mayor's children, he asks, "Mais, avec qui mangerai-je?" 'Well then, whom will I eat with?' (41; 15; 1.5) Neither the old aristocrats, like the marquis de La Mole nor the new, like the baron de Valenod, were willing to concede their claims to social distinction from the commoners everywhere around them, however shrewd and rich the industrialists and financiers might have become. The self-consciously proud stonemasons still enamored of Napoleon stand in the background, since for the moment they do not yet represent any disruption to the lives of the first two orders. By contrasting sharply the lower orders' memories of former glories under the empire with the clergy's and nobility's fears of further loss under the Restoration—"le trône, l'autel, la noblesse peuvent périr demain" 'the throne, the altar, and the nobility may perish tomorrow,' warned M. de La Mole (423; 308; 2.22)—Stendhal vividly portrays the anachronisms among his contemporaries on the eve of another revolution.

Similar contrasts and dangers inform *The Red and the Black*. The Restoration's conflicts were not marked solely by a changing social hierarchy; they were exacerbated by the impatience of the young with the immobility of the old. Was there a Romantic generation of 1820, such as the historian Alan Spitzer defined it and Stendhal portrayed it here in the guise of an ambitious peasant's son in love with a mayor's wife and a marquis's daughter? Was Mathilde de La Mole herself a Romantic youth looking to the future of still more revolutionary upheaval with the same fervor that she dreamed of her sixteenth-century relative, Boniface de La Mole? Observers besides Mathilde's father certainly noted "toute cette jeunesse qui fait des articles incendiaires dans le *Globe*" 'all these young people who are writing incendiary articles in the *Globe*' (422; 307; 2.22).

Contemporaries also remarked on the enormous distance between Paris and the provinces, the latter represented by the Franche-Comté and its small towns like the fictional Verrières and the actual Besançon that the novel describes in disparaging detail. According to the abbé Siéyès, whom Stendhal quotes, the French capital, by contrast, was the focus of political, social, and cultural life directly affecting the rest of France: "On trouve à Paris des gens élégants, il peut y avoir en province des gens à caractère" 'At Paris you will find elegant folk, in the provinces there may be people with character' (93; 54; 1.12). This historical reality is belied perhaps by Julien's emotional preoccupations in Verrières to which he impulsively returns. He dies not in Paris but in Besançon. Yet the exception proves the rule, especially of institutions like Old Sorel's sawmill and the orphanage in Verrières, the seminary near Besançon, and the salons and balls of Paris. The novel was critical of all these locales of Restoration economic and social activity; the nearly penniless Stendhal resented the limited opportunities for promising young men from the provinces who sought their fortunes everywhere on the eve of the 1830 revolution, whatever his more positive personal experiences before and after the publication of his book. Although Stendhal was among "the happy few," his wider world was never altogether of "ce siècle ennuyé" 'this bored century' (287; 202; 2.4).

A rich historical context thus foregrounds *The Red and the Black* and its literary achievement. Its plot, focused on Julien's rapid ascent by ruse and hypocrisy and his even more precipitous descent for emotional and existential reasons, follows a logic that is both historical and artistic. The Restoration provided space for the likes of the novel's protagonist, as Stendhal's life attests, but too little to satisfy all such aspirations. The interruption in the plot's development just as Julien is about to achieve his life's goal, precisely when he learns that his ambition was ruined by Louise de Rênal's letter to M. de La Mole, also marks an historically significant rupture. What may have been possible during the First Republic or the Napoleonic empire was far less plausible during the Restoration. The class resentment that Julien, the future Danton, expresses repeatedly in the novel reveals his character, but it also suggests the revolutionary tradition ironically represented by the Italian count Altamira and his participation in the Carbonari (324; 231–32; 2.8). "Désespérant de l'Europe, le pauvre Altamira en était réduit à penser que, quand les Etats de l'Amérique méridionale seront forts et puissants, ils pourront rendre à l'Europe la liberté que Mirabeau leur a envoyée" 'Having given up all hope of Europe [. . .] poor Altamira was reduced to hoping that when the states of South America became strong and stable, they might be able to return the liberty that Mirabeau sent them' (325; 232; 2.8). How appropriate then is Julien's deliberate, Socratic justification of his ultimate martyrdom, a disillusionment as social as it is amorous.

The same logic applies to Julien's movement from Verrières to Paris and back by the novel's end. His geographic mobility follows a course appropriate to his social rise and demise. From the sawmill upriver to the mayor's household, from Verrières's *mairie* to the Besançon seminary, from the provincial intrigues of petty clerics to the complications of Parisian *salonnières* and conservative ideologues, and finally nearly home again, Julien moves in both space and esteem with well-calculated precision. Although he does not actually return—in jail Julien fears most the inevitable visit from his father—the trajectory of his movements traces a path of discursive truth and historical verisimilitude. Julien's perch on the executioner's scaffold resembles the one in the sawmill where the reader first encounters him, though the falls from each position differ profoundly.

Finally, the novel's play of colors, names, ladders, and gardens complements the historical implications of the plot and setting. The title's hues—the red of life, passion, revolution, and the military and the black of death, failure, formality, and the clergy—suggest among other matters Julien's quest for love, revenge, and position, notwithstanding their conflicted appearance in the Restoration context. Under the empire, just as later under the July monarchy, these colors had different meanings for the likes of Julien, that is, among Napoleon's corporals with marshal's batons in their knapsacks or among Louis-Philippe's railway entrepreneurs on the state payroll. The names of characters and places serve comparable purposes. Verrières does not exist in fact, but its fragile rigidity exists in every small town with an insecure social elite protected only by local habits of deference and shrewd, timely maneuvers against implacable rivals. M. de Rênal is a supposedly decent, upright, royal subject whose renable rectitude fails to convince everyone in town. And the ironically termed Congregationists are as destructive of religious community as they are reactionary in their political goals.

Few such names are altogether innocent in the novel's narrative, just as the ladders erected for Julien to ascend, usually to advantageous bedroom trysts, are not incidental. It is equally no accident that Julien acts more freely outdoors, in the natural settings dear to Rousseau's alter egos, in sharp contrast to the constraints he experiences indoors, whether he is cloistered in the seminary or closeted in M. de La Mole's library. Such spaces resemble too much his father's sawmill, the first prison, like his lovers' bedrooms, from which he flees. The church serves Julien as the only enclosure where he acts decisively, as he does when he finally summons enough courage to shoot Louise during mass. For once, Julien chooses his own confinement.

The critical response to Stendhal's text seems to contradict its apparent historicity. Few readers were as generous in their judgments as the anonymous reviewer in *La revue de Paris* who highlighted the narrative's realism, even though he followed the trend of other reviewers who decried the novel's amoral treatment of an immoral protagonist; it was, the reviewer wrote, little more than "une dénonciation en forme contre l'âme humaine" 'a formal denunciation of the human heart' (quoted in Mélia 77; my trans.). Most critics reading *The Red and the Black* in 1831 deplored Julien's hypocritical calculations in his conquests of Louise de Rênal and Mathilde de La Mole. Nearly all of them also disliked Stendhal's unvarnished, unassuming prose; they found the lexical texture too plebeian, too unpolished, too ill-suited to the pretensions of a long novel about such important matters as the Restoration's institutions, conflicts, and intellectual life. Yet Stendhal's creative work stood counter to his apparent allegiances to the Romantics professed in his essay *Racine and Shakespeare* and his participation in Etienne Delécluze's literary circle. He was very ambivalent about the label he was assigned despite himself. Like Balzac's *Human Comedy*, which took shape in the same period, Stendhal's work belonged to no literary school and thus incurred the wrath of both Romantics and their opponents.

By the 1880s, as Stendhal predicted, critics finally accepted what earlier readers had rejected. A new literary world opened up with the death of Victor Hugo and the birth of the avant-garde; the threat to French cultural identity posed by Romanticism passed, and with it, the obsession to defend neoclassical values. "Unhonored during his lifetime," writes Harry Levin, "[Stendhal's work] would be accepted by the realists and rewarded by the naturalists—recommended by [Hippolyte] Taine and [Francisque] Sarcey, imitated by [Paul] Bourget and [Maurice] Barrès, canonized by the antiquarians of the Stendhal Club, and enshrined by Henri Martineau's bookshop and publishing firm, Le Divan" (84-85). As André Gide noted in his *Journal*, *The Red and the Black* had been written for the pleasure of its twentieth-century readers: "Chaque phrase est tendue comme une corde d'arc" 'Each sentence is as taut as a bowstring' (805; my trans.). At the time Gide wrote, Stendhal's novel had joined the canon, where it has remained ever since, even becoming a staple of lycée instruction, *baccalauréat* examinations, popular cinema, and French government exportation to distant francophone countries.

No serious criticism or scholarship on Stendhal ever vouched for his historical accuracy. Contrary to his epigraph to book 1, chapter 13, likening the novel to "un miroir qu'on promène le long d'un chemin" 'a mirror being carried along a highway' Stendhal's text actually reflects his own curious point of view, that of a professor of nonconformity, in both major and minor matters of fact (398; 289; 2.19). *The Red and the Black* is replete with elemental errors, like Louise de Rênal's plea for royal clemency from Charles X in 1831 and the article in Napoleon's penal code relevant to Julien's case (no. 296, not no. 1342). More important are its misplaced emphases on the conspiratorial activities of the Congregationists after the 1827 election of the 221 liberal deputies. Such conspiracies there were, but they were not as significant historically as those of the Carbonari and their sympathizers. These latter figures Stendhal represents sardonically in the guise of the Italian count awaiting extradition to Lombardy, where the novelist himself had been under Austrian police surveillance. Rather, it is the novel's historicity, not its history, that bears recognition and further consideration by scholars and students alike. In keeping with Stendhal's literary transformation of Mathilde de La Mole from a host of women in his life—Méthilde Dembowski, Mary de Neuville, Clémentine Curial, and Alberthe de Rubempré, among others—*The Red and the Black* offers readers another view of the past.

Nor did the novelist recognize all historical changes since 1789. *The Red and the Black* developed strange gaps in its view of the Other represented by gender, race, and class. However central to Julien's ambitions, women here are intellectually marginal. Stendhal himself sympathized with the Saint-Simonian socialists who sought to establish new gender roles, but he insisted on complementarity rather than equality. In his work women are objects of the male gaze, whether as workers in the nail mills or as lovers appearing through bedroom windows. Louise de Rênal does not read, while Mathilde de La Mole reads self-destructively like Flaubert's Emma Bovary, even though women actually fulfilled important literate functions in Restoration France. Like workers and people of color, whatever their place historically, women literati are virtually invisible in and to this text. This lacuna is all the more glaring given the work's remarkable context of revolutionary change.

Otherwise, as a historical source and a textual narrative, this work takes on a life all its own. It has become a myth. Between history as lived experience and fiction as literary genre, Stendhal's novel inscribes both an actual and an imaginary world in the wake of 1789 and its revolutionary consequences, at least as they were perceived by contemporaries. *The Red and the Black* employs telling details to create a reality that transcends actuality and even artistic achievement—like the empire's exaggerated reputation for Julien and that of the monarchy for nearly everyone else in the text—in a particular discursive moment made possible by the Revolution. That France witnessed a succession of such moments from 1789 onward lends substance to the meanings that readers have given to the novel's subtitle, *Chronicle of 1830*, and to Stendhal's epistolary claim "de peindre la France telle qu'elle est en 1830" 'to paint France just as it is in 1830' (*Correspondance* 2: 186; my trans.). The dramatic changes in regime in 1848, 1851, and 1870 underscore the historical and literary mythos latent in this work completed in 1830. *The Red and the Black* thus captures what the historian François Furet once called the nature of revolution, the profound "dialectic between actual power and a symbolic representation of it" (78). For this very reason, then, Stendhal's novel belongs as much in the history classroom as it does in the French literature course.

The Specters of Revolution; or, Politics at the Concert

Priscilla Parkhurst Ferguson

Politics in a work of the imagination, Stendhal proclaims in one of his most celebrated declarations, is like a pistol shot in the middle of a concert: "Ce bruit est déchirant sans être énergique. Il ne s'accorde avec le son d'aucun instrument" 'The noise is shattering without being forceful. It doesn't harmonize with any of the other instruments.' The characterization of this literary strategy as harmonically imperfect is especially sharp coming from the biographer of Haydn, Mozart, Metastasio, and Rossini. But after stating this dictum, Stendhal blithely disregards it, embarking on a long chapter of labyrinthine political intrigue, supposedly in deference to his publisher's principles of marketing: "Si vos personnages ne parlent pas politique [. . .] ce ne sont plus des Français de 1830, et votre livre n'est plus un miroir, comme vous en avez la prétention" 'If your characters don't talk politics [. . .] then they are no longer Frenchmen of 1830, and your book is no longer a mirror, as you claim [. . .]' (419; 304; 2.22).

One of the most important questions posed by this extraordinarily self-conscious work turns on just the issue raised by Stendhal's putative publisher, who very precisely locates in historical time and place not only the characters in the novel but also, by implication, the readers (and potential purchasers) of the book. Politics does play in the Stendhalian concert, largely in the comic mode, as in the send-up of political intrigue that turns the marquis de La Mole's royalist conspiracy into the most baroque of enterprises. Liberals and conservatives change places without any observable effect on the social order. Stendhal's final novel, *La chartreuse de Parme* (*The Charterhouse of Parma*, 1838), makes the political enterprise even more absurd, politics even more outrageous.

But in the larger sense the political as a mode of apprehending the world supplies the very stuff for the making of *The Red and the Black*. As many critics have noted, it is the political resonance that makes this novel a genuinely historical work because it is the political that roots this novel in the contradictions of early nineteenth-century France. *The Red and the Black* fulfills Stendhal's claim to mirror a wide range of social phenomena ("un roman: c'est un miroir qu'on promène le long du chemin" 'A novel: it's a mirror being carried along a highway' [100; 60; 1.13]; cf. "un roman est un miroir qui se promène sur une grande route" 'a novel is a mirror moving along a highway' [398; 289; 2.19]). The kind of historicity that Stendhal's mirror image reflects has little to do with the background information about contemporary events and terms supplied in notes and introductions of editions aimed at students. A truly historical reading of this novel requires us to look beyond the obvious and often boring, largely irrelevant antiquarian explanations and to consider how history enmeshes the work in a web of textual relations and how, to follow Stendhal's metaphor, history inheres in the music of the text.

Thus the question of revolution that looms so large in discussions of *The Red and the Black*. For the mirror that Stendhal holds up to the France of 1830, before and after the revolutionary days of July, reflects a society defined by politics, about which, true to the publisher's requirement, the characters talk incessantly. And the politics that show up in the Stendhalian mirror depict a society preoccupied by revolution. Just as understanding how the different characters construe revolution gives a key to their characters, so understanding revolution in *The Red and the Black* offers a key to this intensely historical work.

Omnipresent yet elusive, revolution has always presented a problem for reading *The Red and the Black*. If the subtitle proclaimed on the title page of the original edition —"Chronicle of the Nineteenth Century"—invites us to consider *The Red and the Black* in the broadest terms as the annals of a century not yet one-third over, the subtitle for Chapter 1—"Chronicle of 1830"—points us, as it did Stendhal's first readers, for whom this novel dealt with current events, to the July Revolution of 1830 that brought the Restoration to an end, exiled the Bourbon Charles X (brother of the executed Louis XVI), and installed on the throne his Orleanist cousin, the "bourgeois king" Louis-Philippe. Subsequent editions vary between the two subtitles, but both foreground revolution, if differently.

Yet even as the subtitles steer us toward revolution, Stendhal nudges us not so subtly in the other direction. The prefatory note ("Avertissement") rather ponderously places the composition of the novel in 1827, well before "les grands événements de juillet sont venus donner à tous les esprits une direction peu favorable aux jeux de l'imagination" 'the great events of July came along to give all our thoughts a turn away from the free play of imagination' (20; 1; 1.1). (The July Revolution interrupted the typesetting of the novel since the typesetters quit work to join the fighting; Stendhal recounts correcting the proofs of book 1 as the insurrection took place under his windows.) Even though he reworked the manuscript almost until the novel appeared in November 1830, there are no references to the specific political events of 1830. Yet Stendhal makes a point of referring to other incidents in the same period, like the premiere of Victor Hugo's explosive drama *Hernani* in February 1830 (2.9). To complicate the temporality still further, the novel extends beyond historical time. Following the internal chronology scrupulously (which of course Stendhal does not do) sets the beginning of the novel in September 1826 and the date of Julien's execution on 25 July 1831, that is, over seven months after the novel itself appeared (Crouzet, *Rouge* ch. 2). Small wonder that the *Journal des débats*, announcing the novel in December 1830, gave the subtitle as "Chronicle of 1829" (Castex, *Rouge et le noir* 693).

It is nonetheless true that Julien makes a decided assault on the bastions of Restoration society and dies in the attempt. If we are to believe Mathilde de La Mole, much of Julien's attraction lay in "[des] profondes discussions sur l'avenir qui attend la France, ses idées sur la resssemblance que les événements qui vont fondre sur nous peuvent avoir avec la révolution de 1688 en Angleterre" 'profound thoughts on the future which awaits France, his ideas about a possible parallel between the events soon to burst upon us and the revolution of 1688 in England' (395; 287; 2.19). Still, considerable violence has to be done to the novel to make Julien anything like a revolutionary. The blatant injustice of power relations in postrevolutionary society crosses his mind only infrequently and social reform never does.

Nevertheless, *The Red and the Black* is very much a novel of revolution—less because of July 1830 than because of July 1789. For it is the first revolution in France. This novel is a "chronicle of the nineteenth century" because Stendhal defines the entire century, even the years yet to come, by the revolution now commemorated on 14 July. The storming of the Bastille set the stage for Julien's career. It determined his sense of self and destiny, defining both his strategies of confrontation and the maneuvers through which society met that challenge. His overweening ambition and pride, his claims on the social order, and, above all, to invoke a favored Stendhalian term, his *énergie* make Julien emblematic of the social disruption that revolution portends. Julien arouses outrage and fear in both the bourgeoisie of Verrières and the aristocracy of Paris because he figures as an as yet unnamed, therefore obscurely apprehended, threat to the social order.

In the novel as without, society wavers between the dual senses of revolution, at times taking the Revolution as a uniquely defining historical event and at others treating revolution as a sociopolitical concept suggestive of a continuing cycle (Rey). Though people naturally assess its effects differently, they all know full well that the Revolution forever changed the world. (Napoleon, in this reading, completed the original disruption of the social order.) At the same time, they live in fear (M. de Rênal and the marquis de La Mole) or in hope (Julien and the count Altamira) that revolution will come around again. In this sense the novel very much directs us to the Revolution of July 1830. The prospect of radical change suffuses this novel that nevertheless forecloses every avenue such change might conceivably take.

Stendhal weaves the revolution into the text in ways both obvious and subtle. Thus the ten chapter epigraphs attributed to bona fide and well-known revolutionaries: nine of them refer to the orator Barnave (27, 136, 190, 469; 4, 88, 129, 342; 1.2, 1.19, 1.24, 2.31); the abbé Sieyès (93; 54; 1.12); the Italian conspirator Silvio Pellico (317; 225; 2.8), cited at the head of the chapter that focuses on the count Altamira, who has been condemned to death for revolutionary conspiracy in "his own country" (carefully unspecified); Mirabeau (479, 491; 350, 359; 2.33, 2.35); and Napoleon (417; 303; 2.22). It makes little difference that these may be false attributions, as Stendhal's epigraphs often are; they make space for the Revolution by thrusting its personages stage center.

By far the most momentous of these personages is Danton, the fiery revolutionary under whose aegis Stendhal places book 1 ("La vérité, l'âpre vérité"

'Truth, bitter truth' [21; 1; 1.1]) and to whom a chapter title explicitly ties Julien ("Serait-ce un Danton?" 'Will He Be a Danton?'[2.12]). Danton also turns up in conversation with Mathilde and count Altamira (328–29; 234; 2.9), and Julien recalls an observation of Danton when he finds himself facing the guillotine in three days (532, 534; 389, 391; 2.42). Although the guillotine that ends Julien's life has been taken as a figure of the absent revolution (Brooks, "1830"), this quintessential instrument of the Revolution (and the official instrument of execution in France until the abolition of capital punishment in 1981) appears at the outset and is reinvoked, directly and indirectly, throughout this novel virtually haunted by execution and specifically decollation. For starters, in the church on his way to take up employment in the Rênal household, Julien finds a newspaper clipping about the execution of a young man in Besançon, fatefully marked "*Le premier pas*" '*The first step*' (47; 20; 1.5). An early horse ride in Paris takes him to the place Louis XVI (the name given to the place de la Concorde between 1826 and 1828), named for the king guillotined there in 1791 (2.3). The emblematic ancestor Boniface de La Mole was decapitated in the sixteenth century, and Mathilde, thinking about the revolution that might come, immediately imagines herself as Mme Roland, who was executed in 1793, and assigns Julien the role of Mme Roland's husband, who committed suicide at the same time (395–96; 287; 2.19). Even more suggestive, with this reference to the turbulent Danton, who met his end at the guillotine in 1794, Stendhal seals Julien Sorel's fate at the very beginning of the novel and reconfirms it well before that destiny is accomplished. Like count Altamira, Julien is under sentence of death. Not surprisingly, the count fascinates Julien from their first encounter; after the second, at the ball, "Julien était amoureux de son conspirateur" 'Julien was in love with his conspirator' (333–34; 238; 2.9). The "truth" that Stendhal-Danton claims as his credo is realized in Julien, for whom the truth turns out to be bitter indeed, and the bitterness and truth have a great deal to do with Julien's revolutionary promise.

For much of the novel, however, revolutionary potential is obscured by the focus on Julien as a parvenu, an individual who crosses the boundaries that society has set between social classes, an individual concerned above all with making his or her (but, in the novel of manners, more likely his) way. It is as a parvenu that Julien is perceived and even, at times, perceives himself. The parvenu is quite the opposite of the revolutionary, since mobility is a strictly personal enterprise. The many ladders that Julien climbs up (and down) throughout the novel—to the roof in his father's yard, where he is discovered reading; in the library of the marquis to get the books; in and out of his mistresses' bedrooms; at the church to decorate it for a feast day (1.30, 2.16, 2.19, 1.28)—carry him alone. There is no question of collective action, and there is no aspiration on his part to obliterate the boundaries he crosses, to destroy the barriers between social groups, or to reconfigure the social order. On the contrary, not only does the parvenu not call constituted social groups into question, he actually reinforces them: no one has more vested than the parvenu does in assimilation and therefore in the continuance of the social group into which he has managed to climb. The newly ennobled in *The Red and the Black* defend the rights and privileges of rank far more zealously than does the marquis de La Mole, whose time in rank allows him greater latitude in his behavior. Not even the marquis, however, is immune to the temptations of ambition, since he covets the title of duke for himself (242; 169; 1.30) and that of duchess for his daughter (362, 480; 261, 353; 2.13, 2.15).

In many respects *The Red and the Black* tells a classic parvenu's tale. The youngest son of a rich peasant rises into the bourgeoisie through employment as a tutor in the household of a minor provincial aristocrat, is elevated to the position of secretary to a titled member of the Parisian aristocracy, and (almost) marries his boss's daughter, coming into a title, an income. and a regiment. Julien bypasses the monied or commercial bourgeoisie, for which he (like the narrator) has nothing but scorn. Julien's is the bourgeoisie of the knowledge professions, a class that is defined not by property or wealth or birth but by skill and that functions as the dominated fraction of the dominant class (Bourdieu). He must learn the mores and manners of the elite, and Stendhal spends considerable time on Julien's acquisition of "milieu markers," that is, signs that associate an individual with a given group or milieu. Julien has a great deal to learn, and Stendhal has a great deal of fun showing up his hero's ineptitude: the deep bow to an elegant man who turns out to be a tailor, his spelling of *cela* with two ls, his fall from a horse in the middle of Paris (2.2–3). "Tous les usages lui semblaient singuliers, et il manquait à tous. Ses bévues faisaient la joie des valets de chambre" 'All their customs seemed strange to him, and he could not live up to them, His social blunders were the delight of the footmen' (286; 201; 2.3). The marquis immediately sends him off to lessons—riding, fencing, and dancing—and later to the foyer of the opera house to acquire the final Parisian polish (308; 218; 2.6).

What makes Julien dangerous is that he ends up mastering these milieu markers. Designating Julien as an outsider, a stranger, virtually a foreigner in class terms, is the usual tactic by which the milieux to which he aspires endeavor to dismiss him. His peasant birth is often recalled, which is one more way of denying him entry to the bourgeoisie or the aristocracy. When difference is no longer apparent or remarked upon, the parvenu has become a fully integrated member of the group, and Stendhal takes pains to emphasize Julien's mastery of these codes. (The only place where Julien remains obdurately "different" is the seminary, where the majority of seminarians are from the peasantry that he has left behind.) He learns to speak the language that once seemed so foreign to him in the de La Mole salon ("C'était comme une langue étrangère qu'il eût comprise, mais qu'il n'eût pu parler" 'It was like a foreign language he could understand [and appreciate], but which he could not talk' (290; 204; 2.4; brackets in orig.). His behavior in the embassies in London is still cited as a model to young secretaries (2.7), and soon after he becomes "un dandy [. . .] et comprenait l'art de vivre à Paris" 'a dandy [. . .] and understood the art of living in Paris' (317; 226; 2.8); he is "un vrai dandy [. . .] l'un des hommes les mieux mis de Paris" 'a real dandy [. . .] one of the best-dressed men in Paris' (473; 346; 2.31).

Most important, he learns to read society correctly and to judge by his own standards. Julien is a parvenu, but a parvenu who makes it, an arriviste who arrives by obliterating his "foreign" past. Readers often have a hard time understanding Julien's shooting of Mme de Rênal, which destroys his hard-won success, because this rash act counters every notion of the parvenu literature (and life) purveys. A true parvenu would never have risked so much.

Which is precisely Stendhal's point: Julien is not a true parvenu. The abbé Pirard is shocked when Julien asks to be excused from dinner at the La Mole's, but that is because he—not Julien—is the "véritable parvenu" 'real parvenu' (289; 203; 2.4). At one point, when Julien is under the spell of everything that makes Mathilde a "jolie femme du grand monde" 'pretty woman of high fashion,' Stendhal notes that "en cela, Julien était encore un parvenu" 'In this respect, Julien was still an upstart' (357; 257; 2.13). But not for long. Julien escapes social categories, manipulating the codes of all of them without adhering to any. He moves from the "triste habit noir" 'gloomy black suit' (124; 79; 1.18), his ordinary dress as tutor to the Rênal children, to the splendid sky-blue uniform he puts on for the king's visit to Verrières and then, for the high mass on the same occasion, to a cassock and a surplice (which do not quite cover the spurs that he has not had time to remove). He moves still more effortlessly between the black suit that identifies him as the marquis's subaltern and the blue suit that designates him as the younger son of a count, that is, the marquis's equal. The uniform and the suits perform social class all the more effectively by showing it for the fiction that it is (Petrey). For the dandy, moreover, social class is presumed irrelevant since what defines this characteristic nineteenth-century personage is not the conventional components of class (birth, income, occupation) but appearance and behavior. The dandy is all surface.

Julien of course is not. Stendhal places him in a sense beyond social class, and this well before he becomes a dandy. Whence the recurrent association with solitude and heights, from the first glimpse of him reading on the roof (1.4) to his choice of a final resting place on "le point le plus élevé d'une des hautes montagnes du Jura" 'the peak of one of the highest mountains in the Jura' (556; 408; 2.45). In between Julien is consistently shown above the world or alone and frequently both: thus his meditations high in the mountains (1.10, 1.12, 1.13) or when he is comforted by the view from the abbé Pirard's cell in the seminary overlooking the countryside and delighted that his own cell on the top floor is not only solitary but has a splendid view (1.25). This situation is repeated in Paris, where he occupies a "jolie mansarde qui donnait sur l'immense jardin" 'neat attic room looking out on the immense garden' in the de La Mole mansion (277; 194; 2.2). His appointment as tutor in the Old and New Testament gives him the precious right of dining alone and entering the garden by himself (1.29). Perhaps the most emblematic scene comes when Julien helps prepare the church for the Corpus Christi celebrations and, at considerable risk to life and limb, nimbly and adroitly places decorations high over the altar (1.28). Finally, of course, Julien experiences his greatest happiness in the prison cell on an upper story of a gothic tower with a wonderful view (2.36), a "jolie chambre à cent quatre-vingts marches d'élévation" 'pleasant room a hundred and eighty steps above the ground' (507; 371; 2.37).

Thus even as Julien acquires the suitable demeanor and adopts the requisite behavior of the elite, Stendhal insists on his difference. It is this difference that makes Julien far more threatening than any parvenu could possibly be and puts him among the eternal outsiders. Because what is most striking about Julien is that he learns everything—his prodigious memory serves him well—and believes nothing. He has memorized the whole New Testament in Latin along with Joseph de Maistre's ultraconservative tract *Du pape* (*On the Pope*) "et croyait à l'un aussi peu qu'à l'autre" 'and believed as little of one as of the other' (42; 16; 1.5). At the seminary he remains obstinately apart, learning a great deal, all of which leaves him unaffected. He has mastered the codes of each milieu, he has learned the *doxa*, the assumptions, the tacit understandings and beliefs that support any social system. He can memorize a page of the newspaper as easily and credit it with as little import as the directives of the royalist conspiracy in which the marquis de La Mole involves him. Julien moves between "mythologies" (Barthes) as easily as he moves from the black to the blue suit or puts together the disguise the marquis orders up, "à la mode d'il y a deux ans [. . .] l'air peu soigné," 'the fashion of a couple of years ago [. . .] a slightly scruffy look' (413; 300; 2.21). (He scruffs up so well that the marquis cannot help laughing.) He is remarkable for being able to make himself unremarkable. With his cross and his blue greatcoat in Strasbourg, Julien blends into the crowd, utterly fooling the police spies looking for him. His attitudes are as factitious as his attire.

Ultimately Julien does not, cannot, blend in. He stands out the most, he is the emblematic revolutionary personage that he is, because of his capacity to astonish, to do the unexpected. The marquis de La Mole bestows a decoration on Julien instead of his own son precisely because of that capacity (318; 226; 2.8). This talent charms but it also frightens. At the seminary he is accused of the unpardonable "vice" of thinking for himself (209; 143; 1.26). His very brilliance is suspect in the eyes of the church because it signals the independence that creates revolutionaries like the abbés Sieyès and Grégoire, both ecclesiastics who played a notable role in the Revolution: "Qui empêchera l'homme supérieur de passer de l'autre côté comme Sieyès ou Grégoire!" 'Who can prevent the superior man from passing over to the other side like Sieyès or Grégoire!' (207; 142; 1.26).

The apprehension Julien's difference excites in the seminary, like the consternation he provokes generally, is a function of his energy and passion. This society lives under the pall of ennui or boredom (Auerbach)—"ce siècle ennuyé" 'this bored century' (287; 202; 2.4). Norbert de La Mole issues a general warning against Julien: "Prenez bien garde à ce jeune homme, qui a tant d'énergie [. . .] si la révolution recommence, il nous fera tous guillotiner" 'Better be careful of this young fellow who has so much energy [. . .] if the Revolution begins again, he'll have us all guillotined.' Mathilde recognizes that their fear of energy is at bottom the fear of the unexpected: "Dans ce siècle, où toute énergie est morte, son énergie leur fait peur" 'In the age when all energy seems dead, his energy terrifies them' (351; 252–53; 2.12). Mathilde loves Julien because he saves her from boredom: "Du moment qu'elle eut décidé qu'elle aimait Julien, elle ne s'ennuya plus" 'From the moment of her decision that she loved Julien, she was no longer bored' (355; 255; 2.12). Not surprisingly, their relationship deteriorates when she becomes used to not being bored (385; 279; 2.17). In every grammatical form, noun, adjective, and verb, boredom weaves through the entire novel; it is the warp against which energy and passion weave Julien's career and Stendhal's text.

The greatest expenditure of energy, the most extraordinary outburst of passion, is, of course, Julien's shooting of Mme de Rênal in the church at Verrières. There is no end of commentary on the supposed implausibility of this action, which dashes all of Julien's hopes for advancement. Whether individual revenge for honor impugned—Mme de Rênal's letter accuses him in sum of *arrivisme*, of using the basest means for personal advancement—or a state of "demi-folie" 'half madness' (502; 366–67; 2.36), this, the most strikingly unpredictable of his acts, points to the ineluctable conflict on which Stendhal has structured his entire novel. Julien renounces ambition in favor of honor, and that renunciation, in the terms set out by the novel, requires him to cut himself off from the society in which that ambition made sense. He thinks of suicide in prison and effectively commits suicide twice, once through his speech to the jury at his trial (2.41) and the second time when he refuses to ask for a pardon. His death, as his old enemy Valenod recognizes, will be a kind of suicide (543; 397; 2.44). He opts for his "vie idéale" 'ideal life' over the "petites tracasseries, [les] détails de la vie réelle" 'the tricks and details from real life' (521; 381; 2.40), a choice that places him beyond social class once and for all. In his speech to the jury Julien attacks the monied classes, the bourgeoisie, and speaks of himself as a peasant. But, of course, Julien's rhetorical ploy of (re)associating himself with the peasantry denies the social mobility on which the novel is premised. Society wins insofar as it reasserts the primacy of social class determined by birth and punishes the transgressing of its constitutive boundaries.

But Julien wins too insofar as his suicide rejects that society and those boundaries and asserts his integrity against its duplicities. Integrity, honor, and principle have no place in society, and Julien withdraws, like Stendhal's other heroes, Octave, in *Armance* (1827), who commits suicide, and Fabrice, in *La chartreuse de Parme* (1838), who retires to a monastery. Julien's (and Stendhal's) politics is not a politics of revolution but a politics of rejection, dismissal, and, finally, transcendence. The social mobility that has carried Julien from Verrières to Paris and back continues on a rhetorical plane. At Besançon Julien is elevated to the "happy prison" (Brombert, *Romantic Prison*); after his condemnation he is thrown down into a dark, dank dungeon from which, on the day of his execution, he emerges, released, into the open air. His ascent continues after death to the mountaintop that he selected for his burial. From that site, Julien overlooks—*dominates* is the French term—Verrières, the France from which he had risen. Stendhal consecrates the triumph forbidden Julien by Restoration society, placing him once and for all beyond social class, beyond society, beyond the politics that had played such a large role in his life.

Stendhal, indeed, fires a pistol in the middle of the concert orchestrated after the Revolution. The shot that wounds Mme de Rênal rends that society, exposes the contradictions on which it is founded, and prepares the July Revolution. If, as Marx and Engels claimed, the specter of revolution haunted nineteenth-century Europe, nowhere was revolution more intensely present in the social imaginary than in France, and no text makes that imaginary more vivid than *The Red and the Black*, Stendhal's concert with pistol shots written into the score.

Secret Notes and Pistol Shots

Peter Brooks

The episode of "la note secrète" ("the secret note") is for many readers one of the most opaque and baffling moments of *The Red and the Black.* It is as if the atmosphere of concealment and conspiracy Stendhal creates in this clandestine meeting envelops the reader as well and compromises the section's legibility. Yet it is a key moment in the novel. It includes the narrator's famous remark comparing politics in the novel to a pistol shot in the middle of a concert, and it dramatizes the central political issues at stake in both the plot of the novel and the moment of the novel's composition.

That remark about politics in the novel is often quoted out of context to suggest that Stendhal thought politics had no place in imaginative literature. On the contrary, in the context of this imagined dialogue between author and publisher, the publisher has the last word: "If your characters don't talk politics, [. . .] then they are no longer Frenchmen of 1830, and your book is no longer a mirror, as you claim" (304; 2.22). Politics is indeed a dissonant note in the novel but a necessary one. A novel faithful to the year 1830 necessarily contains within itself a dangerous, explosive potential. Julien will by the end of the novel explode his own successful career with his pistol shot at Mme de Rênal, an act that has no rational explanation but may be—as Julien will suggest at his trial—ultimately a political gesture, the act of a "peasant in open revolt against his humble station" (387; 2.41), a personal compensation for the lack of political revolution.

There is more than one paradox here, since the political revolution had in fact occurred in the real world while Stendhal was writing his novel, though it never shows up in the novel itself—except, perhaps, in such displaced forms as Julien's ultimate revolt against his absorption into good society and in the counterrevolutionary conspiracies of the secret note episode. Stendhal tells us in his "Avertissement de l'éditeur," or foreword, that the novel was written in 1827 (even though he's subtitled it "Chronicle of 1830"). The foreword is one more obfuscation, since the novel was written in 1830 and indeed includes allusions to events shortly before and after the July Revolution: the premiere of Victor Hugo's play *Hernani*; Stendhal's own failure to win a position of Prefect from the new minister of the interior, François Guizot; and the French capture of Algiers, in North Africa—part of the cause of the success of the July Revolution, since the crack army divisions were absent on this colonial expedition and thus unavailable to put down the Revolution. We know from other sources that Stendhal was correcting proof for the first book of the novel—with most of book 2 still unwritten—while watching the insurrection take form beneath the windows of his apartment in the rue de Richelieu.

Furthermore, it's clear that Stendhal could not have published his account of the conspiracy of the secret note before the July Revolution: the censorship laws in place at the time would have prevented it. In fact, the July Revolution was in large part touched off by the long-standing disputes over censorship that marked the Restoration. King Charles X's reactionary ministry, led by the Prince de Polignac, had decided to try to impose *la censure préalable*—the censorship of books and articles before they appeared in print—and in the vanguard of the insurrection that broke out on 28 July were journalists and printers. Hence this episode of dark doings by the aristocrats and their allies could see the light of print only after their attempts to muzzle the press had been defeated by Revolution. That Revolution, absent from the text of Stendhal's novel, has a way of making indirect appearances of this sort. It is as if the time of the writing of the novel interjected itself into the time represented in the novel, figuring the political stakes of the year 1830 in ways that the world of the novel doesn't explicitly acknowledge.

What is going on in the pages devoted to the secret note (2.21–23)? The marquis de La Mole and a group of high-ranking nobles—including the prime minister—and notables of the church are engaged in a treasonable conspiracy to provoke conditions that would lead to an occupation of France by the armies of the Holy Alliance, the group of states that fought against and eventually defeated Napoleon, restored the Bourbon monarchy following the Battle of Waterloo, and then, under the leadership of Prince Metternich of Austria, sought to quash any future revolutionary challenges to the status quo. After the fall of Napoleon, France was ruled by Louis XVIII, brother of Louis XVI, guillotined by the Jacobins during the Reign of Terror in 1793. But this restored Bourbon monarch was obliged to accept La Charte, a constitution that created a parliamentary regime, somewhat on the English model, and limited the powers of the monarchy. The story of the Restoration period, 1815–30, is one of struggle between one group, which saw La Charte as the guarantee of representative government, constitutionalism, and basic liberties of speech, association, and the press, and another, which wished to restore a truly absolute monarchy on the model of the Old Regime. When Louis XVIII died, in 1824, he was succeeded by his younger brother, Charles X, formerly the comte d'Artois and well known as the most arrogant and absolutist member of the family, who raised hopes among the ultras—the irreconcilable monarchists—that the Restoration would truly become a reproduction of the Old Regime. It should be remembered that Charles X was sixty-seven years old when he became king: the Restoration was a gerontocracy, nostalgic for the past, out of touch with the aspirations of Julien's generation.

After restoring the monarchy in 1815, the occupying armies withdrew from France in 1817. To the conspirators of the secret note, this was a fatal error: the only way to prevent the spread of revolutionary ideas, and the rise of the lower orders, would have been a continued occupation. If one could create conditions that would provoke the Holy Alliance to invade France once again, then a true Restoration could take place, La Charte could be abrogated, and the king could rule as he saw fit. There were a number of conspiracies of this type during the Restoration. One of the best known arose in 1817, when a royalist group encouraged by the comte d'Artois (the future Charles X) wrote a secret note to the courts of Austria, England, and Russia, urging a prolongation of the occupation to stamp out the Jacobin peril. And in 1829, as the struggle between the king and the opposition—in the legislature, in the press, in the country at large—became ever more polarized and intense, various newspapers carried accounts of similar conspiracies, real or fantasized, which involved secret notes pleading for military occupation of France.

The July Revolution of 1830 was provoked not by a secret note but by actions on the part of the king that made it equally apparent that he had lost his patience with constitutional rule and intended to concentrate all power in his own hands. In 1829 Charles X appointed as prime minister the Prince de Polignac, leader of the ultras—who appears in Stendhal's conspiracy thinly disguised as M. de Nerval—and confrontation with the opposition was inevitable. When the majority of deputies in the Chamber insisted that the king choose a prime minister acceptable to them, the king dissolved the Chamber and called new elections. But the resulting majority was more liberal still. The king responded with "Les Trois Ordonnances" of 26 July 1830: the institution of a strict new censorship of the press; the dissolution of the new Chamber (which hadn't even met yet); and the modification of the qualifications for voting, which shifted power from the industrial and commercial bourgeoisie to the landed aristocracy. It looked like a clear attempt at a coup d'état by the crown. The immediate result was a revolution that swept the Bourbons from power forever.

The resulting regime was not a republic, in large part because the leaders who took control of the upheaval feared that the declaration of a republic would result in a military reaction by the Holy Alliance—and a reoccupation of France. The men who assumed power in July 1830 were on the whole a moderate and cautious lot: bankers and journalists, who also feared an upsurge of the Jacobin spirit and sought refuge in a new constitutional monarchy headed by Louis-Philippe d'Orléans, head of the younger branch of the royal family, reputed for its liberal spirit. Thus it is that the issues under discussion in the secret note episode were ones of burning importance at the moment Stendhal composed these pages: while he is describing an ultraroyalist conspiracy under the Restoration, it is in the context of fears that the new regime created on 31 July 1830 might be smothered in its cradle by the return of the armies that the duke of Wellington had led to victory over Napoleon at Waterloo.

The politics of *The Red and the Black* tend to intrude themselves in this curious manner, bringing to what are supposedly representations of a past moment (1827? pre-July 1830?) concerns of the moment of writing, post-July 1830, in a kind of double vision. Toward the end of the novel, when Julien has been condemned to death, Mme de Rênal considers making a plea for clemency by throwing herself at the feet of King Charles X—who, by the chronology of the novel, had by this point been dethroned and exiled for nearly a year. Indeed, by the novel's chronology we ought to have a representation of the July Revolution itself. We don't—Julien's career takes place entirely under the Restoration. But that unrepresented Revolution insinuates itself into the novel where it has no place: in the episode of the secret note, to be sure, and perhaps also in Julien's trial and execution, where the "peasant in open revolt," as he calls himself, is condemned to die for having attempted a kind of usurpation against those who style themselves the legitimate rulers of France. It's as if the July Revolution were echoed in the novel with an opposite result: the victory of the repressive regime, the sacrifice of those members of the aspiring younger generation who dreamed of change. In a novel characterized by a very talkative narrator, who frequently intervenes to judge the characters and their actions, there may be a more generalized, though subtle, invasion of the "story" by the "narrative discourse." That is, the time and process of the writing itself, its historical context, feeds back into the representation of prior events, giving them a kind of stereoscopic historical presence. If the July Revolution is never represented in the novel, it's nonetheless present. It might be the subject of book 2, chapter 46—the one following the last we in fact have. A pistol shot waiting to be heard.

When in the middle of the discussion about the secret note Julien is told to leave the room, he does so with "great regret" because the conspirators are debating the very questions that form the subject of his "habitual meditations" (422; 306; 2.22). If there were an invasion by the Holy Alliance, could it succeed? If the foreign armies won the first and maybe the second campaign, by the third wouldn't the citizen army that routed the foreign armies during the wars of the original French Revolution once again form into a mighty fighting force? It was the French Revolution that created the "levée en masse": an entire nation called to arms to defend the mother soil—and an army that also offered an intelligent and ambitious young plebeian such as Julien the chance to attain power and glory by talent alone. So that Julien as witness to the discussions of the secret note episode is every bit as interested in the subjects under debate as the conspirators themselves—only from the opposite perspective. For him, the plot of the counterrevolutionaries opens the prospect of a renewed Jacobin revolution and the return of a France where young men like himself would once again have a position as something other than "servant" to the marquis.

"How can they say such things in front of a plebeian?" Julien wonders (427; 311; 2.23), as the conspirators talk of forming a kind of secret militia, commanded by the nobility, throughout France, and of the need to base this militia on the church—which wants the restoration of its lands. Those lands had been confiscated in the French Revolution, and throughout the Restoration the ultras sought their return (eventually, there was an indemnity paid instead). The cardinal who dominates the discussion here argues that the clergy must necessarily take the lead in counterrevolutionary activity—which of course confirms all Julien's (and Stendhal's) beliefs about the sinister conspiratorial role played by the church, especially the confraternity known as *la Congrégation*, in undermining constitutional government. The young bishop of Agde (whom Julien has met earlier at the sumptuous—and fully politicized—religious ceremony at

Bray-le-Haut [1.18]) goes further in ferocity, arguing that the mistake of the English during the Napoleonic Wars was not to have assassinated Napoleon himself and that the only solution is to destroy Paris, the site of intellectual ferment, journalism, and political discussion—a new Babylon that must perish. In fact it was the demon Napoleon who alone knew how to subdue the Paris mob: during his rise to power, in 1795, near the church of Saint-Roch, he turned his artillery on the people.

How, indeed, can they say such things in the presence of a plebeian? The secret-note episode makes explicit—more than any other episode of the novel—the fear and loathing felt by reactionary royalists toward the mass of the French people. Julien states at his trial that even if he were not guilty of shooting Mme de Rênal, he would be convicted by a jury of local notables—not in fact his peers—who would want to punish in him a whole class of inferiors who have sought to rise from poverty and gain entry into the governing classes. He will be guillotined, he implies, not simply in criminal justice but in class warfare. The stark subtext of *The Red and the Black* is indeed class warfare, the struggle unleashed by the French Revolution to decide to whom the country belongs—to a traditional ruling class or to the people? Here again, the July Revolution of 1830 makes its presence felt, as one more episode in the continuing battle over the ownership of the country: an episode that would not of itself resolve the issue, since there were further revolutions in 1848 and 1871, not to speak of those that would come in the twentieth century. One might say that only by the bicentennial of the French Revolution, in 1989, had the forces unleashed in 1789 reached equilibrium.

The "charter of the salon" (detailed in 2.4) declares that above all, one must not talk politics in good company. Politics, to Restoration society, always raises the specter of revolution, of the have-nots rising to claim what they spectacularly gained and then lost over the revolutionary years. When the "author" echoes this charter by claiming that talk of politics is like a pistol shot in the midst of a concert, he appears to align himself, as he most often does, with the tone of good company. The voice of the Stendhalian narrator is usually worldly, witty, unsurprised by the world's knaveries. But as his "publisher" tells him, the French in 1830 do talk politics. Indeed, politics is even talked at the splendid society ball at the duc de Retz's. Political talk in this world, like so much else in the Restoration, is simultaneously denied and practiced. It's a regime based on denial, on the repression of historical evolution and the fact of the Revolution, yet always haunted by that which has been repressed.

Stendhal himself, with a superior awareness, both denies the interest of politics and asserts its necessity. He rules out representing the July Revolution (it of course wasn't part of his original plan for a novel half written before that revolution took place—but it would have fit perfectly with his theme), then smuggles it back in perspectivally. The secret-note episode is in this regard the most noticeable moment in the second half of the novel, which represents a world in the perspective of its doom—its coming overthrow by the forces of youth and of movement, the dynamic created by repression, pressures which will sooner or later break through the surface.

The idea of a secret note recording a conspiracy aiming at an occult action of history also very much appeals to Stendhal's overall conspiracy theory of history. He loved "secret memoirs" of Old Regime court intrigues and Napoleonic warfare (Julien's favorite book, we recall, is the *Mémorial de Sainte-Hélène*, Napoleon's memoirs set down by his aide-de-camp Las Cases), and when the new regime created by the July Revolution finally gave him a diplomatic post, as French consul in the Italian town of Civita-Vecchia, he often sent dispatches to the Ministry of Foreign Affairs that were filled with tales of intrigue and conspiracy—so much so that his superiors apparently regarded them as somewhat novelistic and unreliable. Perhaps it is inevitable that a novelist, concerned with the place of the individual destiny within the social order, should see politics and history as determined by the machinations of actors whose role is hidden from the public. In any case, such a view of history makes it more compatible with the novel and more interesting.

The place of the secret-note episode in the plot of *The Red and the Black* also bears thinking about. Julien is at the nadir of his relations with Mathilde, apparently rejected forever as her lover, and now he is as well the agent of a political conspiracy that stands in direct opposition to his own political aspirations. Yet after delivering the secret note to the great personage just over the French border (presumably in the German town of Mainz), as he awaits his reply in Strasbourg, he encounters the Russian Prince Korasoff. The prince gives him a lesson in how to win back the heart of Mathilde—through addressing an amorous correspondence to Mme de Fervaques—and puts him on the road to an astonishing success: becoming Mathilde's lover again and then, because of her pregnancy, her fiancé, with a new name and title—M. le chevalier Julien Sorel de La Vernaye—a commission as lieutenant in the hussards (the dream of the Red—the military career—finally realized), a putative new noble father, and nothing more to wish for. Until the letter from Mme de Rênal provokes the final disaster. It's as if the political conspiracy, which has no visible results in the novel, created the conditions for Julien's personal conspiracy for real entry into Restoration society. That conspiracy is both extraordinarily successful and subject to being blown to bits by the pistol shots fired at Mme de Rênal, an event that, once again, seems to be a displaced representation of revolution, enacted in the personal rather than the political sphere.

The more one thinks about the initially baffling episode of the secret note, then, the more it discloses its importance in the design and the meaning of the novel as a whole. That it should be initially baffling is of course part of what it is about: the obscure and hidden forces that motivate history and narrative. In one view the machinations of these aristocratic conspirators are about as silly as Julien's courtship of Mme de Fervaques using the volume of ready-made letters supplied by Korasoff. In another view Julien's conspiracy to win back Mathilde by the Korasoff method has the effective force of a conspiracy to change French history. Both plans for action respond to a wish to change the world by exerting intelligence on exterior reality. Both hence concern the intellectual's relation to power. And a novel that claims to be a "mirror" of its time, a "chronicle" of 1830, is very much an intellectual's meditation on the powers that move persons and events. The episode of the secret note may give us a glimpse into the novelist's workshop: into how Stendhal generates the ideas that become plots that claim to motivate action in the world. What we have to expect with Stendhal—one of the most oblique and elusive of novelists—is that the effects of the plots may not come where expected. They may be displaced, in the wrong place—like a pistol shot in the midst of a concert, like a revolution that is absent from the representation but present in the representing.

A Romantic Approach to *The Red and the Black*

Mary Ellen Birkett

My primary goal in teaching Stendhal's *The Red and the Black* is to introduce undergraduates to a fictive world where nothing is absolute or even one-dimensional: from the novel's title (two incompatible, symbolic colors) to its structure (two parts, each containing two settings) to its style (narration interrupted by the double thrust of ironic authorial interventions) to its characters (two heroines, Mme de Rênal and Mathilde de La Mole, and a complex protagonist, Julien Sorel) to its plot (two denouements). We read Stendhal's novel and discuss its many ambiguities within the context of an upper-level French course on the Romantic revolution.

Identity and Opposition

Because of its inner contradictions, French Romanticism provides a framework for *The Red and the Black* that legitimates the bewilderment students often feel on first encountering the text. By 1830, when the novel appeared, French Romantics had been trying for more than a decade to define their doctrine and aesthetics. They all knew that to be a Romantic meant to defy tradition, to reject the classical unities, and to pit inspiration, sincerity, and sentiment against reason and understanding. They all believed that Romanticism was an attempt to arrive at truth by way of literature rather than science or philosophy. But there were few other tenets on which all Romantics could agree.

Stendhal's own attitudes toward Romanticism were equally elusive. In *Racine and Shakespeare* (1823–25) Stendhal equated Romanticism with whatever, in art or life, might give to living peoples "in the existing state of their habits and beliefs, the greatest possible pleasure" (qtd. in Hollier 632). However, in the *projet d'article* that he wrote for *The Red and the Black*, he admitted that his overriding aim was "to disengage as far as possible from the expectations and conventions liable to be imposed on him by his public" (Jefferson 113, *Reading*).

Stendhal's writings focus nonetheless on the discovery of the self that characterizes French Romanticism of the 1820s. But they have none of the disenchantment of Constant's and Musset's prose, the stoicism of Vigny's poetry, the intimacy of Sainte-Beuve's verse, or the spiritualization of Lamartine's works. And if Stendhal's Romanticism reflects the duality promulgated by Hugo's preface to *Cromwell* (1827), it nevertheless rejects Romantic historicism and grandiloquence of the sort practiced by Chateaubriand and Hugo himself. Indeed, Stendhal's art differs from so many aspects of idealistic Romanticism that Eric Auerbach considers him the "founder" of "the serious realism of modern times," in the sense that *The Red and the Black* "would be almost incomprehensible without a most accurate and detailed knowledge of the political situation, the social stratification, and the economic circumstances of a perfectly definite historical moment, namely, that in which France found itself just before the July Revolution [of 1830]" (Stendhal, *Red* 444, 443, 436).

Eye and "I"

The opening pages of *The Red and the Black* do in fact introduce the sociologically precise world that makes the novel a "Chronicle of 1830" (1; 1.1). The picturesque town of Verrières is set in an alpine landscape. A narrator, in the guise of a tourist from Paris (24; 2; 1.1), details Verrières's geographic situation, the state of its industrialization, the self-interest that governs its politics, and the petty rivalries that dominate its society. His clipped, dry voice dispenses with Romantic rhetoric: gone are Rousseau's idyllic internalization of the exterior world, Lamartine's pathetic fallacies, Hugo's verbal virtuosity.

However, from the beginning, Verrières is a world where first impressions are not to be trusted. When the narrator remarks that "la petite ville de Verrières peut passer pour l'une des plus jolies de la Franche-Comté" (23; 1.1), he suggests that appearances are unreliable indicators of truth. The phrase "peut passer" is the clue that this depiction of Verrières might not be realistic, for it proffers opinions rather than facts: "The little town of Verrières *must be* one of the prettiest in Franche-Comté" (1); "*can rightly be considered*" (Pearson 81); "*may be regarded as*" (Turnell 141); "*might pass for*" (my trans.). Stendhal's realism of reflection—the "miroir qu'on promène le long d'un chemin" 'mirror being carried along a highway' (100; 60; 1.13)— depends on the presence of an "I" who interprets visual images as much as it relies on the eye that perceives them.

Stendhal's own interpretive "I" does not reveal itself with the self-indulgence that many Romantics practiced; instead, it weaves its vision of the world subtly into the text of *The Red and the Black*. For instance, frequent authorial commentaries accompanied by constant shifts in point of view pass the reader from a ubiquitous narrator to an opinionated authorial voice whose interventions—sometimes direct, sometimes indirect—further compromise the novel's realism. Verrières is an example, for there authorial commentary confirms the narrator's impression of smallness as pettiness, not prettiness (25; 3; 1.1): "*Rapporter du revenu* est la raison qui décide de tout dans cette petite ville qui vous semblait si jolie" '*Yielding a return* decides everything in this little town which at first seemed so attractive to you' (29; 6; 1.2). This technique both disguises Stendhal's "I" and brings the authorial point of view to bear on what the "eye" sees.

Stendhal also simultaneously introduces his "I" and shields it through irony, the figure of speech in which contrasts between content and context point, again indirectly, to the presence of subjective values. For example, words that appear to condemn indicate authorial approbation: "naïf" 'naive' is a synonym for *innocent*; "vif" 'high-spirited' indicates spontaneity and sincerity; "imprévu" 'unexpected,' energy that cannot be stifled by conventions; "sot" 'foolish,' awkwardness, timidity, emotion, and generosity; "fou" and "folie" 'madness,' imagination, grandeur, grace, and capacity for love (Brombert, *Stendhal et la voie* 51–52; Felman 76–77). Other examples of contradictions between what words say and what they connote for Stendhal at times intensify irony into sarcasm, as when the ecclesiastical society of the seminary at Besançon is indicted for worshipping only "l'idée sublime *d'argent comptant*" 'the sublime idea of *cash on the line*' (213; 146; 1.26) or when the pretentious vanity of Paris's aristocratic salons becomes a metaphor for all life in France under the Restoration government:

> Pourvu qu'on ne plaisantât ni de Dieu, ni des prêtres, ni du roi, ni des gens en place, ni des artistes protégés par la cour, ni de tout ce qui est établi; pourvu qu'on ne dît du bien ni de Béranger, ni des journaux de l'opposition, ni de Voltaire, ni de Rousseau, ni de tout ce qui se permet un peu de franc-parler; pourvu surtout qu'on ne parlât jamais politique, on pouvait librement raisonner de tout. (287)
>
> Provided one didn't joke about God, or the priests, or the king, or the men in power, or the artists protected by the court, or about any part of the establishment; provided one said nothing good about Béranger, or the opposition newspapers, or Voltaire, or Rousseau, or of anything which involves the use of free speech; provided, above all, that one never talked politics, one could talk freely about anything whatever. (202; 2.4)

Irony and sarcasm instill Stendhal's opinions so thoroughly into *The Red and the Black* that even the novel's realism is not indifferent to the claims of Romantic subjectivity.

"Amour de Cœur" and "Amour de Tête"

Stendhal's historically accurate and, at the same time, highly judgmental portrait of Restoration France accounts for tensions between individual and society that are fundamental to the dynamics of both the Romantic movement in general and *The Red and the Black* in particular. Not only is Julien Sorel "l'homme malheureux en guerre avec toute la société" 'an unhappy man at war with his whole society' (364; 263; 2.13): the women who fall in love with him have little affinity with the world in which they live.

Mme de Rênal's aversion to her provincial milieu is intuitive. She never questions or seeks alternatives to Verrières's mores; she simply disregards them: "elle ne donnait aucune attention aux actions des personnages grossiers au milieu desquels le hasard l'avait jetée" 'she paid no attention to the behavior of the gross creatures amid whom fortune had thrust her' (58; 29; 1.7). Her quickly forgotten convent education, "le naturel et la vivacté d'esprit" 'the instinctive quickness of her wit' (58–59; 29; 1.7), her "manière de vivre tout intérieure" 'whole inner life of her own' (59; 29; 1.7), her modesty and "la pureté de cette âme naïve" 'the purity of this innocent spirit' (90; 52; 1.11) make her Rousseau's ideal, maternal woman. Indeed, "[j]usqu'à l'arrivée de Julien, elle n'avait réellement eu d'attention que pour ses enfants" 'Until Julien came she had really paid no attention to anyone except her children' (59; 29; 1.7). Her first reaction to Julien, whom her husband has hired to be their children's tutor, is compassion, because she sees him solely as a "jeune paysan presque encore enfant, extrêmement pâle et qui venait de pleurer" 'a young peasant, scarcely more than a child, very pale and showing traces of recent tears' (48; 21; 1.6). She is totally incapable of foreseeing how extraordinary are the love and happiness that Julien will bring to her:

> Madame de Rênal n'avait aucune expérience de la vie, [. . . son âme était] égarée par une passion qu'elle n'avait jamais éprouvée. Elle était trompée, mais à son insu [. . . L]a présence d'un bonheur que jamais elle n'avait même rêvé, lui donn[a] des transports d'amour et de folle gaieté. (92, 90)

> Mme. de Rênal had no experience of life. [. . . Her soul was] haunted by a passion it had never known before. She was deceived, but unknowingly. [. . .] The presence of a joy such as she had never dreamed of, inspired in her transports of affection and wild gaiety. (54; 52; 1.11)

She naively allows her confessor to rewrite the story of her passion as a sordid tale of seduction (495–96; 361–62; 2.35). She is wrong; her passivity and lack of awareness bring condemnation, imprisonment and death to the man she loves.

In contrast, Mathilde's rebellion against Parisian aristocracy is willful and deliberate. Where Mme de Rênal is governed by her heart, Mathilde is governed by her head: "Madame de Rênal trouvait des raisons pour faire ce que son cœur lui dictait: cette jeune fille du grand monde ne laisse son cœur s'émouvoir que lorsqu'elle s'est prouvé par bonnes raisons qu'il doit être ému" 'Mme. de Rênal always found reasons to do what her heart dictated; this high-society girl lets her heart be moved only when she has found proofs based upon good logic that it ought to be moved' (467; 340; 2.30; see also 397; 288; 2.19). Mathilde expresses opposition to the monotony of salon life through intellectual flight into one of the historical periods the Romantics esteemed for its spontaneity and originality, the French Renaissance (Hollier 639). As she puts it, "Les guerres de la Ligue sont les temps héroïques de la France. [. . .] Convenez qu'il y avait moins d'égoïsme et de petitesse. J'aime ce siècle" 'The wars of the League were the heroic days of France. [. . .] You must agree, there was less self-glorification and pettiness then. I love that century' (342; 245–46; 2.10). She, Mathilde-Marguerite, venerates the dramatic legend of her ancestor Boniface de La Mole, who was beheaded in 1574 for political insurgency, and his mistress Marguerite de Navarre, who subsequently buried his head herself at midnight (339–40; 243–44; 2.10). Her genius for "singularité" 'strangeness' (324; 231; 2.8; see also 407; 296; 2.20) attracts Julien, a stranger to Parisian society (286; 201;

2.3). He ends up falling in love with her, fathering her child, and gaining a new, aristocratic identity solely because he enables her noble bloodline to continue.

Mathilde's rebellion satisfies Julien's desire for advancement and appeals to his imagination but in the end exhausts him: "à vrai dire il était fatigué d'héroïsme. C'eût été à une tendresse simple, naïve et presque timide, qu'il se fût trouvé sensible, tandis qu'au contraire il fallait toujours l'idée d'un public et *des autres* à l'âme hautaine de Mathilde" 'to tell the truth, he was getting tired of heroics. He would have been responsive to a simple, a naïve and almost timid approach, whereas Mathilde's lofty soul always had to be conscious of a public and *other people*' (516; 378; 2.39). She too is wrong, for her insatiable need to impress on others that she is a tragic heroine leads her to confuse love with self-love:

> Tous les jours elle se félicitait du parti qu'elle avait pris de se donner une grande passion. Cet amusement a bien des dangers, pensait-elle. Tant mieux! mille fois tant mieux! Sans grande passion, j'étais languissante d'ennui au plus beau moment de la vie, de seize ans jusqu'à vingt. (355)
>
> Every day she congratulated herself on her decision to indulge in a great passion. It's a dangerous game, she thought; so much the better! A thousand times better! Without a great passion, I was pining away from boredom during the best period of a girl's life, from sixteen to twenty. (255; 2.12)

Mme de Rênal, whose heart sets her, despite herself, against the norms of her provincial society, and Mathilde, whose fearlessness brings her to open defiance of the proprieties of her aristocratic world, represent two kinds of Romanticism: one sentimental, the other intellectual. The contrast of these two approaches shows the inner contradictions of Romantic ideals. Nevertheless, the way in which each woman creates her own destiny suggests that the way to rise above society's constraints in 1830 is to live life as a Romantic.

Ambition and Impulse

Romantic ambivalence extends as well to the novel's protagonist, Julien Sorel. Julien is a contradictory young man, intelligent and awkward, imaginative and calculating, tender and arrogant, sensitive and unstable. Although timid, he is too conscious of his own superiority to hold any but the highest ambitions (132–33, 381; 83, 277; 1.18, 2.16), requiring the greatest energy (351; 253; 2.12). Even that which motivates Julien is equivocal:

> Qui eût pu deviner que cette figure de jeune fille, si pâle et si douce, cachait la résolution inébranlable de s'exposer à mille morts plutôt que de ne pas faire fortune!

> Pour Julien, faire fortune, c'était d'abord sortir de Verrières; il abhorrait sa patrie. Tout ce qu'il y voyait glaçait son imagination.
>
> Dès sa première enfance, il avait eu des moments d'exaltation. Alors il songeait avec délices qu'un jour il serait présenté aux jolies femmes de Paris, il saurait attirer leur attention par quelque action d'éclat. Pourquoi ne serait-il pas aimé de l'une d'elles, comme Bonaparte, pauvre encore, avait été aimé de la brillante Mme de Beauharnais? (45)
>
> Who could have guessed that that girlish face, so pale and soft, concealed an unshakable resolution to die a thousand deaths rather than fail to make his fortune!
>
> For Julien, making his fortune meant, first of all, getting out of Verrières; he loathed his home town. Everything he saw there chilled his imagination.
>
> Ever since he was a boy, he had had moments of secret exultation. He dreamed with joy of one day being introduced to the pretty women of Paris; he would, of course, attract their admiration with some brilliant action. Why should he not win the love of one of them, just as Bonaparte, when still young, had been loved by the brilliant Mme. de Beauharnais? (19; 1.5)

The Romantic figure of young Napoleon, "maître du monde" 'master of the world' (46; 19; 1.5), presides over Julien's hope of winning love and distinction. To achieve his ambitions, Julien adopts a Napoleonic strategy: aggressive offensives (as tutor, he breaches the walls of M. de Rênal's estate; as seminarist, the gates of the theological college at Besançon; as secretary, the portal of the Hotel de La Mole); transgression of class barriers (he rises from provincial bourgeoisie to Parisian aristocracy); and finally usurpation (he seduces the wife of a provincial nobleman and then takes as his mistress the only daughter of an aristocrat). However, Julien's energetic maneuvers turn out to be less effective than do other people's seemingly unrelated emotionally motivated actions, which become turning points in Julien's life. For instance, his first step out of the working-class milieu of the sawmill occurs because M. de Rênal becomes jealous of M. Valenod (33–34; 9–10; 1.3); his escape from the seminary into the La Mole household takes place because the abbé Pirard unpredictably intervenes on his behalf (244; 170; 1.30); his aristocratic rank and commission in the army result from the marquis de La Mole's pride and generosity (490; 358; 2.34).

Similarly, the dreams of heroism that impel Julien vigorously but inappropriately to apply notions of soldierly duty to courting Mme de Rênal (91, 103, 111–12; 53, 62, 69; 1.11, 1.13, 1.15) and to mount a quasi-military campaign to overcome Mathilde's vacillations (445, 467, 470; 325, 341, 343; 2.25, 2.30, 2.31) succeed mainly because they too are promoted by unforeseen outbreaks of emotion: namely Julien's own. He wins Mme de Rênal's affection when his tearful timidity erupts (112; 69; 1.15), and Mathilde falls in love with him when he unguardedly shows a lack of interest in what her social world values (289; 203–04; 2.4) and even in her brilliance and daring (547, 551; 401, 404; 2.44, 2.45). Julien does in the end succeed through the Napoleonic model of conquest—insufficient and even comic as it occasionally appears—because it puts him in a position in which emotional energies secure for him what he wants.

Success so gained is, of course, precarious. On learning from Mathilde that he has been named lieutenant in the army with the title M. le chevalier Julien Sorel de La Vernaye, Julien finds fulfilled "l'ambition de toute sa vie" 'the ambition of his whole life' (491; 359; 2.34). Although he dares to think, "[M]on roman est fini, et à moi seul le mérite" '[N]ow at last the novel of my career is over, and the credit is all mine' (491; 359; 2.34), he could not be more wrong. The idea that his story has ended is as false as his belief that his title and brilliant rise through the social hierarchy are attributable exclusively to his own conscious energies. Indeed, even as he indulges in "transports de l'ambition la plus effrénée" 'transports of unbridled ambition' (494; 361; 2.35), an impulsive act brings that ambition to ruin: Julien shoots Mme de Rênal as she prays in the church at Verrières (496–97; 362–63; 2.35). The same impulsiveness that served Julien's ambition now betrays it. His shocking deed demonstrates more eloquently than words can that a Romantic way of life is vulnerable to the same passionate energies that define it.

Partial Truths and Moral Integrity

Julien's assassination attempt is prompted, but not explained, by Mme de Rênal's letter to the marquis de La Mole depicting her lover as a seducer motivated by greed (495–96; 361–62; 2.35). Its skillful use of half-truths betrays Julien. His violent reaction to this superficially accurate yet profoundly false image of him delivers him to prison, to trial by jury, and ultimately to the guillotine.

In the solitude of his prison cell Julien begins an inner journey on which, for the first time, he experiences emotions untainted by the desire for advancement:

> L'ambition était morte en son cœur, une autre passion y était sortie de ses cendres; il l'appelait le remords d'avoir assassiné Mme de Rênal. Dans le fait, il en était éperdument amoureux. Il trouvait un bonheur singulier quand, laissé absolument seul et sans crainte d'être interrompu, il pouvait se livrer tout entier au souvenir des journées heureuses qu'il avait passées jadis à Verrières ou à Vergy. (517)

> Ambition was dead within his heart; another passion rose from its ashes; he called it remorse for having tried to kill Mme. de Rênal.
>
> As a matter of fact, he was madly in love with her. He found an extraordinary happiness when, in absolute solitude and without any fear of interruption, he could devote himself entirely to memories of the happy days he had once spent at Verrières or Vergy. (379; 2.39)

This remembered happiness, which replaces all his self-interested strivings, endows Julien with a new sense of who he is. Yet when put on trial for his crime, Julien presents only a partially complete portrait of himself to the court: "Messieurs les jurés. [. . .] vous voyez en moi un paysan qui s'est révolté contre la bassesse de sa fortune" 'Gentlemen of the jury. [. . .] you see in me a peasant in open revolt against his humble station' (530; 387; 2.41; see also 341; 245; 2.10). And he insists on a strictly legal, that is, accurate but only half true, interpretation of his crime: "Mme de Rênal avait été pour moi comme une mère. Mon crime est atroce, et il fut *prémédité*. J'ai donc mérité la mort, Messieurs les jurés" 'Mme. de Rênal had been like a mother to me. My crime is atrocious, and it was *premeditated*. I have therefore deserved the death sentence, gentlemen of the jury' (530; 387; 2.41).

Paradoxically, then, the same kind of half-truths that produce Julien's undoing procure for him the nobility that "in the spiritual sense is. [. . .] exactly synonymous with passion" (Girard, "Triangular Desire" 506), for the partial truths he offers to the court bring anew to him Mme de Rênal's love, which now inspires in him an equally selfless "amour fou" 'delirious love' (539; 394; 2.43). All the ambiguities of Julien's character resolve into the spiritual nobility this passion grants to him:

> Jamais cette tête n'avait été aussi poétique qu'au moment où elle allait tomber. Les plus doux moments qu'il avait trouvés jadis dans les bois de Vergy revenaient en foule à sa pensée et avec une extrême énergie. Tout se passa simplement, convenablement, et de sa part sans aucune affectation. (554–55)

> Never had that head been so poetic as at the moment when it was about to fall. The sweetest moments he had ever known in the woods at Vergy came crowding back into his mind, and with immense vividness. Everything proceeded simply, decently, and without the slightest affectation on his part. (407; 2.45)

Here is the true close of Julien's story: not in worldly success but in heroic death, not in the betrayals of self-image but in integrity, not in the falsifications of language but in unspoken poetry.

Inevitably, as narration resumes to frame the silences of Julien's death, so too do partial truths. After Julien's beheading Mathilde realizes the dramatic fantasy of herself as Marguerite de Navarre kissing her lover's severed head and burying his body (556; 407–08; 2.45). Her funerary tribute underscores the role of imagination in Julien's life but cannot do justice to the scope and depth of his passions. And as Mme de Rênal, dying, embraces her children for the last time (556; 408; 2.45), she symbolically enfolds Julien in her love, but the imaginative side of his character eludes even her tender grasp. Furthermore, the final word of *The Red and the Black*—"enfants" 'children' (556; 408; 2.45)

—leaves unresolved the question of what holds most true in a world where passion, poetry, and integrity no longer exist. Is it the selfless love of Mme de Rênal, who has lived for Julien as if he were one of her beloved children? Or is it the vitality of Mathilde, for whose unborn child, Julien's heir, *The Red and the Black* reserves an enigmatic fate?

For all the unanswered questions surrounding *The Red and the Black*'s ending, its final pages nonetheless convey a strong indication of what Stendhal admires: subjectivity, individualism, energy, courage, imagination, the rejection of society's vanity, the happiness of reciprocated love, and the nobility of integrity. Indeed, these qualities—Romantic in essence—underlie more than just the enigma of the denouement: they frame—without explaining or totally encompassing—the novel's many ambiguities. Their widespread presence confirms that Stendhal wrote *The Red and the Black* with attention to Romantic motifs and, even more important, that he wrote with respect for the imperfect, vulnerable, yet ennobling, redeeming moral values of Romanticism itself.

Reading Appearances: The Opening Chapters of *The Red and the Black*

Catharine Savage Brosman

Among the multiple ways in which Stendhal strikes readers as an extremely perspicacious and still modern novelist, a significant one is his emphasis on the role of appearances in social functioning (on both a small and a large scale) and on the relation, sometimes obvious, sometimes subtle, between appearances and reality. The concerns he raises can be subjective (Does one really love? What is genuine feeling?), psychological or social (Are these people and institutions truly as they appear?), or moral (Is this act truly genuine, good, or, in Stendhalian terms, useful?—a question that leads to examination of the act's causes and consequences). To use a word that Stendhal did not know but that some later admirers, such as Nietzsche and Camus, would have found fitting, he even raises existential issues (Who am I? Is this human subject authentic?).

By no means, of course, is Stendhal the first French author to give certain of these topics a major place. One feature of seventeenth-century French classicism, with its preeminent concern for social dynamics, is this very issue of appearances and their crucial importance in a self-conscious and structured upper-class society. Countless characters in drama and fiction of the period are concerned with their *gloire*—their social status, their reputation, or how they appear to others. While some writers, such as Descartes and Corneille, a dramatist whom Stendhal admired for the importance he gave to duty, honor, and integrity, emphasize making the inner person correspond to the outer reputation—that is, making reality and appearance coincide—other writers are concerned simply with appearance, and the challenge of those driven by passion or vice is to conceal appearance. Numerous maxims of La Rochefoucauld concern the distance, which may be psychological or social, between what appears, or what one believes, and what is: "On n'est jamais si heureux ou si malheureux qu'on s'imagine" 'One is never so happy or so unhappy as one imagines'; "Nous aurions souvent honte de nos plus belles actions si le monde voyait tous les motifs qui les produisent" 'We would often be ashamed of our finest acts if people saw all the motives that produce them' (17, 96; my trans.).

In seventeenth-century social relationships, the value of appearances is enormous, underlying much of social mechanics; the elaborate manners and usages of the court and the town imply and act out this value. When La Rochefoucauld writes, "L'hypocrisie est un hommage que le vice rend à la vertu" 'Hypocrisy is a homage that vice pays to virtue' (56; my trans.), he underlines both the distance between vice and virtue and the social strength of the latter, which demands at least ostensible allegiance. In Molière's *Le misanthrope* a central issue is whether recourse to courtesy and other social usages are, when not heartfelt, compatible with virtue; Alceste argues that to give a false impression (as when one praises a mediocre sonnet to please its author) is unacceptable, while Philinte says that society depends on such usages and that to say always what one thinks, to show always the inner reality, would render human relationships impossible. However, in classical literature the absolute monarchy was not questioned, whereas Stendhal's attacks on the benighted and reactionary society of the Restoration implies criticism of the last Bourbon kings and their ossified structures.

More than 160 years after the high moments of French classicism, Stendhal took up in radically different form some of its themes, which had never disappeared entirely from authors' concerns (Voltaire was sensitive to the question of dissimulation and dupery, as *Candide* and other stories show, and Rousseau was in some ways a latter-day Alceste) but had been eclipsed, particularly owing to the powerful waves of Romanticism in the early nineteenth century, which brought to the forefront the concern for individual feeling and made the subject, rather than society, the supreme measure of everything. *The Red and the Black* is built on the conflict between this Romantic individualism and the rule of appearances in a society in which distances between what was and what should be were often enormous and obvious and in which the social structures and usages of the ancien régime, which had confined hypocrisy to accustomed forms, had been both exaggerated under the Restoration and undermined by the changes of the Revolution and the Napoleonic period. This conflict resulted in class paranoia among conservatives. Stendhal's concern in his major novels with placing his characters in social structures (of the sort he knew well) that bear down on individuals, thus obliging them to react, sets him apart from some earlier writers of the Romantic period, who placed their characters in solitude, and makes him an heir of the great classic *moralistes* (writers on society, mores, and human motivation). His imaginary universe differs from theirs, however, in its materialist, nonmetaphysical perspective and its grounding in sense knowledge, an outlook that Stendhal had adopted from philosophers of the eighteenth and early nineteenth centuries such as Condillac, Destutt de Tracy, and Cabanis, who stressed sense impressions and physiology.

While the entire novel is concerned with these issues of what seems and what is, which constitute one aspect of its dualism, Stendhal takes particular care to draw attention to them and illuminate them in the early chapters, giving those who will read further a lesson in reading both his novel and the society and characters it depicts. The depiction frequently involves irony (which can be defined loosely as any qualification to the discourse of the text brought by the text itself): in these chapters literary irony (Stendhal's particular mode of stepping away from what appears—or what has just been said—to scrutinize and correct it) often conveys social irony, as Stendhal qualifies social structures and mechanisms through disclosure of their workings.

A short digression that might be pertinent to a classroom presentation is in order. Although students often find that the France of 1830 seems chronologically and spatially distant and so foreign that they are repulsed by the novel, present-day industrialized society bears significant resemblances to the France depicted by Stendhal. In France and in English-speaking countries class structures are less rigid and there is greater political freedom, but, if one considers variables such as family, education, race, and region, it is clear that some of the same constraints on individual action and obstacles to success exist. Stendhal speaks unfavorably of popular democracy, including that in America, pointing out (1.23) that public opinion in a city such as New York, just as in a small French provincial town, is tyrannical. Social features such as political corruption and graft (which are at the heart of 1.3 and recur later), the struggle for power between political parties (here, the ultras, i.e., extremely conservative royalists, and the liberals, i.e., those of whatever stripe, Bonapartists, Jacobins, and others, who oppose the Bourbon monarchy of Charles X), political interference by the church (perfectly legal under the monarchy but insidious and tyrannical), competition for position and honors, and connections between money and power are so current that any reflective reader can find parallels.

For instance, most readers will recognize such types as the dishonest nouveau riche M. Valenod, who has acquired wealth through skimming off funds intended for public institutions and whose vulgarity cannot be corrected (he and his wife tell their guests the price of their furniture and their wine). The need to follow the correct political line and to avoid offending those who can be of service or are in authority is felt in every social and economic situation. Ceremonies such as that in the church at Bray-le-Haut (1.18), in which the power of state and church, embodied in king, bishop, and retinue, impresses the spectators deeply, have contemporary parallels in huge campaign rallies; and students will be familiar with political maneuvering such as that carried out by M. de Rênal when he wishes to have M. de Moirod promoted to the position of mayor's first assistant so that Moirod will disregard improprieties exercised partially in Rênal's favor (1.17). Even in present-day societies, denunciations of rivals (as when M. de Rênal is said to have been responsible for unjust arrests and worse [1.21]) are not unknown, and it is common for someone to turn against an old friend for social advantage (again, M. de Rênal, in the same chapter). As for the rivalry between M. Valenod and M. de Rênal—the former showing off his splendid Norman horses, the latter the private tutor he has engaged for his children—it is a version of what all today should recognize: the drive to dominate through the prestige conferred by display of material goods and other advantages.

The opening pages of *The Red and the Black* reveal a society whose power structures are built on money and perceived status within a reactionary monarchy supported by the church. While Verrières is said, in the initial sentence, to be one of the prettiest cities of the province and the attractive natural features of the town are enumerated at once, the emphasis is on industrial prosperity, including that of the mayor, M. de Rênal. The novelist presents him as he appears; not named until his nail factory has been described, he is viewed as a stranger would see him: "un grand homme à l'air affairé et important" 'a big man looking busy and important,' "chevalier de plusieurs ordres" 'He wears the ribbons of several orders.' The observer (that is, the reader) may draw appropriate conclusions, which the novelist shapes somewhat by adding that the figure has "un certain air de contentement de soi et de suffisance" 'a certain air of self-satisfaction, perhaps of sufficiency' (24; 2; 1.1). Similarly, a fine and beautifully situated estate described immediately thereafter, whose view "fait oublier au voyageur l'atmosphère empestée des petits intérêts d'argent dont il commence à être asphyxié" 'makes the traveler forget the pestilent atmosphere of petty financial worries in which he has been close to stifling' (25; 3; 1.1), is identified as the mayor's only after it has been perceived.

The association between this lovely property and the complacent mayor, whose true concerns are those of his town—lucre and status—alerts readers to contradictions that characterize the entire section on Verrières. One learns that the house was built not with inherited wealth, although M. de Rênal comes from an old and distinguished family, but rather with profits from the nail factory. Yet since 1815 (the final fall of Napoleon and return of the Bourbon monarchy) he has been ashamed of being an industrial magnate, although he uses his money in ways both ostentatious and self-serving. The examples Stendhal gives include his successful contracting for a sustaining wall (which suggests class fortification [Turnell 145]) to shore up the public promenade, a wall that he imposed on the municipal council with help from Paris and that earned him another award for his lapel; his rerouting to his advantage of the public stream; and his exchange of land with old Sorel (trading four lots for one). All the examples illustrate M. de Rênal's concern for appearances, his recourse to political patronage (after elections in the 1820s), and his fatuity: for old Sorel, who has no social pretentions whatsoever (and thus is less vulnerable to vanity) and depends only on his wits (that is, he has a greater need), has driven a hard bargain, seeing how much M. de Rênal desired the terrain; only Sorel's smile later suggests that the price could have been lower.

Stendhal concludes the first chapter with a few words on the tyranny in Verrières of public opinion, of reputation, even among those who give lip service to the egalitarian principles of the Revolution. This is the stage on which Julien Sorel must play his first role, before he moves to the seminary and then Paris, that "théâtre des grandes choses" 'theater of the world' (245; 172; 1.30). Before presenting his hero, the novelist has alerted his readers to the principal elements of social dynamism with which Julien, like everyone, must deal: he invites them to look behind masks and façades, to identify the motives of actions, discover the complicated manipulations that produce apparently simple results, and assess the truth of professed positions. As Julien reflects much later, "Tout ce qu'il en voyait pouvait n'être qu'une apparence" 'Whatever he had seen of it might be just a pretense' (317; 257; 2.13). Just as, fearful of being duped, he constantly examines words and acts—including his own—the reader is not to take everything at face value. In this society at once politically reactionary and driven by money, Gresham's law would seem to apply, bad money, motives, and character driving away good.

The word *hypocrisy*, used repeatedly, is thus to be weighed with care: while pejorative at first glance, it must be assessed with regard to the milieu and the circumstances in which it is exercised and must be viewed as a means, perhaps a legitimate one, to survive under tyranny and indeed among others' hypocrisies: it can be an antihypocrisy. As Gide, an admirer of Stendhal, wrote in *Les faux-monnayeurs* (*The Counterfeiters*, 1925), "Dans un monde où chacun triche, c'est l'homme vrai qui fait figure de charlatan" 'In a world where everyone cheats, it is the genuine man who looks bogus' (421; my trans.).

Julien, often and justly considered a Romantic hero par excellence, has the tender soul of a poet, moved by beauty in nature and by goodness in actions. An outsider because he is so different in character and physique from his father and brothers (there are suggestions later—although they may simply be a ruse of others or a projection of Stendhal's antipaternal feelings—that he may be illegitimate, thus not what he seems and even more a social pariah), he incarnates, at times, the Romantic loner; he adores Rousseau's *Confessions*, flees his brothers, reads alone at night, and takes refuge in the forest, where in one episode he stands on a high promontory, dominating all nature below him. His sensibility is touched by children, by Mme de Rênal's beauty, by a lovely evening. In this respect he is very close to the mood of early French Romanticism, illustrated in the prose of Chateaubriand and Senancour and the verse of Lamartine; as befitting a sensitive man of the time, he weeps easily. His Romantic taste for nature includes the Stendhalian concept of "le naturel" 'the natural,' which involves nature strictly speaking (gardens, landscapes) but also aesthetics and a moral element, including the spontaneous and sincere (which makes him appreciate Mme de Rênal), as opposed to the artificial and dissembling.

A child of the 1820s, however, he has also been touched, thanks in part to his old major-surgeon friend, by memory of the Napoleonic era, with its great military deeds and its trappings of glory; readers discover early that his favorite book is the *Mémorial de Sainte-Hélène*, which, with Rousseau and the bulletins from Bonaparte's Grande Armée, constitutes his first library. Possessed of energy—unlike the typically languid Romantic hero—he wants to be a man of action, not one of contemplation. This ambition is commensurate with his talents and consistent with the post-1789 transformation of France from an absolute monarchy and a feudal class system to a society involving popular representation and "a social hierarchy" based on money. It is useful to note that Stendhal's frequent references to Julien's *génie*, or genius, need not be taken to mean only extraordinary intelligence or inventiveness, though certainly Julien has a quick mind and an exceptional memory; the French word, suggesting special aptitude, can apply in such fields as politics and the military in addition to arts and sciences; and as Stendhal uses it, sometimes in reflections by Mme de Rênal, it suggests brilliance in speech, conduct, insight, and particularly character.

In practice, however, during the period under consideration, the individual freedoms assured by the 1789 Revolution, which even the Restoration had not dared curtail entirely in principle, were so limited as to mean little for someone without wealth or some other conferred power. "Enrichissez-vous" 'Get rich!' the nineteenth-century historian and politician Guizot said (qtd. in Brogan 90). The recurring vocabulary of combat in *The Red and the Black* can be explained in part by Stendhal's taste for military metaphors, but it also conveys the centrality of social and economic struggle in the novel and the nineteenth century. Given Julien's resolution to advance, there is only one route, that of the church, since military glory (of which, nevertheless, he continues to dream and which he judges honorable) has been brought to an end with Napoleon's defeat, and there is no other outlet or *carrière ouverte aux talents* (career opened to talents). (The enthusiasm that Stendhal attributes to Julien for the army and Napoleon's achievements may surprise present-day readers, skeptical about the notion of military honor and accustomed to view Napoleon as a tyrant and war as disastrous and inhumane; Stendhal's ethics did not include pacifism.)

Thus Julien has taken theology lessons with the abbé Chélan, learned Latin, memorized the New Testament (and Joseph de Maistre's *Du pape*, an extremely conservative volume), and assumed a mask of piety, all as a means of rising in the world. Students are often put off, shocked by this choice, because they do not conceive of the clerical life as a means of acquiring money. Furthermore, religious hypocrisy seems worse than others, approaching sacrilege; Julien must be a monster. However, for centuries it had been customary for families, often the most distinguished, to send a son into the priesthood, partially to protect the rights of primogeniture but often also to acquire family power; bishops and archbishops, whose secular and political influence were frequently enormous, came of such families. Two great political figures of France in the seventeenth century, Cardinals Richelieu and Retz, afford famous examples of the often successful drive for wealth and power among the clergy. The custom had not disappeared: readers will discover that M. de La

Mole has arranged for his nephew to be named bishop of Agde despite the nephew's youth. One may ask whether, if faced with so few choices as Julien has, today's readers would wish to forsake all ambition and, rejecting even the appearance of compromise, resign themselves to utter obscurity, family hostility, and dull routine for their entire lives.

Moreover, Stendhal takes pains to show that hypocrisy and exploitation are the norm among the clergy. The terms *jésuite* and *jésuitique*, which he uses regarding more than one character, call attention to the fact that casuistry (specious reasoning) and dissimulation were made an art by the church. In book 1, chapter 5, one learns that the meddling in civil affairs of a young church vicar, probably a spy for a reactionary party within the church, has led to obstruction of justice. When old abbé Chélan, about whose sincerity and true piety—in the Jansenist mode, that is, he is pure and rigorous—Stendhal leaves no doubt, is removed from his position (another upright priest is similarly threatened later) because he is unwilling to abandon his principles and thus has risked exposing the dishonesty of M. Valenod (1.3), he is replaced by abbé Maslon, who is readier to compromise with the civil authority in their mutual interest and not adverse to helping himself to public property. By a type of preterition, in which the author denies or qualifies something to call attention to it, the narrator (who, speaking in the first person, has called himself a liberal a few lines earlier) observes, in connection with the trees, which are pruned mercilessly, that "les libéraux de l'endroit prétendent, mais ils exagèrent, que la main du jardinier officiel est devenue bien plus sévère depuis que M. le vicaire Maslon a pris l'habitude de s'emparer des produits de la tonte" 'The liberals of the district claim, but they exaggerate, that the official gardener wields a heavier hand since Vicar Maslon has started to engross for himself the products of the shearing' (28; 5; 1.2). The vicar's conduct is no model, but it is less obvious to the reader than Julien's hypocrisy because the vicar is a peripheral character.

Moreover, Stendhal makes it clear in early episodes, such as that in which Julien weeps over the loss of his book, that he is, in truth, not callous. His hypocrisy is of the head, not the heart; he must cultivate it by self-instruction in appearances, including his own, and study of examples around him, as he becomes progressively aware of the contrasts between professed probity and real dishonesty that characterize most of those he can observe— although even after the lessons of Verrières he often has trouble interpreting others' motives. As late as book 1, chapter 22, it is noted that, despite his well-exercised *tartuferie* 'hypocrisy,' "il avait les manières, mais non pas encore le cœur de son état" 'He had the manners, but not yet the feelings, of his social position' (167; 111; 1.22). Physiological reactions, which Stendhal, following his views on the physical basis of sentiment, emphasizes for both Julien and Mme de Rênal, often betray the hero. Julien knows he must hide certain truths—verbs such as *cacher* (to hide), *tromper* (to deceive), *feindre* (to feign), recur frequently, as well as words suggesting the possibility of error, such as *dehors* (exterior), *paraître* (to appear), and *aveuglement* (blindness); significantly, Stendhal uses as an epigraph to book 1, chapter 22 a phrase variously attributed, "La parole a été donnée à l'homme pour cacher sa pensée" 'Speech was given to man to conceal his thoughts' (163; 108). Julien must practice what Jean Starobinski calls the "art of appearing [. . .] a deliberate altering of human relations" (114).

Yet Julien lets his true self burst out frequently; it charms Mme de Rênal during the calm and tender moments they spend together, but he risks betraying himself, as when he praises Napoleon at a dinner attended by priests. His self-punishment (tying down his arm to his chest for two months) is a measure of his severe discipline of his own passions. His visit to the church before he goes to the Rênal estate for the first time, while "utile à son hypocrisie" 'useful to his hypocrisy' (44; 18; 1.5), is chiefly an attempt to gather courage; his terror expresses itself in his trembling, in his emotion at the prefigurative paper relating the execution of Louis Jenrel, and especially in his transforming vision—he sees blood where there are only red reflections (that is, the *appearance* of blood). Following passages, such as his first timid words to Mme de Rênal, reinforce the portrait of a sensitive youth, poor in everything but talents and pride, obliged to beg favors as his only means of rising and sometimes to suffer abuse.

In short, Julien is not what he appears initially—neither to those around him, who are usually taken in by his apparent modesty, humility, and piety, nor to readers who judge him hastily as a scoundrel. When he arrives at Mme de Rênal's gate, his appearance is doubly misleading. She first imagines that this innocent-looking creature who has visibly shed some tears is really a young woman, disguised in men's garb; the idea does not occur to her that he might be the new tutor, who she supposes will be a vulgar, dirty, despotic priest of the sort Stendhal loathed. Learning that it is Julien who will take charge of her children, she is enormously relieved—and rightly so, for he proves to be a devoted and inspiring master. But his ingenuity, which is real, nevertheless hides tremendous pride and a burning ambition, supported by a craftiness not unlike that of his father—although with different aims—which, in certain circumstances, will make him callous and cruel.

The real Julien is not, then, as he may appear at any moment. Where or who is he then? He wonders himself: might he be a coward, a fool, a dupe? a brilliant deceiver and seducer? Although Stendhal continually points out that Julien is acting, playing a role, assuming positions not congenial to him—as when he replies to his father with an air of false piety and when his dread at eating with servants is said to be an effect of having read Rousseau (1.5)—he has assumed these attitudes freely, and, according to the existential perspective that the novel invites, assuming them helps constitute him as a subject: he is what he does. This connection disturbs him at moments when he considers his actions and his future direction; dissociating himself from his acts, he denies that appearances construct him. The conflict between the roles he must play and the implicit real Julien, not yet wholly formed and identified, is central throughout the novel.

Even his affair with Mme de Rênal needs to be assessed in connection with the question of being versus appearing. Though he is outwardly frank and humble with the family, he burns inside, variously, with hurt pride, envy, dismay, and always ambition, and thus his behavior is more often than not deceitful. As students must recognize, neither love nor simple physical attraction makes him take Mme de Rênal's hand, then pursue the attack by further measures; rather, it is a self-imposed duty, an exercise in self-discipline and a means of avoiding scorn and asserting himself. Even at the height of the lovers' happiness, when he drops most of his defenses and allows himself not only to feel but also to express his feelings, he remains vulnerable to any imagined slight from Mme de Rênal and others of her class; in response to anything that seems like coolness or snobbery, he will reassume his own seeming, disguising through outward humility and deference the resentment and ambition that are, without his knowing it, contrary to his deepest nature.

From these multiple ways in which Stendhal reveals the play of reality and appearances, starting with the society depicted in the opening chapters and involving the hero himself, it becomes clear how much, in his fiction, reality is a process rather than a given. His celebrated image of a novel as a mirror carried along a highway emphasizes the linearity of fiction and suggests, suitably, the dimension of development and the question of appearances, although its reflective passivity is inadequate to the psychological reality of Julien's character, which consists so much in reaction. His reactions lead in turn to others' acts and further reactions, through which the real self becomes even more obscured by superimposed layers of pretension and intention, falsehood and truth. In a society characterized by deceit but freed from class definitions that derive authority from divine right, the search for one's essence—no longer a given—is necessarily uncertain. For Julien, it requires an entire novel, since, like those living human beings who reject metaphysical absolutes and question subjective data, he has nothing to go on but appearances, that is, reality as it variously manifests itself; but the reader, to whom the author shows unnoticed aspects of things and may reveal truths omnisciently, can outdistance Julien, knowing from the outset that both error and truth must live by appearances, and that in the manipulation of these appearances and the progressive disclosure of their layers lies one aspect of Stendhal's genius.

A Story of Reading and Writing; or, The Poetics of Self-Reference

James T. Day

> Il faut des spectacles dans les grandes villes, et des romans aux peuples corrompus. [. . .] Jamais fille chaste n'a lu de romans.
>
> Cities require entertainments, and corrupt societies require novels. [. . .] Never has a chaste girl read any novels.
>
> —Jean-Jacques Rousseau, preface to *Julie ou la Nouvelle Héloïse*
>
> Ce roman n'en est pas un. Tout ce qu'il raconte est réellement arrivé.
>
> This novel is not fiction. Everything it relates really happened.
>
> —Stendhal, "Projet d'article sur *Le rouge et le noir*"

Students who first encounter *The Red and the Black* are likely to read it primarily as the tale of a provincial youth who, in the process of seizing opportunities to improve his social station, learns a thing or two about love. The numerous historical and cultural details of setting, the large cast of characters, and the protagonists' sometimes mystifying behavior, may keep students from appreciating the novel's formal complexity. One way to encourage understanding is to investigate how various scenes of reading and writing relate to other aspects of the novel: its exemplarity as a mode of literary realism, its symbolic and psychological dimensions, its devices for plot development, and embedded clues to its reception as a creative literary artifact.

Considering the limited options for transmitting information or providing quiet entertainment in Julien Sorel's world, the total absence of books, letters, gazettes, and so on would be surprising in a novel of the period. Such objects have the same sort of referential value as ladders, horses, dueling pistols, blue suits of clothes, heavily pruned trees, and countless other concrete details that Stendhal was mindful to supply, in lieu of extended descriptions, for a realistic effect. Reading matter, like other things that in themselves are unremarkable, may complement the referential grounding of the fictional decor while contributing to plot development. Just as a common ladder in the garden furthers the plot by enabling Julien to rise to a particular occasion, a letter—a few paragraphs, quickly read—arrives with incriminating statements that forever change his destiny. Various texts that complete the decor and advance the plot may, like other objects, have symbolic value as well. Julien's unexceptional blue suit is significant within the story of his rising status in the La Mole household, and it also fits into a color theme in which blue stands between—or perhaps above—red and black (Godfrey). Similarly, the texts Julien reads so passionately are not only part of the cultural landscape and of the narrative of his ambition; they also signify from the outset that he is a singular individual, one for whom words have uncommon importance. Finally, the abundance of books and readers in the book we are reading may promote worthwhile reflection about our own options for reacting to Stendhal's text and to its ending in particular.

A critical review of significant scenes and passages suggests that one can approach *The Red and the Black* as a story of reading and writing framed by a novel of formation. When we first hear of Julien, the mayor of Verrières is explaining to his wife that the young man would be a worthy tutor for their children because he has become an expert in Latin, thanks to the good offices of an old army surgeon who taught him and later bequeathed to him a collection of books (33; 9; 1.3). When we finally see Julien, he is perched high among the timbers of his father's sawmill, reading his favorite book: Las Cases's account of conversations with Napoleon, the *Mémorial de Sainte-Hélène*. The hero's book is thus initially associated with physical elevation, which will connote loftiness of sentiment throughout the novel. Moreover, it appears near the saw blade, which has been interpreted as suggesting a threat of castration while prefiguring the guillotine of the final pages (Mossman 48). Repeating Napoleon's own trajectory and anticipating Julien's, the volume falls into the stream below when old Sorel jostles Julien to get his attention and discuss with him the mayor's search for a tutor (39; 13; 1.4). Julien's illiterate father has no patience with the bookishness of his son, whom he calls a "chien de lisard" (40; 1.5—*lisard*, a pejorative deformation of *liseur* ["devoted reader"], is not rendered in the Adams translation). The narrative clearly presents the father in a negative light as it encourages sympathy for the son, a fictional reader whose oblique path to the guillotine involves various modes of reading. Julien's literacy affords him a social distinction and a measure of refinement that his coarse father and brothers cannot claim. It also allows him to escape from authority (Kempf 829), to experience the exhilaration of transgression in revering books associated with taboos (Gleize 71–76), and even to play out an oedipal drama in which his predilection for reading and writing is pitted against "paternal logophobia" (Mossman 98). His approach to reading will be an important element in his characterization, as is true of other characters as well.

Julien has reservations about becoming the Rênals' tutor, for he has read Rousseau's *Confessions* and has learned to cultivate an aversion for a status that might not distinguish him adequately from the servants (41; 15; 1.5). This scene introduces the theme, so astutely analyzed by René Girard, of patterning desire on models encountered mainly in books. The memoirs of Napoleon and Rousseau, along with the collected reports of Napoleon's Grande armée, are said to be Julien's "Koran" (41; 15; 1.5). His ambitions seem to draw more heavily on the Napoleonic model, but Rousseau's influence should not be underestimated (Haig 52–53; Crouzet, *Rouge* 47–48). In addition to displaying a "Rousseauist dogmatism," as Dennis Porter has observed, Julien identifies with Rousseau's class background, his resentment of class privilege, and his openness to intimacy with an older provincial woman, while sharing with Rousseau a somewhat paranoid psyche, a love of mountains, and "a desire to retreat from the world" (81).

As Julien prepares to take the first decisive steps of his apprenticeship in the workings of his society, he relies on his venerated "Koran" for inspiration and insight, while considering all other books to have been written by hypocrites who seek advancement (41; 16; 1.5). Yet he himself has memorized the New Testament and studied Joseph de Maistre's *On the Pope*, a defense of papal authority, not because he considers their content significant but merely to enhance his chances for a career in the church (42, 45; 16, 19; 1.5). Julien's plan for success at this stage puts him in precarious moral proximity to the mayor of Verrières, who epitomizes the town's dreary adherence to an ethos of financial self-interest. But Julien is later redeemed by his devotion to privileged books, by his capacity to value flights of imagination inspired by reading over the satisfactions of vanity pursued by M. de Rênal and others. This redemption is perhaps most striking when Julien, shortly after his imprisonment, resolves not to commit suicide but instead to take advantage of his peaceful setting to read books he has sent to him from Paris (504; 368; 2.36). Reading is no longer a means to success in the world; it is an end in itself, or at least a bridge to the kind of *rêverie profonde* or *rêverie tendre* (meditative or nostalgic mental state) that figures prominently in Stendhal's aesthetics.

Julien's earlier reading reflects not only fundamental thematic dichotomies but also structural aspects of the novel as a whole. Before going to the Rênals' to begin his duties as tutor, he hides his books at the mountain home of his friend Fouqué (44; 18; 1.5), then makes a hypocritical visit to the town church, where he reads the fateful scrap of a newspaper article about the demise of a Louis Jenrel, whose name Julien fails to decipher as an anagram of his own (47; 20; 1.5). As Michel Crouzet observes, this scene amounts to a *mise en abyme* of the novel and is replicated much later when Julien imagines Mme de Rênal reading details of his own execution in the newspaper (Rouge 44). In the church, where blood-red curtains evoke the title of the novel and signal a dramatic moment, Julien's act of reading—or misreading—is explicitly linked to his sense of a personal destiny, a destiny that is in fact fated to be put into print.

Julien's success as a reader is a central issue in *The Red and the Black*, and this success will be subject to the judgment of many: Julien himself, those around him, and, inevitably, Stendhal's readers. All will face the problem of choosing among competing definitions of success. At the Rênals', where Julien is soon called on to recite from the New Testament (55; 26; 1.6), his apparent success is applauded. Through repeated reading he has memorized the sacred text and can reproduce it orally without regard to its meaning. But what are we to make of the "success" of this kind of inauthentic reading and repeating? This is the first of seven formal recitations (Kempf 836–37; others include interrogations at the seminary and dinner-table performances, including lines from Horace) that Julien undertakes in hopes of winning the approval of his audience. As his final performance Julien recites a portion of the conservative journal *La quotidienne*, which he memorizes to prove himself worthy of the secret-note mission (411–33; 299–316; 2.21–23). Most of the texts that Julien learns by heart, including the secret note itself, seem at odds with his religious and political convictions. The climate of judgment surrounding Julien's formal recitations centers primarily on the accuracy of his memory but also on the acceptability to right-thinking individuals of the texts he has chosen to memorize. Prendergast, for whom literary mimesis represents "not the world but the world as already organised in discourse" (68) discerns in these recitations "an implicit statement about the novel's own relation to the received idioms of narrative representation" (133). In the process of raising the question of success, Stendhal commends the originality of his own refusal to offer his reader yet another rehearsal of the conventional.

Julien's public recitations and private raptures derive from very different types of reading matter: the type reflected by his potentially subversive "Koran" and the Latin poets who inspire original ideas and the unsubversive or "socially useful" (Jefferson, *Reading* 123) texts that Julien studies hypocritically with the subversive intention of penetrating the higher social classes (Gleize 81–86). This division reflects not only the dichotomies that complicate Julien's search for an authentic identity but also the narrator's own explicit and implicit concerns with his readers' critical reception of a narrative that he hopes will be perceived as both acceptable and stimulating.

Stendhal's novel, paradoxically, alludes frequently to the supposed dangers posed by novels, whether as corrupting influences or inducements to inauthentic behavior. Julien and Mme de Rênal are unable to act on their feelings in the initial phases of their strong mutual attraction because they have not read the novels that would have provided models to follow (60; 30; 1.7). When Julien, accompanied by Mme de Rênal, goes for the first time to the town bookseller's shop, he is amazed by the sight of so many books and, in a move that is emblematic of his will to power, devises a scheme to get M. de Rênal's name on the bookseller's subscription list. Julien states, however, that novels should not be allowed in the household (64; 33–34; 1.7). He does this in part to placate M. de Rênal but also to give his "Rousseauist dogmatism" the appearance of moral authority. During the period when Mme de Rênal's developing affection for Julien remains chaste, she considers that the portraits of passionate love she has encountered in just a few novels must surely be aberrations (67; 35; 1.8). Julien himself takes note of some of Napoleon's comments about women and fashionable novels (75; 41; 1.8). Art may be unlifelike, but this does not keep (fictional) life from imitating it: after Julien has finally read Rousseau's *La Nouvelle Héloïse*, he recites passages to charm Amanda Binet in Besançon (194; 132; 1.24) and Mathilde in Paris (381; 276; 2.16), instead of simply being himself. At the Hôtel de La Mole Julien finds Mathilde's racy historical readings surprising, since her mother does not allow Mathilde to read Walter Scott's historical novels (341; 245; 2.10). The tension between fiction and historical writing is great in *The Red and the Black*, to which the author ascribes a historical dimension by declaring it a "chronicle of 1830" on the title page. Mathilde seeks out models of passionate love as portrayed in memoirs and similar types of historical writing, yet also in novels such as "*Manon Lescaut, la Nouvelle Héloïse*, les *Lettres d'une Religieuse portugaise*, etc., etc. [. . .]" (348; 251; 2.11).

Stendhal's various cautionary statements about novels may appear disingenuous in *The Red and the Black*, but in fact they fit well within a characteristic pattern of irony, analyzed in Brombert's *Stendhal et la voie oblique*, in which Stendhal often presents apparent criticism that must be taken as praise. If novels are at all dangerous, it is for one reason only: they are compelling. Like effective historical writing, they touch the imagination, a faculty that is celebrated in the novel itself (a search of the ARTFL project electronic database indicates 48 occurrences of the word *imagination* in *The Red and the Black*, as against 13 in *Les illusions perdues*, 10 in *Madame Bovary*, and 3 in *L'éducation sentimentale*). Both Julien and Mathilde, as character-readers, serve as examples of the powerful responses that mental constructions of written texts can elicit. As internal readers who react to texts, they mirror Stendhal's readers and contribute to a self-conscious dimension of the novel, as do a variety of discursive features (Day). Are they intended as models to be followed? No, if you consider that this would undermine the reading process by freighting it with the perils of imitation (Jefferson, *Reading* 126). No again, if you judge that the protagonists never consume "reading material proposed as healthy, sane, and politically acceptable" (Mossman 97) or that Julien makes grievous errors in selecting books on which to model his ambitions (Haig 56). But insofar as Julien and Mathilde read with the level of passion that Stendhal displays in his personal writings, insofar as their reading is at times associated with longings for transcendence, they surely have something in common with the readers Stendhal hopes for.

In the idyllic setting of Vergy Julien is subjected by his passion for reading to the seductions of writing. His social and sentimental education progresses along with his story of reading, but it will be a while before Mme de Rênal inspires as much emotion as his favorite book (91; 53; 1.11), and his first romantic encounters are with books in the nearby highlands. Reading continues to uplift Julien's spirits, but as Stendhal observes in a volume of memoirs, "Pour qui a goûté de la profonde occupation d'écrire, lire n'est plus qu'un plaisir secondaire" 'For someone who has enjoyed the profound occupation of writing, reading is only a secondary pleasure' (*Souvenirs d'égotisme*, 149; my trans.). And so on a solitary visit to the mountains, where the altitude and a bird of prey symbolize his sense of freedom and superiority, Julien retreats to a small grotto. There, in an exalted state, he writes down his thoughts (96; 57; 1.12). When he fantasizes a glorious life in Paris with the most cultivated and beautiful of mistresses, the narrator intervenes with an ironic remark about Julien's naiveté at "ce point de son roman" 'at this point in his daydream' (97; 57; 1.12; *fantasme* 'fantasy' was not current until later in the nineteenth century—Stendhal sometimes uses *roman*, 'novel,' in this sense). Even though Julien, for the sake of caution, burns the pages he has just written, Stendhal has established clear relations among Julien's imagination, the desire to author a text, and the determination to maintain authority over his destiny.

Julien has recourse to writing again a bit later, when he writes out a detailed plan for achieving his amorous goals with Mme de Rênal (106; 64; 1.14). His plan, paradoxically, is based on the only love stories he has read, those in the Bible—a book that advances Julien's ambitions in unorthodox ways throughout *The Red and the Black*. His reading, here as elsewhere, inspires his chosen course of action, while the written plan is further evidence of the close association of action and authorship.

The price of success is unanticipated competition between the old passion and the new. Once Julien's affair with Mme de Rênal is no longer platonic, he worries that she may come to his room and find him immersed in compromising books that he has obtained through his friend Fouqué (120; 75; 1.17). After the anonymous letter affair, Julien becomes so cautious that Mme de Rênal reproaches him in a letter for appearing to love her only on those days when he has not received "quelque livre amusant" 'some amusing book' from Fouqué (147; 95; 1.20). Books are liberating for Julien, but they threaten his affairs of the heart. Not only do they entail the risk of exposing his ambitions, but they also appeal to a part of him for which love is primarily a means to an end—the achievement of his rise in society—whereas love, as he ultimately realizes, should have been an end in itself.

Julien would have done better to follow the example of abbé Chélan, a reader who is faithful to the righteous precepts found in his books. Julien's mentor, obliged to vacate his presbytery after having been relieved of his functions for political reasons, has moved to smaller quarters that are cluttered with his books. Julien, on an extended leave in Verrières, resolves to build old M. Chélan "une sorte de bibliothèque" 'a sort of bookcase' (163; 108; 1.22). This project amounts to a kind of revenge on Julien's father in the area of woodworking (Kempf 829), while enabling the young man to assume, somewhat self-consciously ("voulant montrer à Verrières ce que c'était qu'un prêtre" 'wanting to show Verrières what it was to be a priest' [163; 108; 1.22]), the biblical pose of a persecuted carpenter as he carries the boards on his back the entire length of the main street.

As a seminary student in Besançon, Julien often encounters the adversarial relation between various texts and established power. He intuits that the church considers books to be its enemies (207; 142; 1.26), since they encourage independent thinking and the questioning of authority. Abbé Pirard himself will later remark that in the north of France "le voisinage des journaux de

Paris fait peur aux petits tyrans" 'having the Paris newspapers near at hand makes the petty tyrants fearful' (273; 191; 2.1). This allusion to the contemporary controversy over freedom of the press, despite the contextual ironies, is another affirmation of the emancipatory virtues of the printed word. Books can challenge authority in part by exposing its arbitrariness, as in the scenes where Julien displays his knowledge of Horace and other profane Latin authors. For his heterodox taste in books he first earns a reprimand from the examiner at the seminary (230; 160; 1.29), then praise from the bishop of Besançon, who gives him an edition of Tacitus (237–38; 165–66; 1.29).

Julien's occupations as a tutor at the Rênals' and as a seminarian often require him to be a reader. In Paris, as the marquis de La Mole's secretary, he will serve as a writer. His future in this endeavor seems less than promising, however: in his first assignment, the copying of some documents, he astounds his employer by misspelling a common word, writing *cella* for *cela* (278; 195; 2.2). Books will still retain considerable importance and appeal, however. Julien will work in the La Mole library, where he delights in the great number of books (277; 194; 2.2). He will continue to be called on to recite memorized text, an activity that stresses the mechanical side of reading as the reproduction of someone else's words. Yet writing, a more creative activity, will occupy him more and more, whether literally or figuratively. When Julien improvises commentary on Horace and Latin poets, the relation between original improvisation and authorship is made explicit by the narrator's remark that Julien has expressed ideas which the academician "n'avait lues nulle part" 'had never seen in print' (451; 197; 2.2). Improvisation allows for a level of authenticity that is absent from recitation (Gleize 85), and the value of speaking with spontaneous sincerity is unmistakable in Julien's remark about his courtroom speech late in the novel: "J'improvisais, et pour la première fois de ma vie!" 'I was improvising, and for the first time in my life' (534; 390; 2.42). Julien has, we will recall, "improvised" earlier, but never in such a way as to reveal his innermost sensibility.

In one of the salons of the Hôtel de La Mole, abbé Pirard warns Julien about the marquis's antipathy for "écrivailleurs" 'scribblers,' whereupon Julien rushes to his room to burn the eight or ten pages he has written about his mentor the surgeon-major (296–97; 209; 2.4). For the powerful, writing represents a more direct threat than reading, while for the likes of Julien, writing represents a greater measure of freedom. At this stage of his ambition, Julien is evidently prepared to renounce certain convictions and basic freedoms for the sake of success. And his inclinations may have evolved in the process, for the narrator reports that Julien has begun spending his spare time riding rather than reading (310; 212; 2.5). An encounter in one of the salons with the revolutionary conspirator Altamira recalls Julien, at least for a while, to his initial values: the marquis's ambitious secretary stays up the rest of the night reading a history of the French Revolution (334; 239; 2.9).

How should Julien interpret the puzzling character of Mathilde de La Mole? Since she too is an avid reader, can he rely on his knowledge of historical and other books? When he discovers that she devours Voltaire and surreptitiously removes from the marquis's private library the works that Julien recognizes as most hostile to the crown and the church, he is charmed by her unorthodoxy (358; 258; 2.13). Yet when Mathilde plays on Julien's capacity for jealousy, the narrator remarks, "On voit que Julien n'avait aucune expérience de la vie, il n'avait pas même lu de romans" 'It's clear that Julien had no experience of life; he had not even read novels' (392; 285; 2.18).

Now, we have already seen that Julien knows *La nouvelle Héloïse* well enough to recite whole passages and that he knows other novels at least indirectly. His knowledge of plays and theatrical traditions, moreover, is considerable (*Tartuffe* [363; 262; 2.13], *Le Cid* [372; 270; 2.15], *Othello* [500; 365; 2.36], the melodrama [387; 281; 2.17], operas, etc.), but the narrator chooses not to mention it here. Finally, the connection between experience of life and having read novels is, on reflection, quite tenuous. How reliably, in real-life situations, can one apply solutions encountered in fiction? And why would the narrator not consider that the numerous memoirs and historical works Julien has read would be of greater value than novels for understanding real life? One answer is that, in a novel, the explicit juxtaposition of novels and real life blurs the distinction between fiction and reality and thus constitutes a self-reflexive wink to the reader. This hypothesis is supported by the passage a few pages later (398; 289; 2.19) in which the narrator, in one of the "intrusions" for which he is known (Blin 179–322), compares a novel—his own—to a mirror that inevitably reflects not just the beauty but also the ugliness of the highway that it faces. Such a disclaimer cannot be taken at face value, since most readers are fully conscious that a novel is certainly not a mirror but a product of an imagination that is free to "reflect" whatever it wants. The narrator's disclaimer signifies something else: his awareness that the reader holds him accountable for the success of the narration and that the referential illusion of his novel, so ardently defended by Crouzet (Rouge 57–80), not only remains intact but indeed is reinforced by various evocations of fictional works to which Julien, as a potential reader of them, may appear superior by virtue of occupying a higher existential plane.

The narrator, as evidenced in particular by his intrusions, betrays his sensitivity to the reader's scrutiny, just as Julien is keenly aware of the critical gaze of others. In this book in which the main characters' self-consciousness is often manifest amid a climate of judgment, in which the hero's recitations and improvisations are a series of minor trials that anticipate his final appearance before the jury, the narrator displays occasional performance anxiety as he seeks to win the reader's approval. In addition to intermittent intrusions or disclaimers, he is mindful to fill his book with images of reading as a source of lofty emotion and with allusions to the immense appeal of books, especially novels. Julien's readings are plausible for his time, if not necessary representative (Gleize 88–89). The numerous book titles in the text have documentary value, and as Crouzet and other scholars have maintained, they are significant elements of the conscientiously constructed inventory of descriptive and historical details. Reflexivity in Stendhal's novel overlays his mode of realism and furnishes a poetic dimension in which images of reading and writing, linked to desiring, bespeak the text's own literariness.

The connection between reading and writing is often explicit. Julien and Mathilde, in particular, are inclined to create scenarios they have adapted from their readings. These inventive scenarios may be spoken, or perhaps only imagined, as when Julien fantasizes at length, in the manner of Benjamin Bart's parastories, what might be or might have been (e.g., 479, 509–10; 349, 372–73; 2.32, 2.38). For Stendhal, who sometimes dictated his prose, writing did not necessarily involve holding a pen. When Julien does put his musings on paper, his concern for privacy is likely to prompt him to burn the paper. Mathilde is bolder: she dares to write the first love letter, which Julien hides in a large Bible and sends to Fouqué (364; 264; 2.13). After receiving her second letter, Julien jokes to himself, "Il paraît que ceci va être le roman par lettres" 'It looks as if this is going to be an epistolary novel' (370; 268; 2.14). He copies her third letter ("Quelle manie d'écrire! se dit-il en riant" 'What a craze for writing she has! said he, with a laugh' [371; 269; 2.14]) as well as the second and hides the copies in a volume of the Voltaire collection. Julien himself writes out a "mémoire justificatif arrangé en forme de conte" 'apologetic memoir, arranged in the form of a story' (375; 272; 2.15), which instead of burning he sends to Fouqué. Julien reacts intensely to what he reads and even more intensely to what he composes: the narrator observes that Julien's overstimulated imagination prompts him to envision further scenarios, so that he is "[é]mu de son propre conte comme un auteur dramatique" '[s]tirred by his own story like a playwright by his play' (375; 272; 2.15). Significant here is Julien's tendency to interpret the events of his life as something to be read ("roman par lettres," "conte") or put into a book (symbolically, the letters hidden in Voltaire or the Bible). Julien's intense emotion suggests that verbalizing these events and in the process representing them mentally are perhaps more thrilling than living them.

The authorial imagination portrayed in this passage anticipates the observation Julien makes after his dreams of achieving rank and glory seem to be fulfilled: "mon roman est fini, et à moi seul tout le mérite" 'the novel of my career is over, and the credit is all mine' (491; 359; 2.34). Stendhal, of course, has other plans, and he offers the briefest of summaries of Julien's success as an officer in Strasbourg (493; 360; 2.35) before changing the course of things with Mme de Rênal's fateful letter. So what are we to make of Julien's enigmatic affirmation of narrative authority? We might see it as an echo of a passage from Scott's *Waverly* and account for it in terms of psychological portraiture and conventions of intertextuality (Crouzet, Rouge 51–55). We might conclude that "the artist-writer in Julien [does] not come to fruition" (Haig 57) and more specifically that when he reaches a certain point in the composition of his personal narrative, Julien becomes dissatisfied with his fabrication and takes steps to disengage himself from it: he shoots Mme de Rênal but still has to work out the complicated matter of closure (Gormley). It may appear that Julien, not having read novels so as to be able to imitate fictional heroes, yields his authorial power to Stendhal and Mathilde, so that his death is emblematic of his failure (Viti). Yet we may also reach a more upbeat conclusion. Could it not be that Julien's narrative bent leads him to negate his inauthentic writing project—the "roman par lettres" with Mathilde—in favor of a more genuine and satisfying narrative for which he composes a dramatic death worthy of a Romantic hero (Kaplan)? In this light, Julien courageously writes his demise and presents a supremely "poetic" head to the crowd assembled to watch it fall (554; 407; 2.45); his burial site is the grotto where, in a moment of writing, he felt free. In prison, a womblike space recalling the grotto, he found an opportunity for unhypocritical reading, reached an understanding of love, and revised his definition of success, after which he was ready to die happily ever after.

Few undergraduate readers today are likely to identify as strongly with Stendhal's hero as did one student I heard proclaim, "Julien Sorel, c'est moi." But most should be able to appreciate Julien's story as an exaltation of the human spirit in search of knowledge and guidance not only for achieving success but also for defining success. This story of reading and writing, in which Julien must learn to discriminate between fantasy and reality, copying and creating, the rhetoric and conventions of books and the more subtle workings of the heart, lends itself to lively classroom discussion. With its countless texts, titles, literary allusions, scenes of reading, images of books and libraries, and scenarios composed on paper or in the imagination, Stendhal's novel presents a favorable image of itself as a source of mental stimulation. At the same time it raises crucial questions of boundaries: those between verbal freedom and political authority, between history and fiction, and between authentic and derivative modes of reading, writing, and desiring.

How Julien Loses His Head; or, Stendhal and the Politics of the Imaginary

Juliet Flower MacCannell

> La marche ordinaire du XIXe siècle est que, quand un être puissant et noble rencontre un homme de cœur, il le tue, l'exile, l'emprisonne ou l'humilie tellement que l'autre a la sottise d'en mourir de douleur.
>
> It's a general rule in the nineteenth century that when a man of power and position meets a man of feeling, he kills him, exiles him, imprisons him, or humiliates him until the other is stupid enough to die of grief from it.
>
> —Stendhal, *The Red and the Black*

The Man of Power: The "Political" in 1828–30

Power is the political, the form by which one person rules another. In *The Red and the Black* Stendhal sees autocratic power, despite its presumed demise in the French Revolution, continuing its operation by other means. Under the Restoration the king was returned to the throne and the nobility, still trembling from the Reign of Terror that had guillotined so many of its members, was again free to reenter France. These other means involve the nobles' manipulating public opinion and, in a more complex way that Stendhal brilliantly unravels, having their manners and mores adopted by those who serve them. Julien Sorel is directly affected by this latter strategy. Nowhere has the political been depicted as more intensely personal than in Stendhal's novel, in which the politics of 1830 are no mere backdrop to the events of Julien Sorel's life and death but their fabric. Politics shape Julien's subjectivity, his psyche, his soul. As such, they command our scrupulous attention.

Sensitive, poor, ambitious, Julien Sorel lives a life that is one long dying of grief, as he stifles his feelings while trying to outwit each man (and woman) of power he encounters by donning the mask of power. In the course of the novel he is spiritually and ultimately physically exiled, imprisoned, and killed. Dreams of power and of resistance to it coexist in Julien; the conflict between them shapes his life. But not, perhaps, his death. For on the eve of his actual demise, Julien experiences an extended period of happiness with Mme de Rênal that renders his powerful adversaries nil in his eyes. The question put forward in this essay is this: Does the man of power defeat the man of feeling if Julien dies not of grief but of joy?

The Nobles

The chapter "The Discussion" (2.22) depicts politics in such minute detail the narrator feels compelled to comment on it: politics in an imaginative work is like a pistol shot in the middle of a concert, yet necessary in 1830. Stendhal had a long-standing adherence, though he ironizes it, to this tenet of Destutt de Tracy's *Idéologie* (1800): the forms of governance, or power, mark human subjects in deep, often unconscious ways, determining their relation to enjoyment, love, and desire. This idea appears in Stendhal's unfinished *Lamiel*, in which fear of 1793 (never far from everyone's lips) sets the course of the heroine's life; of *Armance*, in which the aristocrat Octave's lawsuit to restore revolutionary land seizures is linked to his sexual faltering; and in Stendhal's favorite writing, *De l'amour*, which asserts a materialist *idéologie*, contending that a government's form shapes the love life of its citizenry.

Following Napoleon's fall in 1815, the émigré nobles began returning to France. Their political goals were to restore the monarchy (which they did, but under La Charte or a constitution) and to prevent the recurrence of the Reign of Terror they had fled. Although they briefly retaliated with their own *Terreur blanche* in 1815–16 (at the start of Louis XVIII's reign, royalists purged those who had rallied to Napoleon), force on a mass scale was unthinkable. The émigrés also sought to regain their redistributed land and restore the church—in order to reign again and rein in the "revolutionary" masses—but they had to do so nonviolently or risk a return of terror.

Stendhal depicts how the nobility reclaimed sway over those briefly empowered after the Revolution—peasants and bourgeois—by dominating their imaginations. Depleted in numbers and hampered by new constitutional constraints on the monarchy, the nobility regained ruling-class status by shaping public opinion—especially in the provinces, from which the soul of the French Revolution had sprung—in the service of their interests, asserting themselves as the model and pattern of behavior for all other classes. Stendhal describes the country aristocrat M. de Rênal, mayor of Verrières, for example, as holding his power, limited by a constitution that requires him to stand for election, this way: "Au milieu d'une ville de vingt mille habitants, ces hommes [comme M. de Rênal] font l'opinion publique, et l'opinion publique est terrible dans un pays qui a la charte" 'In a town of twenty thousand inhabitants [. . .] people [like M. de Rênal] make public opinion, and public opinion has terrible power in a country with the charter [a constitution]' (176; 118; 1.23). To maintain the fiction of his hereditary privilege, the mayor has people refer to his house as the manor house; to keep his political prominence, he fosters an illusion of dwelling in aristocratic loftiness. He devotes a large portion of his (or his wife's) wealth to diverting the river, enlarging his estate, and heightening its walls, to create the impression of a top-down power that, technically, no longer exists: after the Revolution, ultimate power resides in the people, who must be perpetually duped to make them believe its source lies elsewhere.

Those duped are legion, most of all when they believe that aping the upper classes will put them closer to power, when in fact it puts power further out of reach. Stendhal distinguishes among dupes, however. He systematically lays down class and religious lines that differentiate ex-bourgeois-wannabe-aristocrat dupes like Valenod from the similarly situated ex-peasant Julien. The restored clergymen, servile and power seeking, the Jesuitical abbé Castanède and abbé Frilair, differ from the Jansenist and spiritual abbés Pirard and Chélan, who serve power without seeking to flatter it by imitation.

The Peasants

When the imitation of the nobility takes perverse root in the politics of the upper bourgeois classes, alert to fill the shoes of the ancien régime, the naked power politics at its heart is exposed. But in the theories leading up to the Revolution, no one foresaw a convergence in the ruling powers, whereby the nobility and the bourgeoisie would end up dividing their rule at the expense of "the people": the peasant, craftsmen, laboring, and servant classes—but chiefly the peasants, in Julien's view. Hence the distinction between a Valenod and a Julien. The bourgeois Valenod, an energetically crafty, noisy "faraud" 'bold-faced slob' (173; 116; 1.22), becomes a baron in the course of the novel, refines his tastes, and plays the lady-killer. This refinement is inessential to his rise: Valenod is after power, not happiness. He pursues Mme de Rênal, for example, to assert power over her, not to find happiness with her.

In contrast, the apparently power-seeking peasant, Julien Sorel, for whose class the Revolution of 1789 was first undertaken, remains the political odd man out because his desire for political success is tied, at the deepest and least conscious level, to his desire for something other than power. If he attaches himself to the aristocratic classes, it is partly because—unbeknownst to himself— he is seeking happiness, not merely power. Stendhal likens Julien to "un jeune homme pauvre qui n'est qu'ambitieux que parce que la délicatesse de son cœur lui fait un besoin de quelques-unes des jouissances que donne l'argent" 'a poor young man who is ambitious only because the delicacy of his heart makes absolutely necessary for him some of those pleasures that only money can buy' (61; 30; 1.7). Those pleasures remain unknown to us (and to him) until he is about to meet his fate.

Julien's rise also differs from Valenod's because it springs from a different class basis. Julien is a peasant, born of peasants (despite hints that he is the natural son of an aristocrat). His father, Old Sorel, is described as a close cousin of the Egyptian fellah, a descendant of slaves with the freed slave's cunning air "de fausseté et presque de friponnerie" 'of falsity and almost trickery' (37; 12; 1.4), continuously plotting revenge against a former master. He bests M. de Rênal in every deal. At his trial, Julien emphasizes his own peasant roots: "vous voyez en moi un paysan qui s' est révolté contre la bassesse de sa fortune" 'you see in me a peasant in open revolt against his station' (530; 387; 2.41), and he says he is being unfairly judged because "je ne suis point jugé par mes pairs. Je ne vois point sur les bancs des jurés quelque paysan enrichi, mais uniquement des bourgeois indignés" 'I am not being judged by my peers. I do not see in the seats of the jury a single rich peasant, only outraged bourgeois' (530; 388; 2.41).

Now, in the zero-sum game of the Restoration, one man's gain seemed to mean another's loss. Julien's enrichment meant one noble or one bourgeois had less. The peasant class was supposed to have made permanent gains over the aristocracy and the oppressive power of the clergy once these groups had lost their lands and were stripped of power: Rousseau's *Second Discourse* had stirred that pot well. But the gain was not simply in wealth, nor was it the peasant's alone: every individual citizen's stake in the Revolution was enormous: *liberté*. The Restoration jeopardized both.

Before the English, French, and American revolutions, kings had absolute power to dispense life and death unfettered by liberal constraint—the charter (or constitution). In postrevolutionary France the individual had gained a civil society ruled not by the law of the strongest but by the principle of freedom from arbitrary power, tyranny, and injustice, such as the infamous lettres de cachet: once sealed by the king they had often sealed someone's death sentence without benefit of a trial by a jury of peers. That Julien is denied a jury of his peers marks a return of autocratic power in the form of a manipulated public opinion.

But students will wonder if Julien had not already lost a measure of his freedom and of his class pride much earlier: had he not become like the nobility? For the nobility, imposing its private tastes and manners on its inferiors was more important in renewing its rule than control of public opinion. Julien has scrutinized the nobles' ways closely and has succeeded in adopting them. The aristocrats might intrigue and conspire away on into the night, as in the tedious discussions of book 2, chapter 22, but it is by their studied restraint in intimate social intercourse that they really hold sway. How? The aristocracy made itself the indisputable pattern for everyone else, less by grandly impressing the public imagination than by strictly policing behavior and talk, by restricting the range of emotional expression.

It is in the realm of manners and morals (*mœurs*) that the nobles triumph—at least the Parisian nobles. A mere *provincial* like M. de Rênal is humiliated first by the peasant Sorel *père*, and, later, Sorel *fils*, and remains a notable failure in the private realm. But in the Parisian drawing room the art of power is cultured. Self-control in the nobles commands the same in their inferiors. See how Julien admires the maréchale de Fervaques for her "calme patricien qui respire une politesse exacte et encore plus l'impossibilité d'aucune vive émotion. L'imprévu dans les mouvements, le manque d'empire sur soi-même, eût scandalisé Mme de Fervaques presque autant que l'absence de majesté envers ses inférieurs" 'patrician calm which breathes an air of perfect politeness and especially the total impossibility of any keen emotion. Any spontaneous gesture, any lapse of complete self-control would have scandalized Mme de Fervaques almost as much as a failure of dignified condescension towards one's inferiors' (448; 327; 2.26).

The effect on Julien is numbing, not only because he must constantly mask his feelings but also because the arbitrary exercise of autocratic power really does demand an inhuman coldness. The patrician calm of the aristocratic salon had become its proving ground. It is the ethic behind the sheer boredom of that salon. When Julien, flushed with a new authority, decides to indulge in a bit of arbitrary exercise of power, he soon has both cause to regret it and occasion to stifle his conscience. M. de La Mole tells Julien to appoint the new director of the lottery in his hometown of Verrières. Julien makes this appointment into a little joke, granting it to M. de Cholin on a whim. Later he discovers that he has, by this gesture, precipitated two families to their ruin, the widow of the former lottery director and M. Gros, the mathematician (named after Stendhal's own beloved teacher), who had counted on the post to continue his charitable support of the widow and her children. Horrified, Julien steels himself with the thought that "il faudra en venir à bien d'autres injustices, si je veux parvenir" 'There are plenty of other injustices I will have to commit if I'm to be successful' (317; 225; 2.8): he thinks he must be cold. He is right. The devices of policing feeling and of intimate social control Julien finds exemplified in a Mme de Fervaques are indeed the foundation of an imaginary but almighty autocratic and aristocratic power in the novel. As Pascal and Montaigne said, and Stendhal's novel demonstrates, the imagination is the dominant faculty in man.

The Bourgeoisie

The other presumptive beneficiary of the French Revolution, counterpart and opposite to the peasant and laborer, was the bourgeois. He, too, had found freedom. But it was less a *freedom from* than a *freedom to*—modernize, industrialize, pursue profits. The bourgeoisie are called "Liberals" in *The Red and the Black*. They are utilitarians, constitutionally opposed to the nobility in manners and morals. Their access to power is finance, not land. But they ultimately aspire to the same absolutist power that the aristocracy desires, even as they lay claim to the mantle of the revolution and its new democratic freedoms. The "revolutionary" count Altamira is among these: "Le regard de Mathilde se moquait du libéralisme d'Altamira [. . .] mais elle l'écoutait avec plaisir. Un conspirateur au bal, c'est un joli contraste, pensait-elle. Elle trouvait à celui-ci, avec ses moustaches noires, la figure du lion quand il se repose; mais elle s'aperçut bientôt que son esprit n' avait qu'une attitude: *l'utilité, l'admiration pour l'utilité*" 'Mathilde's glance mocked the liberalism of Altamira [. . .] but she listened to him with pleasure. A conspirator at a ball makes a pretty contrast, she thought. She thought that this one, with his black moustaches, resembled the features of the lion in repose; but she quickly noted that his mind had but one consideration: *utility, admiration for the useful*' (325; 231–32; 2.8). Altamira's utilitarianism falls flat with Mathilde as he falls in with the nobility he is supposed to oppose, much like Ferrante Palla in Stendhal's *The Charterhouse of Parma*, the regicide rebel poet whose revolutionary ode calls for establishing a bicameral legislature and a budget.

The tip-off that the nobles and the acquisitive bourgeoisie differ all too little can also be seen in the very type of "the liberal," M. Valenod, director of the poorhouse in Verrières. Julien, arriving early for a dinner with the director and his family, finds Valenod "étalant son importance au milieu d'une foule de cartons. Ses gros favoris noirs, son énorme quantité de cheveux, son bonnet grec placé de travers sur le haut de la tête, sa pipe immense, ses pantoufles brodées, les grosses chaînes d'or croisées en tous sens sur sa poitrine, et tout cet appareil d'un financier de province, qui se croit homme à bonnes fortunes, n'imposaient point à Julien. [. . .]" 'exercising his importance in the midst of a pile of papers. His thick black whiskers, his enormous head of hair, his Phrygian cap cocked crossways on his head, his huge pipe, his embroidered slippers, the thick gold chains strung every which way across his chest, and all that apparatus of a provincial money man who thinks himself a lady-killer made no impression on Julien [. . .]' (166; 110; 1.22).

The Phrygian cap is an emblem of the sansculottes who stormed the Bastille. It sits crossways atop Valenod's head, just as he sits crossways atop his poor: he seemingly acts on their behalf but really lives off them As Julien dines with the Valenods he thinks to himself about the poor prisoners on the other side of the wall:

> Ils ont faim peut-être en ce moment, se dit-il à lui-même; sa gorge se serra, il lui fut impossible de manger et presque de parler. Ce fut bien pis un quart d'heure après; on entendait de loin en loin quelques accents d'une chanson populaire, et, il faut l'avouer, un peu ignoble, que chantait l'un des reclus. M. Valenod regarda un de ses gens en grande livrée, qui disparut, et bientôt on n'entendit plus chanter. Dans ce moment, un valet offrait à Julien du vin du Rhin, dans un verre vert, et Mme Valenod avait soin de lui faire observer que ce vin coûtait neuf francs la bouteille pris sur place. Julien, tenant son verre vert, dit à M. Valenod:
>
> —On ne chante plus cette vilaine chanson.
>
> —Parbleu! je le crois bien, répondit le directeur triomphant, j'ai fait imposer silence aux gueux. Ce mot fut trop fort pour Julien; il avait les manières, mais non pas encore le cœur de son état. Malgré toute son hypocrisie si souvent exercée, il sentit une grosse larme couler le long de sa joue. (139)
>
> Perhaps they are suffering from hunger at this very moment, said he to himself; his throat choked up, he found it impossible to eat and almost to talk. It was much worse a quarter of an hour later; in the distance there were heard various phrases of a popular song, rather vulgar it must be admitted, being sung by one of the inmates. M. Valenod cast a glance at one of his servants in full livery who disappeared; shortly thereafter the song stopped. At that moment a valet offered Julien some Rhine wine in a green glass, and Mme Valenod seized the occasion to observe that this wine cost nine francs a bottle direct from the grower. Julien, holding his green glass, said to M. Valenod:

> —They're not singing that miserable song any more.
> —Blast 'em, I should think not, replied the director in triumph. I've had the beggars shut up.
> The phrase was too much for Julien; he had the manners, but not yet the feelings, of his social position. Despite all his much-practiced hypocrisy, he felt a tear flow down his cheek. (111; 1.22)

The bourgeois Valenod, who begins as M. de Rênal's underling (the particle *de* denotes noble birth), ends by acquiring a title of his own (by the time of Julien's trial, he is the baron *de* Valenod). As a bourgeois liberal, Valenod is for "freedom" and against church and throne. But his aspirations are betrayed even in this first encounter. Note his ostentatious emulation of the nobility's style (the liveried servant, the gold chains) under the symbol of the sansculottes (the cap). In the end, mistakes about Valenod's political sympathies are partially responsible for Julien's condemnation: Mathilde and the lawyers do not realize that, under the cover of liberalism, there has been a simple handoff of autocratic power from one ruling class to another—a confusion Valenod exploits. The lot of the peasant—and Julien underscores his class consciousness about being a peasant in his speech to the jury—has not ultimately changed.

Yet students will surely object that Julien seems to be fully taken into the camp of the reactionary nobility and the church. At every opportunity, he has made his home among these forces and stood against the liberals, whom Marx would later call the rising bourgeoisie. Students often surmise that Julien has chosen to live with the nobles because he is one. Despite his fierce class consciousness ("I am a poor peasant from the Jura, he kept repeating to himself over and over" [262; 2.13]) even Julien begins to half-believe the fiction, concocted by the marquis de La Mole to explain the boy's privilege in the La Mole household, that he really is the illegitimate son of the duc de Retz, which would explain his natural aristocratic tastes. Yes, but this may also be only political—an index of the aristocracy's success at winning the mind of the peasant to its side. For Julien maintains throughout the novel that he is a hypocrite in his politics, that some part of him does not go along with what he seems to be doing. Now, if he is not for the liberals against the nobles, in what way is he a hypocrite?

For one thing, it could be noted that only selected features of aristocratic manners move Julien—a certain sweet softness—Mme de Rênal's but not M. de Rênal's taste; M. de La Mole's polished speech, but not the "masculine" harshness of Mathilde de La Mole's voice. Julien makes distinctions; the aristocracy has not fully imposed its style on him. His political hypocrisy has nothing to do with noble versus bourgeois values. Nor, we shall see, with the church.

The Church

Though internally divided, the church plays all the classes against one another in the novel. This said, it is vital to remind oneself that the church's seeming omnipotence in Julien's mind is overstated, considering how precariously the church sits after the Revolution. Even before 1793, the policy of Gallicanism, which was finally codified under Louis XIV in the seventeenth century, created a liberalized French Catholic Church that was permitted to depart from the doctrine of papal infallibility. Gallicanism made the French church very different from others in western Europe, which were rigidifying under the Counter-Reformation of that period.

The French Revolution nevertheless disestablished the church. The Restoration of 1815 brought it back. The brand new church for Verrières, built when Julien is fourteen, symbolizes its return, but as a mere symbol: its core is rotten, it answers no spiritual needs, it is only a semblance of the former church. Nevertheless, the extreme youth of its hierarchy seizes Julien's imagination as a signpost to his own future. Indeed, Julien feels kinship with the young bishop of Agde he comes upon practicing to look bishoplike (104; 83; 1.18): akin to today's yuppies, the bishop is as insecure, and as adept in the art of self-fashioning, as our hero. Julien learns from the church lessons in hypocrisy, in assuming the outer trappings of power.

Julien's heart, however, is drawn to pastoral figures who acknowledge inner life—abbé Chélan, Pirard and his Jansenist friends in Paris, the bishop who is fond of the pagan Latin authors Julien also knows by heart. These ecclesiastical figures are ranged against what is in Julien's mind the monstrosity of the Jesuitical abbé de Frilair, the abbé Castanède, the vicar Maslon. It is less their doctrinal differences than their attitudes toward power that make the difference to Julien: Jansenists must submit to external authority, but they seek inner freedom; the Jesuits must appear submissive while hypocritically seeking power.

As the aristocrats and the church each attempt to make Julien theirs against the liberals—a process he tries desperately to go along with—he is personally drawn only to the portion in each of them that coincides with a determining factor in his own subjective makeup: his relation to his real father figure, the old surgeon-major, and to the legacy this man handed down to him. It is a legacy of narrative and myth concerning a crucial but forgotten moment: the years between 1796 and 1815, when Napoleon seemed destined to spread liberty (rather than liberalism) to every corner of Europe. Julien's hypocrisy often troubles students, and its source and rationale are extremely puzzling. It is the surgeon-major's legacy that really makes Julien a hypocrite.

The Man of Feeling

The Years 1796–1815

The surgeon-major, who lived with the Sorels and taught Julien Latin and the love of liberty, had immersed the boy in genuine, not bourgeois, liberalism; the depths of Julien's personality are imbued with its ideals. This part of recent French social history, which none of the three camps—noble, church, liberal—

can afford to recall, has formed Julien's personality and shaped his soul. The half-generation of 1796–1815 spans the initial promise of the revolution invested in a liberal Napoleon and its Waterloo. When Stendhal writes about the preimperial Napoleon, about figures like the old surgeon-major, about those like himself who fought in Italy in 1796 in *The Charterhouse of Parma* and *The Life of Henry Brulard* (his autobiography), he speaks of and for his own microgeneration. He says he is the only author to have come of age in this brief epoch who survived to document it. This generation, unique in Stendhal's—and Julien's—eyes, believed in and stood for the liberation of feeling, the pursuit of happiness, and the freedom from injustice that the French Revolution was supposed to bring. Where politicians might see only a roller-coaster succession of conservative, then liberal, then conservative decades at the turn of the eighteenth and nineteenth centuries, Stendhal saw moments shaping a young man's soul. The drama of the democratic moment when the armies of General Bonaparte sought to spread "liberalism" (i.e., toppling crowned heads throughout Europe), succeeded by the crushing realization that the Emperor Napoleon had become as autocratic as Europe's former masters, appointing his own brothers and sisters to the thrones of vanquished nations—these were the traumas of Stendhal's youth. But for Julien, only the first Napoleon exists; in Julien's personal hagiography, made out of his reading the *Mémorial* and hearing the tales of the surgeon-major, Napoleon dies a martyr decimated by the forces of arch reaction orchestrated by the conservative Austrians under Metternich, having spent his days in exile on Saint Helena.

Stendhal experienced this period, while Julien could see it only through the surgeon-major's mythified memories. Julien is fiercely loyal to this vision. But he also deeply believes this happy period can never return in the face of the powers ranged against it: the nobles, the church, the bourgeoisie. Although what sets Julien on the path to his execution is the class conflict I have extracted from the novel here—peasant against aristocrat, church, and bourgeoisie alike—Julien experiences this social conflict within himself as a mourning for a lost joy, a lost freedom to desire and to feel he believes he will never experience.

Once we see that Julien, learning how to "choose the uniform of [his] century" (363; 262; 2.13), plans from the start to stash away his ideas of happiness inside social contexts completely hostile to them, we can better understand his belief in his own hypocrisy. Julien faithfully buries symbols of freedom, feeling, and joy in each situation he enters: in his father's house, the *Mémorial de Sainte-Hélène*; at the Rênals', the portrait of Napoleon; at the seminary, the barmaid Amanda's address; and at the Hôtel de La Mole, his reminiscences of the surgeon-major. Julien hides in caves, boxes, trunks, and mattresses these memories not his own, passed on to him by the surgeon-major as souvenirs or regrets, really, over another way things might have gone. One by one Julien finds he must eradicate, burn, destroy them in the course of the "novel of [his] career" in order to prevent his being discovered— not for being, like Valenod, a political liberal, but for being a real one, a man with a heart attuned to love, liberty, and the pursuit of happiness.

The sham contest between liberals and aristocracy, the meaningless internal struggles in the church, fraught with such seeming significance, are only so many diversions from what Julien apprehends viscerally, not rationally: the loss of the human heart in his time. The surgeon-major has taught him a completely different meaning of the French Revolution from the one the restored aristocracy, the rising bourgeoisie, and the reactionary church unanimously assign it, and therefore he is unfit for his era. Julien's heart is political, but it is the political fate of the *liberté* of 1796–1815 that is its essence.

The Enlightenment Legacy

Feeling now requires a much stronger reading, after years of Victorian and twentieth-century sentimentality and modern reactions against the term. *Feeling* in Stendhal means that portion of human life tied to its material interest. *Material* in Stendhal does not connote what it does today, consumerism and greed. It describes everything related to the pursuit of emotional happiness. With the materialists of the eighteenth century, including Rousseau, Destutt de Tracy, and Helvétius, Stendhal believed feelings are the material level. Characters with a direct relationship to feeling have Stendhal's greatest sympathy; for example, Mme de Rênal, who has that "instinct for happiness natural to all living creatures" (58; 29; 1.7). Julien resists this instinct, yet he is unconsciously ruled by it. He compares Mathilde de La Mole negatively with Mme de Rênal on the basis of feeling: "Mme de Rênal trouvait des raisons pour faire ce que son cœur lui dictait; cette jeune fille du grand monde ne laisse son cœur s'émouvoir que lorsqu'elle s'est prouvé par bonnes raisons qu'il doit être ému" 'Mme. de Rênal always found reasons to do what her heart dictated; this high-society girl lets her heart be moved only when she has found proofs based upon good logic that it ought to be moved' (467; 341; 2.30).

Julien always responds to a refinement of feeling—almost an effeminacy—wherever it appears: in the aristocratic Mme de Rênal and in the Jansenist Pirard; never in Mathilde de La Mole nor most of the men. He revolts against the crudeness and vulgarity of the bourgeoisie and the Jesuits in the church less from snobbery than from his dim awareness that they stifle their feelings much more than the aristocracy does, without the same cause: they do not yet rule, or no longer rule; they religiously practice a repression they have no need of. Julien's heterodox, contradictory politics can be reconciled once his pattern of opposing the man of power to the man of feeling is understood. Julien does not will this opposition, but it positions him precisely.

Yet students don't immediately think of Julien as a man of feeling; they see him as ambitious and calculating. Or if he is a man of feeling, he has carefully controlled and repressed this side of himself, policing it as the upper classes do. Still, he harbors a man of feeling in the classical revolutionary style within him despite himself. Its expression—the attempted murder of Mme de Rênal —is feeling's counterthrust to the imaginary politics that has invaded Julien's subjective life. A real pistol shot in the middle of a church, it rings out against the political pistol shot in the middle of a concert.

Who Kills Julien Sorel?

The opposition of feeling and power does not seem fully creditable where it first appears in the novel (148; 118; 1.23). It relays the narrator's acidic critique of the mayor of Verrières, a man of power, for taking into his household a man of feeling (Julien) rather than a servant. Rênal is actually quite limited in his power: he cannot decide the life or death of his citizens; his only power is an artificially inflated reputation. The references to Shakespeare's *Othello* that abound in the first part of the novel (the handkerchief, for example) betray Rênal's incapacity to vent rage at his wife's adultery, unlike the Moorish general. Very much in the spirit of the new aristocracy, he holds himself in check. However much he might like to kill, exile, imprison, or humiliate Julien, Rênal can practice such acts only against a person's reputation, not against his person. M. de Rênal would never kill Julien because his own reputation is at stake: he would be revealed as a cuckold.

Power in *The Red and the Black*, then, is exercised on an imaginary plane in the Pascalian, Hegelian, and Lacanian senses: it has reality, but it does not touch the Real, the passions of its subjects. Determining who has the power to put Julien to death requires a recalibration of *which* man of power can kill a man of feeling under circumstances in which all struggles are only for prestige. Julien's understanding of society has come to him through books. When, for example, Julien expresses his fear that he will be made to eat with the servants in the Rênal household, the narrator tells us that Julien is horrified not because of snobbery but because "il puisait cette répugnance dans *Les Confessions* de Rousseau. C'était le seul livre à l'aide duquel son imagination se figurait le monde" 'he had picked up his notion from Rousseau's *Confessions*. It was the only book his imagination had made use of in constructing a picture of the social world' (41; 15; 1.5).

This picture may be fictional, but its consequences are real. It announces Julien's susceptibility to the imaginary version of power and politics in which the struggle for prestige, though not lethal, is still a Hegelian struggle for power or mastery. The staged or stagy combat between the three ruling powers (nobles, bourgeoisie, church) has real effects on a powerless subject like Julien: it gives him a sense that the social world offers no options, no escape from its seamless totality of forced choices. Julien, reared on "liberty," will, however unwittingly or unwillingly, ineluctably forge just such an escape.

What sends Julien to his death, I suggest, is not the reactionary, pre-Napoleonic religious code and the autocratic authority ironically masquerading as secular liberal constitutional law that the novel analyzes in all their simulated silliness. It is first of all Julien's pleading his capital criminal case as a political one. Arguing that he has not been allowed a "jury of his peers"—rich peasants—and will thus be misjudged, he makes a case that real interclass conflict and intraclass envy do exist. De facto he demands that he be judged, and if necessary, sent to the guillotine, not for a religious or criminal trespass but because of a hidden political code against rising above one's class, a code that gives the Revolution and democracy the lie. His bold references, in his opening and his summation, to a class struggle between peasants and the rest that is more fundamental than the one between the right and left wings of the ruling coalition finally alienates the twinned forces of church and nobility and outrages the bourgeoisie. His speech amounts to a denunciation of their unholy alliance and a pronouncement of his own death sentence.

He stubbornly maintains this outrage to the bourgeoisie throughout the appeals urged on him by Mathilde. Such deeply unpolitic comportment seems mystifying. Stendhal leaves open several explanations for Julien's unexpected behavior and for the sentence so out of proportion to the crime—Mme de Rênal not only lives but forgives him. They include Julien's self-destructive propensity (as if the sentence were the culmination of a long series of acts in which Julien "blows it") and the Greek-like fatality of the oracle (the torn article he finds in the church about his anagram—Louis Jenrel—being sentenced to death). His drive toward death may unconsciously correspond to Mathilde's belief that only a death sentence confers distinction on a man (323; 230; 2.8)—like Rousseau, Julien desired distinction for himself (and liberty for everyone [333; 238; 2.9]).

But can we not argue that Julien's defiant attitude is actually his way of taking power back into his own hands alone—the power to kill him? He wrests it from the forces that have converged to place him in jeopardy and thereby announces their nullity.

Julien, after all, escapes the fate assigned him by the man of power. He does not die of grief; he dies of happiness. Facing himself in the prison cell, the storm and drama of pseudo-politics and the shallowness of religious piety are put aside. He faces the famous feeling—liberty, the instinct for happiness—that he had convinced himself he could ardently long for by prudently hiding its symbols from others. It had not remained uncontaminated; he had yielded on his desire. When he is alone in prison, it returns with absolute insistence:

> Et pourquoi être encore hypocrite en maudissant l'hypocrisie? Ce n'est ni la mort, ni le cachot, ni l'air humide, c'est l'absence de Mme de Rênal qui m'accable. [. . .] Voilà ce qui m'isole, et non l'absence d'un Dieu juste, bon tout-puissant, point méchant, point avide de vengeance. Ah! s'il existait je tomberais à ses genoux. J'ai mérité la mort, lui dirais-je, mais grand Dieu, Dieu bon, Dieu indulgent, rends-moi celle que j'aime! (548–50)

> And why be hypocritical still, even as I curse hypocrisy? It's neither death, nor the dungeon, nor the damp air, it's the absence of Mme. de Rênal that is crushing me. [. . .]

> That is what isolates me, and not the absence of a God who is just, good, all-powerful, who is not malignant, not hungry for vengeance.
>
> Ah! if He existed. . . . Alas! I should fall at His feet. I have deserved death, I should tell him; but, great God, good God, kind God, give me back the woman I love. (402–03; 2.44)

Losing his head, he regains his heart.

The Crystallization of Love

Mary Anne O'Neil

It is difficult to think of a nineteenth-century novel that treats love in greater detail than does *The Red and the Black*; Stendhal not only brings classical conceptions of love to the surface of his text but also foreshadows future variations on the same theme. In Stendhal's extensive reflections on the conflicts between erotic desire and ambition, the lover's quest for happiness and the fear of jealousy, as well as the inevitable problems that arise between the lover and society, he harks back to the classical moralists the duc de La Rochefoucauld and Mme de Lafayette. In his interest in the actual process of falling in love, Stendhal is Proust's predecessor. All three of the novel's main characters—Julien Sorel, Mme de Rênal, and Mathilde de La Mole—develop and act as they do because they experience a powerful passion unknown to the mundane souls around them. Stendhal drew heavily from his earlier theoretical essay *On Love* (*De l'amour*; 1822) to depict love in *The Red and the Black*, especially his description of a phenomenon he termed crystallization.

A radical departure from Stendhal's earlier, historical writings, *On Love* is a classification and description of the many forms of erotic love experienced by both sexes. The author adds personal anecdotes, frequent comments on lovers from fiction, and observations on how different climates, cultures, and even languages shape this most complex of human emotions. Because of its blend of narratives, psychological analysis, and the study of customs, critics have long connected *On Love* to *The Red and the Black*. René Girard has pointed out common themes, such as illusion, vanity, and imitation (*Deceit* 18). For Ann Jefferson, Stendhal's concern to create a discourse capable of an authentic and original presentation of love informs each book ("*De l'amour*" 149, 154). She calls *On Love* "novelistic," for, like *The Red and the Black*, it appeals to the imagination by offering multiple perspectives of desire (160). Lawrence Schehr goes so far as to consider *On Love* Stendhal's first novel, since it is "a sustained anecdotal narrative that has a theory of the novel in it" (55). Schehr adds that, like *The Red and the Black*, *On Love* replaces the sentimental treatment of love common in eighteenth- and early-nineteenth-century European fiction with a convincing analysis of love (56). Given the obvious similarities, it should not surprise the reader to find in *On Love* the foundations of the discussion of passion conducted in *The Red and the Black*.

Crystallization is the key concept from *On Love* that Stendhal uses in *The Red and the Black*. In chapter 2 of the earlier work, Stendhal explains crystallization through the following analogy:

> Aux mines de sel de Salzbourg, on jette, dans les profondeurs abandonnées de la mine, un rameau d'arbre effeuillé par l'hiver; deux ou trois

> mois après on le retire couvert de cristallisations brillantes: les plus petites branches, celles qui ne sont pas plus grosses que la patte d'une mésange, sont garnies d'une infinité de diamants, mobiles et éblouissants; on ne peut plus reconnaître le rameau primitif.
>
> Ce que j'appelle cristallisation, c'est l'opération de l'esprit, qui tire de tout ce qui se présente la découverte que l'objet aimé a de nouvelles perfections. (8–9)

> In the salt mines of Salzburg a bough stripped of its leaves by winter is thrown into the depths of the unused workings; two or three months later it is pulled out again, covered with brilliant crystals: even the tiniest twigs, no bigger than a tomtit's claw, are spangled with a vast number of shimmering, glittering diamonds, so that the original bough is no longer recognizable.
>
> I call crystallization that process of the mind which discovers fresh perfections in its beloved at every turn of events. (6)

This original conception of love, which rings truer to common experience than "le coup de foudre" (love at first sight), suggests that true affection grows slowly, often without the lover's knowledge or acquiescence.

Like all metaphors, this one is imperfect. Schehr has pointed out that Stendhal unconsciously misleads the reader by comparing the birth of love to the dead branch that has become the core of a solid mineral formation (69). The reader may easily understand the finished object as a symbol of full-blown passion, whereas Stendhal actually wishes to suggest the initial stage of desire, when the discovery of new perfections in the beloved first opens the heart. Jefferson also insists that the principal value of the crystallization metaphor lies in its focus on discovery. Crystallization explains, above all, the expansion of perspective that allows movement out of the self, a shift necessary for any true passion. Just as the eye of the agent who carelessly tossed the branch into the Salzburg mine is dazzled by the brilliant lights emanating from the unexpected crystals, so also the lover's imagination is stimulated to perceive in a thousand different ways the beloved's superior qualities (159) and, thus, is inclined toward love.

In a somewhat different vein, the word "perfection" caused René Girard to deny any real similarity between the love described in *On Love* and that which concludes *The Red and the Black*. In *Deceit, Desire, and the Novel* Girard argues that the bestowal of superior qualities results from the lover's self-deception:

> Could it be authentic passion, in the novels, which is accompanied by crystallization? All Stendhal's great pairs of lovers contradict this point of view. True love, such as that [. . .] which Julien finally knows with Mme de Rênal, does not transfigure. The qualities which this love discovers in

> its object, the happiness it expects from it are not illusory. [. . .] The real Mathilde is the one he does not desire. In the first case, it is a question of passion, in the second of vanity. It is indeed, therefore, vanity which transforms its object. (19)

The description of crystallization Stendhal himself gives, however, in no way implies a falsification. It presents falling in love, rather, as a moment of psychological acuity. The lover discovers the beloved's unique virtues, virtues that eventually cause the lover to lose all previous desires and to invest all hopes of happiness in the beloved alone. Crystallization provokes the lover of *On Love* to esteem his mistress thusly: "Elle me donnerait des plaisirs qu'elle seule au monde peut me donner" 'She would give me pleasures that she alone in all the world can give me' (11; 8). Stendhal almost seems to have anticipated Girard's objection, for in the initial pages of *On Love*, he draws a distinction between "l'amour passion," passionate love that requires crystallization, and "l'amour de vanité" 'vanity love' (5–6; 2–3), whose transports sometimes mimic those of a true sentiment but are fundamentally different.

Before turning to *The Red and the Black*, we should note two final important characteristics of crystallization. First, doubt plays a beneficial role in the consolidation of passion, and it is, in fact, necessary in order to focus the lover's attention on the beloved. Second, more than one crystallization is required for a permanent passion: "Ce qui assure la durée de l'amour, c'est la seconde cristallisation pendant laquelle on voit à chaque instant qu'il s'agit d'être aimé ou de mourir" 'The thing that ensures the duration of love is the second crystallization, during which at every moment one realizes that one must either be loved or perish" (12; 11).

It is most effective to start the study of love in *The Red and the Black* with Mme de Rênal, the first of the three main characters to fall in love and the one whose emotional development most clearly demonstrates crystallization. When she meets Julien, her heart is a sentimental tabula rasa, since she has experienced only maternal love. Stendhal presents her, however, as a heroine: "Douée d'une âme délicate et dédaigneuse, cet instinct de bonheur naturel à tous les êtres faisait que, la plupart du temps, elle ne donnait aucune attention aux actions des personnages grossiers au milieu desquels le hasard l'avait jetée" 'Since she was gifted with a delicate and lofty soul, her instinct for happiness which is natural to all living creatures provided that mostly she paid no attention to the behavior of the gross creatures amid whom fortune had thrust her' (58; 29; 1.7). Her love begins with her admiration of Julien's intelligence and her scorn for money. She seeks him out during her daily routine, often accompanied by her children. Her chambermaid Elisa's proposal of marriage to Julien simultaneously sickens her with jealousy and informs her of her heart's novel condition. "Elle était profondément étonnée. Aurais-je de l'amour pour Julien, se dit-elle enfin?" 'When she was revived and taken to her room she sent everyone away.—Can I be in love with Julien? she said to herself at last' (70–71; 38; 1.8).

Crystallization has begun, but it requires a second shock to force Mme de Rênal's recognition of Julien as the unique agent of her happiness. When he asks her to rescue the hidden portrait of Napoleon, a portrait she believes is that of another woman, she suffers the agony of jealousy. Julien's reassurances then flood her soul with "la présence d'un bonheur que jamais elle n'avait même rêvé" 'the presence of a joy such as she had never dreamed of' (90; 52; 1.11). Her hopes for happiness settle forever on Julien as the crystals settle on the branch in the Salzburg mine.

Mme de Rênal's passion for Julien never wanes, as she amply demonstrates during her reunions with him after his stay in the seminary and in the Besançon prison before his death. Even the remorse that causes her to write the condemning letter to the marquis de La Môle actually bears witness to the strength of her love: "La lettre qui lui avait été imposée par son confesseur [. . .] avait donné le dernier coup à cet être affaibli par un malheur trop constant. Ce malheur était l'absence de Julien; elle l'appelait, elle, *le remords*" 'The letter that had been required of her by her present confessor [. . .] was a final blow to the poor woman, weakened already by excessive grief. Her grief was in fact the absence of Julien; she called it *remorse*' (498; 364; 2.36). It should not surprise the reader that Mme de Rênal dies so soon after her lover's execution. One of the rare "femmes tendres" 'sensitive one[s]' (69; 76), whom Stendhal praises highly in *On Love* because their souls, made for love, find solace in no other pleasure, she cannot survive the loss of Julien.

Julien's second mistress, Mathilde de La Mole, obviously differs in temperament from her provincial predecessor, but she falls in love in much the same way. She too is innocent in affairs of the heart. Overwhelmed by boredom, this haughty nineteen-year-old first admires Julien when he expresses scorn for the privilege of dining with her family: "Celui-là n'est pas né à genoux, pensa-t-elle" 'This fellow wasn't born on his knees, she thought' (290; 204; 2.4). Mathilde soon becomes obsessed with her father's secretary. She invites him to sit near her in her parents' salon; she favors him at the ball, preferring to eavesdrop on his discussion with count Altamira than to dance; and she chooses the moments Julien works in the library to browse there. The strange enthusiasm for life she feels, thanks to Julien, sheds light on her emotions:

> Une idée l'illumina tout à coup: J'ai le bonheur d'aimer, se dit-elle un jour, avec un transport de joie incroyable. J'aime, j'aime, c'est clair! A mon âge, une fille jeune, belle, spirituelle, où peut-elle trouver des sensations, si ce n'est dans l'amour? (348)
>
> Suddenly an idea struck her: I must be in love, she said one day in a transport of incredible delight. I'm in love, I'm in love, it's clear! At my age, a girl who is young, beautiful, clever—where can she find sensations, if not in love? (250; 2.11)

Crystallization has begun. Mathilde finds Julien not only handsome but even capable of the same reckless courage as her heroic ancestor Boniface de La Mole (367; 265; 2.14). Julien's indifference to her only strengthens her infatuation until she wagers her virtue by inviting him to a nighttime tryst in her bedroom.

Why do matters go awry once Julien and Mathilde make love? Here, *On Love* is very helpful to our understanding of Mathilde's change of heart. Stendhal suggests in the theoretical work that an adolescent, whose desires are uninformed by experience, cannot develop a true passion (21; 23). Their premature sexual liaison further undermines their relations, even though the woman, Mathilde, instigates their union. Her bitter reproach to Julien, "J'ai l'horreur de m'être livrée au premier venu" 'I am horrified at having given myself to the first comer' (387; 281; 2.17), echoes Stendhal's caution in the chapter on modesty of *On Love* that physical liberties, far from reassuring the woman, can make her doubt and even hate her lover. Although Stendhal is no prude, he understands very well the value of modesty, which he calls "la mère de l'amour" 'the mother of love' (66; 73), because it protects an immature passion from unsettling shame.

More fundamentally, however, a conflicting passion occupies Mathilde's heart. She offers the perfect example of what in *On Love* Stendhal terms "l'amour de vanité" (6; 2), egotistical love that cannot crystallize around another person since vain lovers seek perfection only in themselves. When such a passion ends, the lover does not suffer from an irreplaceable loss but simply regrets that the future may not afford any greater excitement (6; 3). Vanity is the opposite of tenderness, and it occupies the head rather than the heart. Stendhal observes, moreover, that vain women are likely to approach love as a soldier might engage in battle, warily, with calculation, always parrying the adversary's blows to their pride (74–75; 82–83).

As soon as she envisages the possibility of loving Julien, Mathilde dreams of the admiration she will elicit when she spurns her noble suitors for a commoner. Dramatic in thought and deed, she attempts to demonstrate the force of her character by exposing herself to ever greater risks. Julien's role in this passion seems almost insignificant: "Du moment qu'elle eut décidé qu'elle aimait Julien, elle ne s'ennuya plus. Tous les jours elle se félicitait du parti qu'elle avait pris de se donner une grande passion. Cet amusement a bien des dangers, pensait-elle. Tant mieux! mille fois tant mieux!" 'From the moment of her decision that she loved Julien, she was no longer bored. Every day she congratulated herself on her decision to indulge in a great passion. It's a dangerous game, she thought; so much the better! A thousand times better!' (355; 255; 2.12). Alternately sick with fear of submission and exhilarated by her success in humiliating Julien, she seems relieved when he departs on his diplomatic mission: "Mathilde l'avait presque oublié pendant son voyage. Ce n'est après tout qu'un être commun, pensait-elle, son nom me rappellera toujours la plus grande faute de ma vie" 'Mathilde had almost forgotten him while he was away. After all, he is only a common creature; his name will always remind me of the blackest blot on my life' (445; 325; 2.25).

Girard's chapter "Master and Slave" in *Deceit, Desire, and the Novel* offers the best explanation of Mathilde's renewed obsession with Julien on his return to the Hôtel de La Mole (107–12) by attributing it to pride. It is easy to mistake the genuine misery she experiences when Julien feigns indifference toward her during his courtship of Mme de Fervaques as evidence that she has finally fallen in love. Her sacrifice of reputation and social position to marry Julien reinforces this interpretation, as do Stendhal's comments, at several points in the conclusion, that for the first time this proud soul was in love (474; 346; 2.32). Her excessive emotions, her public displays, and her need to control Julien's fate should, however, alert the reader to the falseness of her sentiments. *The Red and the Black*'s final paragraphs offer irrefutable proof that Mathilde's admiration for Julien has not crystallized into passionate love and remains infected by vanity-love, or *l'amour de vanité*. She never mourns her lover's death but rather, exalted by the possibility of proving that she equals Marguerite de Valois in daring and nobility, turns Julien's funeral into a self-serving spectacle. As Jefferson has aptly noted, vanity love inevitably results in imitation ("*De l'amour*" 150). Since Mathilde has never experienced authentic passion, she naturally resorts to old family tricks to satisfy her desires. Julien is right when he tells Mathilde that her love could bring neither of them permanent happiness: "dans quinze ans vous regarderez comme une folie excusable, mais pourtant comme une folie, l'amour que vous avez eu pour moi [. . .]" 'in fifteen years you will regard the love you have borne me as an excusable folly, perhaps, but still a folly [. . .]' (520; 380; 2.39).

In his own development as a lover Julien combines the experiences of his two mistresses. At the outset he is the least knowledgeable of the three in sentimental matters. He is even prouder than Mathilde, and his heart has little room for any passion other than vanity. While he finds Mme de Rênal attractive and of a superior character, he does not even seem to admire her until after he seduces her. With his vanity satisfied by this conquest and his ambitions temporarily forgotten thanks to Mme de Rênal's obvious affection, Julien begins to experience pleasure in her company. When her remorse and the gossips of Verrières threaten his happiness, a first crystallization occurs. Julien admits to his mistress, who blames her son's illness on her adultery and begs Julien to leave her, "[J]amais je ne t'ai tant aimée, mon cher ange, ou plutôt, de cet instant seulement, je commence à t'adorer comme tu mérites de l'être" '[N]ever have I loved you so much, my darling, or rather, it's only at this moment that I've begun to love you as you deserve' (140; 91; 1.19). Although preoccupied by intrigues in the seminary, Julien never stops loving Mme de Rênal, as proven by his reaction to her unexpected appearance in the Besançon cathedral and by his secret visit to Verrières on his way to Paris. Stendhal suggests by the title he gives to this latter episode, "Un ambitieux" 'Ambition' (1.30), that Julien's vanity causes him to seduce once more his repentant mistress. But the suggestion is misleading, for Julien only tricks his way into Mme de Rênal's bed when she repulses his sincere attempt to revive their past happiness.

How, then, can Julien fall in love with Mathilde? To return to Stendhal's analysis of love, a second crystallization, much more powerful than the first (11; 8) and necessary to transform Mme de Rênal into the unique guarantor of Julien's pleasure, has not yet taken place when Julien arrives at the Hotel de La Mole. Once in Paris, Julien directs his instinct for happiness toward his employer's daughter because she incarnates the noble, cosmopolitan world that it is now his ambition to conquer: "Tout ce que la civilisation la plus élégante peut présenter de vifs plaisirs, n'était-il pas réuni comme à l'envie chez Mlle de La Mole?" 'Everything that the most elegant civilization can offer in the way of brilliant delight, isn't it all perfectly present in Mlle de La Mole?' (411; 298; 2.20). Stendhal gives the reader several indications that Julien's desire for Mathilde never develops into passionate love. He finds little except beauty to admire in Mathilde initially and, as the novel progresses, recognizes her defects rather than her perfections. More important, Julien is seldom happy with Mathilde, except for brief moments when his pride has overwhelmed hers or he has bested her aristocratic suitors. Eventually, even such power bores him. When she throws herself at his feet, Julien feels "plus étonné qu'heureux" 'more astonished than happy' (464; 338; 2.30), a sentiment that dominates his attitude toward Mathilde in the days before his death.

Unbeknownst to Julien, a second crystallization of his passion for Mme de Rênal begins even as he consciously pursues Mathilde de La Mole. In his frequent comparisons of his two mistresses, he invariably judges the second inferior to the first. Julien notes that Mathilde's exceptional eyes betray a cold cruelty, while Mme de Rênal's gaze reveals her warmth and virtue (280; 196; 2.2). The Parisian lacks the provincial noblewoman's modesty and natural grace. Julien soon recognizes the differences in their capacities for love: Mme de Rênal follows her heart's dictates, whereas Mathilde "ne laisse son coeur s'émouvoir que lorsqu'elle s'est prouvé par bonnes raisons qu'il doit être ému" 'lets her heart be moved only when she has found proofs based upon good logic that it ought to be moved' (467; 340; 2.30). These comparisons have the greatest bearing on Julien's happiness, the need for which is much harder to satisfy, it turns out, than that for ambition.

The second crystallization occurs after Julien's attempt to kill Mme de Rênal and in almost precisely the manner Stendhal describes in *On Love*: if ever the lover seriously fears losing the beloved woman's affections, he will simultaneously lose interest in all other pleasures and place all happiness in the beloved alone. Love truly becomes the focus of existence. When Julien awakes in the Besançon prison, convinced that Mme de Rênal loathes him for his crime, "Il n'avait plus d'ambition" 'Ambition was dead in him' (503; 368; 2.36). At the same time, he recalls Mme de Rênal's face and knows that the time he spent with her at Vergy was his period of greatest happiness. Although he at first mistakes his emotions for remorse, his memories of Mme de Rênal, which make him even less tolerant of Mathilde's extravagances, soon clarify the state of his heart. When Mme de Rênal finally gains entry to his cell, Julien declares an honest passion free of all vanity: "—Sache que je t'ai toujours aimée, que je n'ai aimé que toi" '—You must know that I've always loved you, I never loved anyone but you' (538; 394; 2.43). This love remains firm in the face of death, which Julien fears less than his mistress's absence.

The theory of love Stendhal propounds in *On Love* provides insights into the novel's conclusion, specifically as to why Julien does not avoid execution when he could easily do so. The reader who has followed the hero's dizzying social ascent may find his ready acquiescence to death incomprehensible, but it makes more sense if we connect it to the notion of crystallization. As Jefferson explains, crystallization transports the lover out of the social sphere, and the lover's vision, which accords all perfection to the beloved, may easily be opposed to the general opinion ("*De l'amour*" 154–55). Throughout *On Love* Stendhal insists on the superiority of passionate love to every other form of human pleasure. In his novel's final chapters Julien adopts the same attitude. Julien comes to favor the hours he spends with Mme de Rênal over worldly success or a long life. He eventually equates loving with living. As he reminds himself in prison, his most important task is "de vivre et d'aimer, quand il me reste si peu de jours [. . .]" 'to live and love, when I have so few days left [. . .]' (539; 395; 2.43). This does not mean that Julien deliberately tries to shorten his life. In fact when Mme de Rênal suggests a double suicide during their first reunion in prison, he declares it foolish to sacrifice two months of certain joy (540; 395; 2.43). In a later scene he also longs for five more years—if he could spend them with Mme de Rênal (494; 403; 2.44). He does not, however, want to live under his past circumstances, either under Mathilde's authority or as Mme de Rênal's occasional, secretive lover, which would be his inevitable choice after a successful appeal or escape. Love allows Julien to become heroic at the end of his life. He disengages his soul from petty ambition, asserts his independence from society, and decides his fate. Through Julien, Stendhal convinces the reader of the superiority of the instinct for happiness over all other human impulses.

Stendhal most commonly speaks of the rewards of love as "happiness," "joy," and "pleasure." What exactly does he mean by these terms? He means the satisfaction resulting from the assurance of the beloved's affection and from the constant contact with the beloved that increases our self-understanding as well as our understanding of the other. A true passion can release the lover from the negative sentiments of fear and vanity. It heightens the lover's awareness of beauty, intensifies the emotions, and produces a harmony of the senses and intellect. In *On Love*, Stendhal explains that passionate love, however powerful, is a simple happiness. It nourishes itself on the lovers' ability to remain natural, spontaneous, and lucid: "Tout l'art d'aimer se réduit, ce me semble, à dire exactement ce que le degré d'ivresse du moment comporte, c'est-à-dire, en d'autres termes, à écouter son âme" 'The whole art of loving reduces itself, it appears to me, to saying exactly what the degree of intoxication of the moment suggests, that is to say, in other words, to listening to the dictates of one's heart' (96; 106–07). In *The Red and the Black* Stendhal creates in Mme de Rênal and Julien Sorel two rare, "tender souls" capable of such passion. Almost as soon as she falls in love, Mme de Rênal becomes able to live each moment fully. In one of the noteworthy glimpses into her modest soul that Stendhal offers the reader, the scene in the Vergy garden where an overwrought Julien hardly enjoys the hand he has seized: "[. . .] Mme de Rênal, la main dans celle de Julien, [. . .] ne pensait à rien; elle se laissait vivre. Les heures qu'on passa sous ce grand tilleul [. . .] furent pour elle une époque de bonheur" 'As for Mme de Rênal, with her hand in Julien's, she thought of nothing at all; she allowed herself to live. The moments passed under the great linden tree [. . .] were for her a whole age of happiness' (78; 44; 1.9). Although it takes Julien a lifetime to do so, through love he finally learns to live in the present, an achievement far more significant than his social successes.

FORMAL APPROACHES

A Narratological Approach to *The Red and the Black*

Gerald Prince

One way to approach a novel narratologically is to study some of its salient narrative features (for instance, the point of view, the modes of discourse, the speed of the narration, the reliability of the narrator), offer a provisional description of their functioning, and explore how they illuminate and are illuminated by (other features of) the novel as a whole, the meanings it generates, the responses it provokes, and the values it foregrounds.

The feature of *The Red and the Black* that many critics—and most of my undergraduates—consider perhaps its most striking formal trait is its use of (interior) monologue. If the frequency with which Stendhal resorted to that discourse mode was probably unprecedented, the distribution of monologues in the novel is just as noteworthy, and so is the number of functions they perform. More than a dozen characters have monologues—from Julien and Mathilde to Amanda Binet, Tanbeau, the chevalier de Beauvoisis, and the ex-lieutenant of the Ninety-Sixth—and there are nearly as many monologues as there are pages in the novel. Indeed, monologue appears even in the midst of dialogue:

> —Ce mot n'est point de mise ici, lui dit-il. [. . .] Dans cette maison, entendre, mon très cher fils, c'est obéir. Combien avez-vous d'argent?
>
> Nous y voici, se dit Julien, c'était pour cela qu'était le très cher fils.
>
> —Trente-cinq francs, mon père.

> —Ecrivez soigneusement l'emploi de cet argent; vous aurez à m'en rendre compte. (204)

> —That expression has no meaning here, said he. [. . .] In this house, my very dear son, to hear is to obey. How much money have you?
> Here we are at the point, said Julien to himself; this was the reason for the *very dear son*.
> —Thirty-five francs, my father.
> —Keep careful track of how you spend that money; you will have to account for it to me. (139; 1.25)

Moreover, monologue does not only play an important role in thematization (the dialectic of understanding and action; the seductions of silence) and in characterization (Mme de Rênal shows much less affection for it than either Julien—who constantly needs to assess his situation—or Mathilde); it is also, more generally, a fundamental ingredient of Stendhal's psychological discernment, of his celebrated clearness, and—because of the agility with which he handles the mode—of the very buoyancy associated with his narration (see Attuel; Castex, Rouge et le noir *de Stendhal* 178–80; Crouzet, Rouge 67–71; Trouiller).

Many critics—and undergraduates—also agree that narratorial intrusiveness is another important trait of *The Red and the Black*. Here Stendhal did not innovate: he inherited the technique from such eighteenth-century authors as Sterne, Fielding, and Diderot. But his narrator does intervene with undeniable panache, and the abundance of explicit commentary on the narrating and the narrated as well as the multiplicity of epigraphs, footnotes, metanarrative passages, and disnarrated elements have given rise to an impressive critical literature. Critics have seen the intrusions, for example, as signs of Stendhal's egotism or of his desire to establish complicity with his reader. They have also said the intrusions contribute to readability, emphasize the arbitrariness of narrative, increase realistic illusion, and, most generally, add to the self-consciousness and self-reflexiveness of the world the novel depicts (see, in particular, Blin; Bolster 25–27; Brombert, *Stendhal et la voie*; Day; and Haig 26–50).

The novel's predilection for both narratorial intrusions and (interior) monologues may seem paradoxical, especially when—as often happens in *The Red and the Black*—the two techniques are conjoined or fused: "Quelle pitié notre provincial ne va-t-il pas inspirer aux jeunes lycéens de Paris qui, à quinze ans, savent déjà entrer dans un café d'un air si distingué? [. . .] [I]l faut que je lui dise la vérité, pensa Julien" 'What pity will be felt for our bumpkin by those Paris schoolboys who at fifteen already know how to enter a café in such distinguished style! [. . .] I must tell her the truth, thought Julien' (192; 130; 1.24). One technique implies the narrator's absence whereas the other asserts his or her presence; one stresses story information and the other the discourse informer. But (seeming) paradoxes may not be that paradoxical in a novel in which major events are elided and incidental ones accentuated (Genette,

"Stendhal" [*Figures of Literary Discourse*] 169–71), jail proves a locus of freedom, the hero is a tender hypocrite, and a scandalous shooting occurs (from which I never quite recovered). Besides, perhaps following the lead of Georges Blin, who attempted to show the compatibility in Stendhal of narratorial intrusions with "restrictions of field" (internal focalizations), critics have stressed the complementarity of interventions by the narrator and monologues by the characters: the subjective voice of the former joins the subjective voice of the latter, experience accompanies youthfulness, and prose mingles with poetry (Trouiller). Whatever the differences between the two forms may be, they have in common an equivocal relation to narrative (both to events and to their narration). If the intrusions replace story with discourse and thus signal the disappearance of narrative (it cannot exist without story), the monologues mark the replacement of "pure narrative" (in Plato's sense) by "imitation," of narrating by something akin to dramatic style.

There are a number of other (formal and thematic) features in *The Red and the Black* that reveal a similarly problematic attitude toward narrative. Or at least toward what Hayden White called "narrativizing": making the world speak itself as a story, imposing "story form" on events instead of simply reporting them. Stendhal surely enjoys the telling of actions and happenings. Didn't he say somewhere that the very basis of a novel lay in the multiplication of incidents? Anyhow, the abundance of episodes in *The Red and the Black* (many of which—like Julien's meeting with don Diego Bustos—prove far from essential to the action) is eloquent. But contrary to his protagonist, Stendhal does not appear to enjoy plotting, to value its mechanisms. In fact, he may well be wary of *récit* (recital), which is linked, etymologically, to repetition and which, in French generic taxonomies, designates a homodiegetic narrative whose narrator retraces what has already been said and done. (Isn't it notable that Henri Beyle, the great "egotist," never wrote a first-person novel?) The *récit*—as opposed to the *roman*—is a reciting; it reaccounts for what is over; it services the rehearsed (Fernandez 60–61).

An important formal characteristic of *The Red and the Black* (one that underlines its strongly episodic nature) is its penchant for chronological order, for a "natural" rather than "concerted" order. To be sure, there are quite a few analepses (retrospections, flashbacks) in the novel: my students regularly isolate over one hundred of them. But most are brief (e.g., 49, 58, 63; 22, 28, 33; 1.6, 1.7) and most—not to say all—do not decipher time, compose it, or impose meaning on it (by insisting, for example, that the future illuminates the past or vice versa). Rather, they merely purvey information (e.g., 47, 59, 72; 21, 29, 40; 1.5, 1.7, 1.8), they facilitate the depiction of simultaneous events (e.g., 91, 96, 150; 53, 56, 98; 1.11, 1.12, 1.21), or they stress the narrator's graceful ease: "Le lecteur est peut-être surpris de ce ton libre et presque amical; nous avons oublié de dire que depuis six semaines le marquis était retenu chez lui par une attaque de goutte" 'The reader is perhaps surprised at this free and almost friendly tone; we have neglected to note that for six weeks the marquis had been kept within doors by an attack of the gout' (309; 219; 2.7). Moreover, there are very few prolepses (anticipations, flashforwards) in the novel. In class we counted fewer than a dozen and found none pertaining to important events. Indeed, as the absence of repeating prolepses (phrases like "We shall see in due course" or "The reader will see later") suggests, anticipatory passages in *The Red and the Black* are not only strange (e.g., "Elle dansa pour échapper à la conversation sur l'apoplexie, qui n'en était pas une, car le surlendemain le baron reparut" 'She danced to get away from the discussions of apoplexy, though indeed it wasn't really such, for a few days later the baron turned up again' [328; 234; 2.9]); they are also perhaps dispensable. At any rate, the hyperfunctionalists among my undergraduates repeatedly fail to uncover the distinctive function of the novel's prolepses and usually end up regarding them as so many more signs of Stendhal's naturalness.

If on the level of form *The Red and the Black* appears to resist plotting or the concerted order of the already known, it manifests the same kinds of distaste on the level of content. Whereas Mme de Rênal's straightforwardness and spontaneity are honored, for instance, the repetitive, the rehearsed, and the predictable (in the language of fiction, the seminary, and the courtroom, in provincial dinners and Parisian balls) are privileged targets for Stendhal's wit. As for the protagonist, whose first job consists in reciting lessons or making others recite them (169; 112–13; 1.22) and whose second job involves writing letters that merely develop M. de La Mole's instructions (269; 187–88; 2.1), he is not particularly admirable for knowing the Bible in Latin by heart and being able to repeat it aloud (that is good for the inhabitants of Verrières [102, 168; 61, 112; 1.13, 1.22]) or for quoting snatches from *La nouvelle Héloïse* to Amanda Binet or Mathilde (194, 381; 132, 276; 1.24, 2.16). Nor is he admirable for plotting or for trying to conform to the Napoleonic stories he has heard or read. On the contrary, he is truly eloquent when he improvises (281, 530; 197, 387; 2.2, 2.41) and he is most attractive when (and because) he proves different, capable of taking unexpected turns and of standing outside convention or propriety, impossible to contain in the straitjacket of the ready-made. At the end of the novel he gives up his models as well as his fascination for his own future. Our hero, who has by nature "cette mine froide et *à mille lieues de la sensation présente*, que nous cherchons à nous donner" 'that cool expression, *a thousand miles from the sensation of the moment*, which we are all eager to acquire' (313; 222; 2.7), finally becomes able to live "au jour le jour" 'from day to day' (554; 406; 2.45); he no longer sees the present as a mere transition from past to future, follows established plans, or worries about programs to come. He has renounced his ambitions (500, 517; 365, 379; 2.36, 2.39), and, as Georges Poulet argued forcefully, "the person who renounces the life of ambition gives up consciousness of his life in the form of the past as in the form of the future. And, suddenly, his life becomes a life without past or future. It is a life reduced to the present, a merely momentary life" (471).

Julien's opting to live for the present finds a parallel in the novel's seeming bias for "presentification." "[U]n roman est un miroir qui se promène sur une grande route" '[A] novel is a mirror moving along a highway' (398; 289; 2.19). Whatever meanings may be attributed to the narrator's (or Saint-Réal's!) famous definition, it seems clear to me that such a mirror, in particular, captures neither the past nor the future but the present, one moment after another. There is also the relative paucity—and lightness—of foreshadowings in the novel (I know: there are the church of Verrières, the family romance, Danton, Boniface de La Mole, Valenod, and Louis Jenrel; but *The Red and the Black* is surely more surprising than not; and I have to point out to my students—as it was pointed out to me—that *Louis Jenrel* is an anagram of *Julien Sorel*). Furthermore, there is the matter of Stendhal's style, which Nathalie Sarraute neatly characterized as "a dry style, direct, perfectly natural, as if it goes without saying, free from all redundancy, shorn of affectation, stripped to the extreme, transparent, invisible"(Sarraute 3, qtd. in Haig 71). Aside from Julien's (and the narrator's) delightful assaults against periodic style (450–55; 328–32; 2.26–27), Stendhal's predilection for parataxis and asyndetic expression at the level of the sentence (e.g., "Ses combats étaient bien plus pénibles que le matin, son âme avait eu le temps de s'émouvoir" 'His inner conflict was far more painful than it had been that morning; his spirit had had time to mobilize itself' [469; 342; 2.31]) but also at the level of the paragraph and of the very structure of the novel strikes me as especially revealing: a series rather than a sum, many dots as opposed to one continuous line, the staccato and not the legato. There is, moreover, the novelist's well-known distaste for detailed descriptions and lengthy portraits. What do we know, for example, of Mme de Fervaques's drawing-room, aside from the fact that "[il] était de la plus haute magnificence, doré comme la galerie de Diane aux Tuileries, avec des tableaux à l'huile aux lambris" '[it] was of the utmost magnificence, gilded like Diana's gallery at the Tuileries, with oil paintings in the panels' (454; 331; 2.27)? and what do we know of the physical attributes of M. de Luz and M. de Caylus, abbé Chélan and old Sorel, or even Mme de Rênal and Mathilde de La Mole? There is the very brevity of the novel's seventy-five chapters, which have an average length of seven or eight pages and often run no longer than three or four. There is the deftness of the narration, the nimbleness with which it goes from one mode to another, from dialogue to monologue to straight reporting to commentary:

> —Eh, grand Dieu! pourquoi toutes ces précautions? dit Mathilde étonnée.
>
> A propos de quoi est-ce que je mentirais? pensa Julien, et il avoua tous ses soupçons.
>
> —Voilà donc la cause de la froideur de tes lettres! s'écria Mathilde avec l'accent de la folie plus que de la tendresse. (380)

> —Good Lord! Why all these precautions? said Mathilde in amazement.
>
> Why should I lie? thought Julien, and told her of all his suspicions.

> —So that's the reason your letters were so cold! Mathilde exclaimed, with an expression more of madness than of affection. (276; 2.16)

There is what might be called the novelist's impatience (like Gide, Stendhal has no capacity for boredom: *il ne sait pas s'ennuyer*), the recourse to *et ceteras* (234, 525, 541; 163, 384, 396; 1.29, 2.40, 2.43), the partiality for ellipsis, the syncopated narration—hopping, skipping, jumping—that so baffled Stendhal's contemporaries (Imbert, "Quelques" 31). There is, finally, the frequent use of the present tense itself, which brings us back (of course!) to monologues and intrusions since the present tense figures in both techniques.

Monologues in *The Red and the Black* have been viewed as the clearest indicators of the novel's presentness. Signifying the bursting forth of the private as opposed to the public person, they put us in the presence of the characters' inner speech and allow us to become immersed in their intimate beings, away from the narrator's mediation (Trouiller). There is considerable justification for that view, but it should perhaps be qualified. After all, a mediating narrator usually stands near the soliloquizing character: not only are most of the monologues quite short; most of them consist of tagged—rather than free—direct discourse and, as such, are not quite liberated from narratorial patronage. Moreover, some monologues are clearly exterior as opposed to interior (e.g., "Eh bien! elle ne m'aime plus, se répétait-il en se parlant tout haut comme pour apprendre sa position" 'All right! so she doesn't love me any more, he kept saying to himself, speaking aloud as though explaining his position to himself' [409; 297; 2.20]), and it is difficult to determine whether many others represent inner or outer speech: Julien, for instance, "exclaim[s] inwardly" (466; 340; 2.30; trans. modified) and "exclaim[s]" (204; 140; 1.25); he "sa[ys] [. . .] to himself" (170; 113; 1.22) but also "sa[ys] [. . .] with a sigh" (190; 129; 1.24) or simply "sa[ys]" (182, 388; 123, 281; 1.23, 2.17); he frequently "add[s]" or "[goes] on" (373; 247, 270; 2.10, 2.15), and he even adopts a Gascon accent in reflection (373; 270; 2.15). Indeed, Stendhal shows no effort to make interior monologues stylistically more "realistic" than exterior ones or, at least, different from them; nor does he make a sustained attempt to distinguish them stylistically from one another (or from utterances in dialogue). Ultimately, the novelist seems less interested in rendering the singularity of specific presents than their typicality, less interested in depicting particular moments than representative ones, and this attitude becomes manifest in the frequent conjunction of monologue and iterative narration (116, 212, 344; 72, 146, 248; 1.16, 1.26, 2.10).

If the presents of the monologues are problematic (they often have less to do with specified points in time than with unlocalized points through time, less to do with a particularized world than with a generalized technique), the presents of the narrator's intrusions prove equally tricky. The narrator identifies himself as a temporal being (one who is a "liberal" and has often looked at the valley of the Doubs); moreover, he temporally situates his act of telling (it occurs in the nineteenth century after the fall of Napoleon); and, on occasion, he even stresses his temporal *presence to* this telling (167, 346, 469; 111, 249, 342; 1.22, 2.11, 2.31). But he also usually acts as an omniscient, ubiquitous, godlike narrator, a "traditional" narrator free from the order of time (e.g., 58, 73, 104; 29, 40, 63; 1.7, 1.8, 1.13), and, though his narration has a loosely calculable date, it does not have any measurable duration.

It is that kind of atemporal, present-transcending present which Julien desires without knowing it and which he reaches at the end of the novel when he is finally able to withdraw beyond signs and history: a present out of time, liberated from past and future, a moment forever. It is also, I think, the kind of present to which Stendhal's novel itself aspires and that it approximates with its famously imprecise chronology (moments count but not their exact temporal relation to one another) and its speed (it has no time; it is out of time). Finally, this present is certainly the kind for which the "happy many" treasure *The Red and the Black*: one that is timeless but ever new.

On Not "Yielding a Return": Plot and the Concept of Freedom in *The Red and the Black*

Michal Peled Ginsburg

In the opening pages of *The Red and the Black* the narrator introduces us to the small town of Verrières, where the plot of the novel is about to begin. Having led us through a short tour of the town, the narrator tells us of the mayor's practice of trimming the town's trees regularly. The mayor justifies the practice in these terms: "J'aime l'ombre, je fais tailler *mes* arbres pour donner de l'ombre, et je ne conçois pas qu'un arbre soit fait pour autre chose, quand toutefois, comme l'utile noyer, il *ne rapporte pas de revenu*" 'I am very fond indeed of the shade; I have *my* trees trimmed in order to give shade; I don't suppose a tree is really good for anything else, unless, like the useful walnut, *it yields a return.*' And the narrator comments: "Voilà le grand mot qui décide tout à Verrières: RAPPORTER DU REVENU. A lui seul il représente la pensée habituelle de plus de trois quarts des habitants" 'There now is the grand phrase that decides everything at Verrières: YIELD A RETURN. That phrase alone represents the mental life of three quarters of the townspeople' (29; 6; 1.2; emphasis in the orig.). The principle of yielding a return is an economic principle according to which, as the example of cutting back the trees makes clear, a loss produces a gain. Not only is the priest Maslon rumored to make money from the trimming of the trees in the public square, but the trimming enables the trees to give more shade, which, according to the mayor, is the economical function of trees that, unlike the "useful walnut," do not bear marketable fruit.

Students can easily grasp that in the opening pages of the novel the principle of yielding a return is attacked most directly as an example of the sacrifice of aesthetic pleasure for economic gain. The beauty of the trees is sacrificed for their utility just as the beauty of the town as a whole is regarded as a money-making asset. The narrator uses the opposition between aesthetic pleasure and economic gain to create complicity with the reader since he can count on the reader's preferring the former: no reader will willingly admit to being a philistine ready to destroy beauty for money:

> *Rapporter du revenu* est la raison qui décide de tout dans cette petite ville qui vous semblait si jolie. L'étranger qui arrive, séduit par la beauté des fraîches et profondes vallées qui l'entourent, s'imagine d'abord que ses habitants soient sensibles au *beau*; ils ne parlent que trop souvent de la beauté de leur pays: on ne peut pas nier qu'ils s'en fassent grand cas; mais c'est parce qu'elle attire quelques étrangers dont l'argent enrichit les aubergistes, ce qui, par le mécanisme de l'octroi, *rapporte du revenu à la ville*. (29)
>
> *Yielding a return* decides everything in this little town which at first seemed so attractive to you. The stranger, as he arrives, is so entranced

> by the beauty of the cool, deep valleys that he imagines the natives are themselves responsive to beauty. It is true that they talk, even to excess, of how beautiful their town is; they make a great to-do over it. But the reason is simply that the scenery attracts various outsiders, whose money enriches the hotel keepers and thus, through the tax-collecting machinery, *yields a return to the town*. (6; 1.2)

The cutting back of the trees has also political connotations, since those who practice and profit by it are the reactionary mayor and priest whereas the one who openly opposes it is the "chirurgien-major de l'armée d'Italie" (28; 6; 1.2), a representative of the army that for Stendhal is the emblem of the passion for freedom. The narrator himself only wishes the trees were left "free" to grow as they do in England: the opposition between French and English gardening becomes a metaphor for the opposition between the reactionary politics of the Restoration and the ideal of a "monarchie d'après la charte" 'constitutional monarchy' represented by England. (Our students may be dismayed to learn that Stendhal was never an advocate of democracy, as his numerous remarks on the United States make clear.) Stendhal does not explicitly oppose reactionary and liberal politics since he cannot count on his readers' endorsement of his political opinions in the same way that he can count on their embracing aesthetic pleasure as a realm of freedom. If anything, the sliding from the aesthetic to the political can be seen as a rhetorical ploy designed to persuade the reader who has opted for beauty of the desirability of political freedom.

The critique of yielding a return is more than a critique of philistinism or of conservative politics since what opposes both is a certain notion of freedom. Freedom, of course, is a key concept for Stendhal. It is normally understood as the opposition either to social constraints (that is, as the equivalent of spontaneity, opposed to role-playing or codified behavior) or to tyranny (familial or political). The analysis of the opening description can serve to show another, more problematic and ultimately, I argue, more important understanding of freedom: to be free for Stendhal is opposed to being determined by goals or ends. To accept the principle of yielding a return means to accept incurring a loss with the aim of gaining something—later, elsewhere. Since what is gained is presumably better than what is lost (or else why accept the loss?), this principle generates and depends on a hierarchy of values. If Stendhal criticizes the inhabitants of Verrières it is not simply because their hierarchy of values is false (they esteem money more than beauty); rather, it is because he refuses hierarchization and its complement, subordination. To want the trees to remain free to grow as they will, to see them as first and foremost beautiful, is to resist subordinating their existence to some "higher" goal that lies outside them. In other words, the opposition between those who seek profit and those who cherish beauty is between the valorization of usefulness and that of freedom, defined as the rejection of subordination to an end. Up to now it seems as if in linking freedom to beauty the narrator simply presents us with the classical privileging of the aesthetic as disinterested, as a separate sphere, well demarcated from mundane social life, from which it can serve as a refuge. But the violent end of the novel suggests that this cannot be quite so. To understand the end of the novel we need to see what Stendhal's understanding of freedom means on the level of plot.

The subordination of means (or middle) to a goal (or end) is the basic assumption of the traditional novelistic plot. Students of the novel learn that every act in the well-constructed plot contributes to an end; a pistol purchased at the beginning of the novel means a pistol shot at the end. The economy of the plot is that episodes, incidents, and conversations are harnessed to a goal, are "useful" because they give us clues, foreshadow, create parallels or oppositions, and so on. (Of course, those incidents that are not useful for the plot may be useful for another goal—such as thematic content or symbolic depth.) An episode that is not useful in any of these ways appears meaningless—excessive or wasteful. Even a cursory reading of *The Red and the Black* shows the extent to which its plot is not well constructed in this traditional way. The most spectacular instance of "useless plot" is the conservative plot in which Julien gets involved as a messenger—a plot that is soon forgotten, its end is never told, and that remains totally irrelevant to the fate of the hero and the other characters.

The duel between Julien and the chevalier de Beauvoisis (2.6) is another example, one which can be read as an emblem for the "freedom" of the middle, in *The Red and the Black*, its independence of an end. As D. A. Miller shows in his detailed analysis of this scene (259–64) the episode consists of a series of displacements that completely undermine the scenario of a duel. Moreover, the duel itself is treated almost in passing, whereas the conversation on the way to the duel between the chevalier, Julien, and their seconds, becomes the focus of interest, pleasure, and narrative investment. As Miller emphasizes, this episode is not simply an instance of a shift in emphasis from the center to the margin, a common device in realistic fiction whereby "accessory circumstances, or objects, stand in for other more central and less explicit concerns" (162). The conversation on the way does not stand, metonymically, for the duel; rather it manifests how in Stendhal the middle and the means are the locus of pleasure and interest, so much so that they become independent of the goal they presumably were designed to serve. This episode allegorizes the way in which in Stendhal the middle frees itself of an end, refuses to be useful or yield a return, and remains an enclave of "useless" pleasure.

But this, of course, is not the whole story. Though *The Red and the Black* is not a traditionally well-constructed novel, it is not a rambling, digressive, series of pointless (that is, more or less autonomous) episodes that lead nowhere and ultimately reach an uninteresting (weak, unmarked) end. Unlike the duel episode between Julien and the chevalier that ends with a whimper (since all the energy of the characters and the narrator has been invested in the conversation on the way), the novel as a whole ends with a bang—a resounding pistol shot, a fiery speech in court, and an execution. Moreover, this end is almost classically well prepared from the outset: though we don't see Julien buying a pistol in the first chapter, we do see him at the very beginning of his life journey (1.5) visiting the church at Verrières where the attempted murder of Mme de Rênal will eventually take place. In the church, which seems to be spotted with blood because of the play of light and the red curtains on the water in the baptismal font, Julien sees a piece of paper on which he reads: "*Détails de l'exécution et des derniers moments de Louis Jenrel, exécuté à Besançon, le...* Le papier était déchiré. Au revers, on lisait les deux premiers mots d'une ligne, c'étaient: *Le premier pas*" '*Details of the execution and last moments of Louis Jenrel, executed at Besançon, on the* ——— The paper was torn. On the other side were the first words of a line: *The first step* . . .' (47; 20; 1.5; emphasis in the orig.). At first sight it seems as if this piece of paper functions as an oracle announcing, at the very beginning, what will inevitably happen at the end: the church that only seemed spotted by blood will end up really so and just like his namesake, Julien will be executed. At the end of the novel we should be able to recognize how "the first step" (of both Julien and his double, Jenrel) started a chain of events that led with some logic and necessity to the last step—the violent murder attempt and the execution.

But this reading is totally unconvincing. Why would the totally formal resemblance between Julien Sorel and Louis Jenrel (their names are the anagrams of each other—a formal resemblance that Julien does not even fully grasp) predict a similarity in their fates? And in what sense can we say the two men are similar since neither we nor Julien know anything of Jenrel (who is thus very different from other role models Julien sets out to imitate, such as Napoleon and Tartuffe)? What Julien reads on the piece of paper he picks up is, on one side, the end of his namesake (his execution) and, on the other side, the words "The first step . . ." In other words, this oracle-text is presented as almost pure form, as empty of content as possible: on one side, a beginning, on the other side, the end. The "oracle" says that there was a beginning and there will be a (violent) end; here the parallel between the ur-text and its repetition begins and ends. The events that will create the space between beginning and end, the pages that will "separate" the two sides of the paper and will fill out the empty form with some kind of semantic content, are those of the novel we are going to read. While the matrix is predicted and predictable (as is the codified scenario of the duel), the middle is not. The violence of the end is not so much a semantic content (a theme) as an expression of the end's arbitrariness: an end that is not organically produced by all the steps that "lead" to it is "violent."

Students can see then that if Stendhal undermines the idea of an end-dominated plot he does not propose its opposite—a totally open-ended plot in which contingent events bring about an unforeseen ending. Certainly, if Julien's end strikes us as problematic (unconvincing, not sufficiently motivated) it is not because his end has been unpredictable. On the contrary. But that a certain event is revealed in retrospect to have been predictable or predetermined does not entail here that the chain of events that led to it was produced by internal or logical necessity—that it was, in fact, a chain. In Stendhal the end meets the beginning, but the events that mediate fail to constitute a coherent sequence. The predictability of an end that remains, nevertheless, external (or even "foreign") to the story thwarts our attempts to reconstruct a continuous, motivated sequence.

What we call in the analysis of narrative "closure" is a certain metaphorical relation between beginning and end whereby the end is already present at the beginning as a retrospective first cause and the beginning, read from the point of view of the end, is seen as full of meaning. The middle is the space where the relation between beginning and end gradually unfolds. But that does not happen in *The Red and the Black*, as the episode with M. Appert shows (Brodsky 218–22). In the early chapters of the novel we hear about a certain M. Appert, whose visit to the town prison under the wings of the marquis de La Mole and the abbé Chélan is much frowned upon by M. de Rênal. Now as the notes tell us M. Appert is the name of the activist who tried to act on behalf of Antoine Berthet, the real-life model of Julien Sorel. The reason that Appert is visiting Verrières is never given, as indeed it cannot be—if he is there, it must be to visit Berthet's fictional double, Julien Sorel, who, however, has not yet shot Mme de Rênal—in fact, he has not yet met her. Indeed, Appert's visit in some complicated way is the reason Julien meets Mme de Rênal at all. (M. de Rênal cannot or does not want to answer his wife's question of why he objects so much to Appert's visit and is saved from answering by seeing his son climbing on the parapet; this dangerous activity determines him to hire Julien as a tutor to his children.) The relation between beginning and end (both in the sense of the relation of the origin of events to their outcome and of the relation of a real-life source to its fictional representation) is present here but in a way that defies the construction of a logical chain and the achievement of closure.

So even though the end of *The Red and the Black* is elaborate (unlike the hasty end of *The Charterhouse of Parma* or the missing end of *Lucien Leuwen*), it does not function in the traditional way. In the traditional novel, the end retrospectively endows everything that precedes it with meaning. It is from the point of view of the end that we see previous incidents as a sequence of episodes (or "actions" as a sequence of "functions," to use Vladimir Propp's terms) leading toward a certain outcome. The end is also the point at which the protagonist typically looks back at his or her life and finally understands it. This moment of recognition very often consists of the realization that the past consisted of a sequence of errors, shortcomings, missed opportunities, moments of blindness, and so on. But we also assume that this very recognition redeems faulty experience. In short, the moment of recognition we find in so many nineteenth-century novels dramatizes the logic of yielding a return in yet another way by claiming that the loss in experience (or the experience of loss) is made good by the gain of knowledge of this experience (and of this loss). Knowledge is gained at the expense of experience but the loss of experience is recuperated or redeemed through knowledge. Not only do many traditional novels narrate the process by which characters, at the end, gain knowledge of their by-now lost experience; we, in reading these novels, also transform their "lost time" into an understanding that "regains" it. Our reading of the novel duplicates the protagonist's reading of his or her past life—we both learn something from "reading." Indeed, if reading did not yield a return, why would one read (or, even more poignant, teach students to read)?

The resistance of *The Red and the Black* to the economy of yielding a return may suggest that according to Stendhal reading should never be made to serve a purpose, that it should remain what it essentially is—a pleasurable experience. Certainly, a whole tradition pointing out the dangers of reading can be interpreted in this light: the danger comes not from what one reads but from indulging in useless, unproductive pleasure. The pleasure-seeking element in Stendhal (his definition of character as one's particular way of going "à la chasse du bonheur" 'in pursuit of happiness' rather than as one's quest for knowledge; see Stendhal, *Vie* [Divan] 42, 128, 399 and *Lucien Leuwen* 2: 67) should not be underestimated. But the violence of the end of *The Red and the Black* suggests that this is not the entire story. What then of reading in *The Red and the Black*?

To approach this issue we have to look at the fundamental tension in the representation of Julien as a character. When Mathilde de La Mole teases her father for giving Julien the decoration he has denied his own son, the marquis answers that "Julien a de l'imprévu, c'est ce qui n'est jamais arrivé au La Mole dont vous me parlez" 'Julien is capable of the unexpected, and that has never occurred to the La Mole you mention' (318; 226; 2.8). Julien's ability to do the unexpected is the basis of his mystery; "Je ne sais pas encore ce que c'est que votre Julien, et vous-même vous le savez moins que moi" 'I don't yet know what your Julien is, and you know even less than I do' (490; 358; 2.34), writes the marquis to his daughter. Julien's unpredictability is interpreted in the novel in contradictory ways. On the one hand, it is read as the sign of true aristocracy (the only reason the aristocrat gives for his actions is whim—"tel est mon bon plaisir" 'Such is my wish'), which the actual aristocracy of the Restoration can no longer achieve. On the other hand, it is seen as a sign of plebeian origins. Thus Mathilde sees Julien both as the true ancestor, Boniface de La Mole, and as the future Danton or Robespierre.

But the contradiction goes even further, because this Julien who is so unpredictable is also a simple memory machine: he can memorize everything and anything, from the New Testament to the classified ads in the *Constitutionnel*, and hence can be a pious student of theology, an excellent humanist, a passionate lover, a faithful political agent. His unpredictability is not a sign of authenticity or spontaneity, let alone of genius, but rather of his complete emptiness, of his ability to be everything or anything.

It would seem, then, as if Julien has the most utilitarian possible relation to reading since his rise in the world largely has to do with his memorizing texts and reproducing them: "Avec une âme de feu, Julien avait une de ces mémoires étonnantes si souvent unies à la sottise. Pour gagner le vieux curé Chélan, duquel il voyait bien que dépendait son sort à venir, il avait appris par cœur tout le Nouveau Testament en latin, il savait aussi le livre *du Pape* de M. de Maistre et croyait à l'un aussi peu qu'à l'autre" 'With a very fiery spirit Julien united one of those astounding memories which are so often joined to complete stupidity. In order to win over the old priest Chélan, on whom he could see his future depended, he learnt by heart the whole New Testament in Latin; he also knew M. de Maistre's book *On the Pope*, and believed as little of the one as of the other' (42; 16; 1.5; trans. modified). This passage presents Julien as a consummate hypocrite who learns by heart texts in which he does not believe to please a person who he thinks can help him advance. It is interesting to note that Robert Adams's English translation adds what the French original does not quite say—that Julien's calculation proved effective (the English translation reads: "*he had won him* [the priest Chélan] *over by learning* the whole New Testament"; my emphasis). The truth, of course, is that in keeping with Julien's characterization as a rather bumbling Tartuffe, his recitations have mixed results. Thus when he is left alone with Mme de Rênal, not knowing what to say—having, in fact, nothing to say—he recites to her the accounts of operations that he has heard from his friend the surgeon-major. This does not do and so in his next attempt at seduction—of Amanda Binet—he resorts to another text which proves more appropriate: *La nouvelle Héloïse.* Since this text seems to work on this occasion he uses it again in his seduction of Mathilde. Similarly, Julien commits an error of judgment by reciting the texts of Horace and other classical authors during his examination; not knowing when and where the recital of these texts may prove useful, he tries again in front of the bishop and is in luck this time. Again, once he performs with success, he knows in which situations the performance is suitable and can repeat it; he thus recites from the classics during the dinner in the Hôtel de La Mole and earns approval. It seems, then, as if Julien's memorizing (and not only his reciting from memory) is almost automatic; he does not choose to memorize certain texts intending to use them in particular circumstances for his advancement. Indeed, he is not sure whether and in what circumstances what he memorizes is useful. What he memorizes becomes useful—and thus acquires meaning, makes sense—on a future occasion unknown to him at the moment of memorizing.

Though Julien is described as a passionate reader who prefers reading his books to anything else (even to the company of Mme de Rênal), we don't see him being formed by any other books except the three that constituted his "Koran" at the beginning of the novel (Rousseau's *Confessions*, the "bulletins de la grande armée," and the *Mémorial de Sainte-Hélène*, 41; 15; 1.5). He inherited from the surgeon-major some forty books, read more through the library service at M. de Rênal's, and had at his disposal the entire library of M. de La Mole, and yet we are never told or shown that these books had an effect on him, or changed him, that he "gained" something from reading them.

But we are told of the different texts that he recites and that are more or less explicitly described as meaningless to him or even as contradicting his deep convictions (as with the secret note and the Bible). These texts, paradoxically, have a huge effect on his life.

Neither process conforms to what we normally call reading. If Stendhal implicitly presents Julien as a reader who finds immense pleasure in reading without apparently gaining anything from it, he also presents through Julien the incredible power that texts have over our lives. But this power comes not from the truth or knowledge we gain from texts but rather from their social circulation, of which we are the more or less unconscious agents (Julien memorizes texts without believing in them, without even fully understanding them). In relation to texts, the opposite of yielding a return is, then, on the one hand, our reading for sheer pleasure and, on the other hand, our being subject to (rather than being the subject of) cultural discourses that determine our lives. The aesthetic is just the other side of (a certain understanding of) the social. Both the valorization of pleasure and the representation of human agents as the more or less unconscious vehicles of social discourses posit a human subject without interiority, made entirely of surfaces (and thus "beautiful"). Thus, one can say, in opposing the notion of yielding a return Stendhal opposes the main tenets of bourgeois ideology: usefulness, interiority, and the autonomous subject.

Approaching a Major Novel through Its Minor Characters

Pauline Wahl Willis

One problem students regularly face when tackling nineteenth-century novels is their length. Covering all 408 pages of Adams's English translation of *The Red and the Black* is no easy task, but completing the 533 pages of the Garnier-Flammarion French edition is even more difficult for Anglophones. Given this demand on their time, some students choose to forgo the delicious irony and tender allusion of Stendhal's prose in favor of more questionable labor-saving devices. It is rather easy and possibly quite fun for instructors to catch the little *jésuites de robe courte* at their own game; for instance, by inquiring solemnly about an incident sufficiently far along in the novel to cause some discomfort: "When Julien fears that he may be imprisoned or even killed in his tragicomic attempt to visit Mathilde de La Mole's room, does he send an account of his situation to (a) Fouqué, (b) Foucault, or (c) Fokine?" The less industrious readers may admit to bluffing but, in the end, could very well echo the Shakespearean epigraph at the beginning of book 1, chapter 21:

> Alas, our frailty is the cause, not we:
> For such as we are made of, such we be.

It would seem that the only remedy for these students lies in better preparation for advanced literature courses or—dare it be suggested!—more time spent on homework.

Thus it is not this type of delinquent student that I deal with in what follows. Instead, I focus on the diligent reader who nonetheless may have trouble dealing with such a large, demanding novel as *The Red and the Black*. After all, even top anglophone students with excellent comprehension strategies and strong background knowledge of nineteenth-century French fiction in general and Stendhal in particular can attain a reading speed in French of only approximately twenty pages an hour. This figure, which my good students have reported consistently year after year, indicates that they have to spend nearly twenty-four hours of high concentration to read the novel from cover to cover just once. It is therefore somewhat unrealistic to expect that even the committed students will come fully prepared to study the book in its entirety during the first class or possibly even the first few classes. What to do? One can, of course, begin by analyzing key scenes that occur early in the novel, and certainly there is no shortage of such gems in *The Red and the Black*. The narrator's opening description of Verrières; the reader's first glimpse of Julien, sitting on the saw's superstructure; the hero's brief visit to the church; his arrival at the Rênal home; and, of course, the episode in which he first takes

Mme de Rênal's hand are only a few of the many wonderful early scenes that spring to mind. While this approach can be useful indeed, it does have the drawback of promoting a certain amount of repetition concerning the protagonist and a certain inevitable tendency to refer to later passages that students may not yet have read.

As an alternative or a complement to such analysis, I would suggest the study of certain minor characters. Besides keeping pace with the students' reading, this method allows for a variety of critical approaches and displays the depth and richness of the novel in a way that a steady focus on the protagonist may not. At the same time, of course, it also provides a perspective from which to view the main characters more subtly. There are many minor characters to whom this approach may fruitfully be applied: the surgeon-major, Chélan, Fouqué, Valenod, and Pirard are obvious choices. I deal in this essay with three who, perhaps, do not immediately suggest themselves: Geronimo, the singer who turns up mainly in book 1, chapter 23, during his brief visit to the Rênal household; Mme Derville, who appears episodically until she and Mme de Rênal see Julien in the Besançon cathedral and then reappears only at his trial; and the duc de Chaulnes, who is never actually present but who is mentioned, albeit ambiguously, in the last part of the novel.

Geronimo

The Neapolitan opera singer Geronimo briefly steals the scene when he stops en route to London to visit the Rênal family in Verrières (180–83; 121–23; 1.23). His short stay permits the introduction of useful background information for the study of *The Red and the Black*. The descriptions of Zingarelli, of the Naples conservatory, and of the San Carlino theater lead neatly to the presentation of Henri Beyle as a well-known opera historian and commentator of his era. Biographical material is always important in Stendhal's novels, and this little episode provides some excellent examples. Geronimo is modeled on the famous basso Luigi Lablache (*Red and Black* 121n1; see esp. *Rouge* [Marsan] 1: 424–25n to 261), who was born in Naples of French parents and who could well have been a real-life prototype for "Arrigo Beyle, milanese." Certainly, he brings a breath of fresh Italian air to an otherwise morose French provincial evening. In addition, by mentioning that Mme de Rênal knows Italian, Geronimo links her immediately to Beyle's mother, Henriette Gagnon, thereby reinforcing the naturalness and goodness of the heroine's character.

However, Geronimo's real importance lies in his playing the role of a parasite. He thereby elucidates some important features of power relations in the novel and serves as a measurement of Julien's conduct within this general framework. Jean-Jacques Hamm alludes to Geronimo's parasitic role when he explains the mechanism of the parasite as envisioned by Michel Serres in *Le parasite* and applies it generally to *The Red and the Black*. The French "parasite" designates a biological or social parasite, as it does in English; in addition, it means "static"

(Serres 8). Analyzing the implications of this homograph, Serres observes that the social parasite fulfills the same function as static: he interrupts the flow of relationships, changes their direction, and gives rise to new systems (14). The parasite is thus an exciter or catalyst (190–91), for without him there would be only a deathlike order (127).

Let us examine briefly, then, how the concept of Geronimo as parasite enables one to approach the novel. After bursting in on the Rênals, Geronimo literally sings for his supper, tells stories, and turns the evening from one of bitter ruminations on petty politics to a convivial and relaxing interlude. He is the classic parasite as described by Serres. His presence opens up the novel to the contemplation of a world where music, happiness, and spontaneity are possible. Because of the visit, we see that Julien is no longer the outsider he was at the beginning of his tutoring contract: Geronimo the parasite has, at least momentarily, replaced Julien the parasite. Furthermore, Julien has replaced M. de Rênal insofar as it is the young preceptor and not the mayor who Mme de Rênal hopes will be cheered up and distracted by this unplanned soirée. Geronimo is the yardstick by which the reader can measure two conditions that will ultimately prove to be contradictory: Julien's social ascension and his attainment of happiness. Geronimo, the embodiment of Serres's joker (67), is unpredictably both positive and negative.

It would also be useful to refer at some point to Geronimo's other brief appearances in the novel because they enable the reader, through the same mechanism of the parasite, to measure Julien's fall from grace. Julien and Geronimo next meet when, after the duel, Julien is invited to the opera by his erstwhile opponent, the chevalier de Beauvoisis (whose name is almost identical to that of the French diplomat and cousin of Mme de Rênal, the chevalier de Beauvaisis, who had written a letter of introduction for the singer) (308; 218; 2.6). It is interesting that, in this small world and in view of how memorable the evening with Geronimo in Verrières had been, Julien never lets on that he had already met the singer. Obviously, Julien wants to play the role of the chevalier's friend and equal to the hilt and he does so by hiding the earlier incident, in effect by snubbing Geronimo. Their last meeting completes Julien's betrayal of his noble ideas. They are thrown together in a small village near Metz, where the Congregation tries to prevent Julien from delivering the secret note (429–32; 314–15; 2.23). It is Geronimo who first realizes that there is a plot afoot and proposes an escape plan to Julien. Later that night, Julien does indeed do everything possible to arouse Geronimo from a drug-induced stupor, but in the end he abandons the singer in favor of his royalist mission. Geronimo, in contrast, forfeits his chance to sing for the seven sovereign princes to sleep off the sedative. At this moment, by behaving completely naturally, Geronimo forgoes the role of parasite and the advancement it could bring him. The contrast between his behavior and Julien's emphasizes the latter's single-minded ambition and self-aggrandizing adoption of the parasitic stance.

Madame Derville

Mme Derville, like Geronimo, serves to elucidate power relations. In particular she sheds light on what women are and are not allowed to do in the society of *The Red and the Black*. Her position is ambiguous and therefore interesting. She is, of course, a distant relative of Mme de Rênal, her school chum from their convent days and currently her best friend. Obviously, she comes from the same background as the heroine. Adams describes her as "cool, sensible, and unparticularized" (40n5; 1.8); yet it is exactly her featurelessness that is significant. Mme Derville can come and go as she pleases, rush to the side of her troubled friend, and travel about precisely because she is "unparticularized": we know nothing of a M. Derville (is he dead or alive? old or young? interested in her whereabouts or not?) or of any children she may have. Because she is not fictionally tied down by family responsibilities yet has the means to live comfortably she is able to do as she pleases, or so it seems. We must not forget that she is also "cool" and "sensible," that she has internalized the norms of behavior expected of decent upper-middle-class women.

Her function in the early scenes of the novel illustrates this tension between freedom and duty, for she is both helper and opponent to Julien and Mme de Rênal. Although one tends to think of her as the spoilsport who tries to keep the lovers apart, it is equally true that without her presence they probably would not have got together in the first place. Her visit to Vergy allows Mme de Rênal an initial extended stay there without her husband about; her presence affords Julien the breathing space he needs to carry out his seduction; and finally, Julien and Mme de Rênal could never have remained in the garden together after dark without the company of Mme Derville. Of course, cool, sensible Mme Derville is not blind to the goings-on around her. She censures the lovers' behavior, not so much because she believes it to be immoral as because she feels that it will bring unhappiness to her friend. This reasoning shows that her thoughts are shaped completely by the prevailing ideology of her time. She has so utterly internalized its moral code that she perceives any deviance from it in emotional, not legal or moral, terms. Her departure sums up the inherent duality of her position. She cannot stand to see Mme de Rênal persist in what she believes to be disastrous behavior, so she simply leaves without offering any explanation for her sudden departure, a course of action she has the economic and social liberty to pursue.

Mme Derville's ambiguous position is often presented in terms of her gaze. On the one hand, from the beginning she appreciates Julien's grandeur of vision:

> Dès l'arrivée de Mme Derville, il sembla à Julien qu'elle était son amie; il se hâta de lui montrer le point de vue qu'on a de l'extrémité de la nouvelle allée sous les grands noyers; [. . .] C'est sur les sommets de ces rochers coupés à pic, que Julien, heureux, libre, et même quelque chose de plus, roi de la maison, conduisait les deux amies, et jouissait de leur admiration pour ces aspects sublimes. (74)

> When Mme. Derville arrived Julien was at once convinced that she was his friend; he hastened to show her the panorama that opens up at the end of the new walk under the walnut trees. [. . .] Atop these tumbled rocks, Julien, happy, free, and, moreover, king of the household, guided the two ladies and delighted in their admiration of the magnificent view. (41; 1.8)

On the other hand, being an astute observer of Julien and Mme de Rênal, she is soon able to figure out what is afoot.

If one studies Mme Derville's subsequent appearances, at the cathedral in Besançon and at Julien's trial, one realizes fully the importance of the gaze in connection with her. First, in the cathedral, Mme Derville herself draws attention to the power of the gaze by entreating Julien not to let Mme de Rênal see him when she regains consciousness: "—Fuyez, Monsieur, fuyez! lui dit-elle avec l'accent de la plus vive colère. Que surtout elle ne vous revoie pas. Votre vue doit en effet lui faire horreur [. . .]!" '—Leave us, sir, leave us! she said to him, in accents of the most passionate anger. She must not see you again, whatever happpens. The sight of you ought to be horrible for her [. . .]!' (225; 156; 1.28). Finally, at Julien's trial, Mme Derville's disapproving gaze is vanquished: she seems once again to share Julien's point of view. At the trial the positioning of Mme Derville is very important. Seated high up in a small balcony, she occupies a position akin to that of the overseer of Bentham's panopticon, as described by Foucault (*Discipline* 200–03). True, she is not invisible to Julien; nevertheless, he does not notice her until she is pointed out to him. The trial thus begins with Mme Derville in a commanding position: the conative function of her gaze (Argyle and Cook 74–80) is to make Julien blush deeply (528; 386; 2.41). As the trial progresses, Julien finds Mme Derville's eyes brilliant, as though she might have been crying (529; 387; 2.41): her gaze is no longer transparent but translucent, the first sign that her power over Julien has diminished and that her emotions are freeing themselves from the grip of the prevailing ideology. Finally, after Julien's address to the jury, Mme Derville's gaze is completely blocked by her handkerchief and, moments later, "Mme Derville jeta un cri et s'évanouit" 'Mme. Derville gave a little cry and fainted' (530; 388; 2.41). At this point her cool, sensible side has completely surrendered. She is as free emotionally as she is financially and domestically. Of course, she attains her emotional freedom in a fainting spell, in a sort of pseudodeath, much as Julien attains his in prison and then, finally, in death itself.

The Duc de Chaulnes and the Duc de Retz

Because of certain ambiguities that arise from Stendhal's use of the duc de Chaulnes's name, a study of this character can be undertaken properly only by students reading *The Red and the Black* in an edition that faithfully reproduces the original printed text. Robert Adams has not done so, choosing instead to follow the example of Stendhal's handwritten annotations to the Bucci edition of the novel by changing the character's name to Retz when necessary to maintain a logical narrative (x). Nevertheless, for students using the Adams edition or a French edition based on similar editorial principles, a brief discussion of the editor's choices would be worthwhile. In addition, they can certainly study the significance of the name Retz, as I do here. Crouzet's French edition, which follows the original published text, lends itself admirably to an analysis of the duc de Chaulnes. In fact, precisely because it is a mass-market book, it does not contain the critical apparatus necessary to elucidate some of the confusion surrounding this character, a situation that may cause the students undue bewilderment. I must, therefore, limit myself to the French edition in some references to the text below.

Not only does the duke never actually appear in *The Red and the Black*, but when he is mentioned it is in a very confusing manner indeed. He is first introduced as the marquise de La Mole's father (271; 189; 2.1). Then, only a few pages farther on, when her husband proposes to treat Julien as an equal, he tells his young secretary the blue suit will indicate that the wearer is the youngest son of the duc de Chaulnes (310; 2.7)—a rather curious slip on the part of the son-in-law of the duke, but a slip he nonetheless maintains at the end of the chapter (315; 2.7). This state of affairs is sustained until, in another slip, no less curious and probably no less Freudian than the first, the duc de Chaulnes seems to become the father of Mathilde or possibly of the marquis de Croisenois; it is not entirely clear (367; 2.14). Finally, the old duke again takes on the identity of the marquise de La Mole's father (488; 356; 2.34).

Whatever the source of this confusion, and it could well stem from other occurences of the name Chaulnes in the works of Stendhal, the ambiguity results in an incestuous situation: the marquise de La Mole, Julien, and even Mathilde and perhaps Croisenois seem to have the same father. If the reader believes even for an instant that this could be true, it means that Julien could join the aristocracy only by transgressing a biological and social taboo. The ambiguous presence of the duc de Chaulnes thus emphasizes the insurmountable obstacle of birth and class that stops Julien's social ascension dead in its tracks.

We may continue to analyze the palimpsests (Genette) of this character by turning our attention to the surname Retz, which, in the Bucci copy, Stendhal used for the presumed father of Julien. This appellation too is a prominent name often mentioned in Stendhal's other works. Obviously, the choice of this particular name is motivated primarily by the role this gentleman plays in the novel. Julien's rapid social ascension makes it imperative that he belong to a family that suits his new position. Who could better play the role of his father than the aristocratic personage who, more than any other noble in the book, seems to represent the apogee of French aristocracy?

Julien's entrance to the ball at the Hôtel de Retz serves to emphasize the nature of this presumed lineage:

> Le soir, en arrivant au bal, il fut frappé de la magnificence de l'hôtel de Retz. La cour d'entrée était couverte d'une immense tente de coutil cramoisi avec des étoiles en or: rien de plus élégant. Au-dessous de cette tente, la cour était transformée en un bois d'orangers et de lauriers-roses en fleurs. Comme on avait eu soin d'enterrer suffisamment les vases, les lauriers et les orangers avaient l'air de sortir de terre. (320)
>
> That evening as he came to the ball he was struck by the magnificence of the Hotel de Retz. The courtyard by which one entered was covered with an immense canvas awning painted scarlet and studded with gold stars: nothing could have been more elegant. Beneath this awning, the courtyard had been transformed into a grove of orange trees and of flowering laurel bushes. As pains had been taken to set the garden pots into the earth, the laurels and orange trees seemed to rise naturally from the ground. (227; 2.8)

The symbols of birth, genealogy, and magic all work toward creating Julien's miraculous presumed lineage. It seems that Julien has engendered his own origins. However, his ascendance is merely superficial and illusory, like the potted trees that decorate the duke's courtyard.

Nevertheless, Stendhal is careful to emphasize how magical the decor and the evening itself are, a strategy that makes the ball seem to transcend the confines of the Paris winter of 1830. In this way, the duc de Retz and behind him the palimpsest of the duc de Chaulnes seem to melt into a sort of superhuman character, one whom Genette might have called the ur-duke; that is, the general idea of the duke that is at the origin of all the particular ducal manifestations and that seems to soar above the novel. This notion is reinforced by the marquis de La Mole's dream of becoming a duke himself or seeing his daughter become a duchess through marriage to the future duc de Croisenois. As we read in the epigraph that serves as a transition to Julien's Parisian adventure, "Il n'y a plus qu'une seule noblesse, c'est le titre de *duc*; marquis est ridicule, au mot *duc* on tourne la tête" 'There's only one really noble rank left, that's the title of *duke*; marquis is ridiculous, at the word *duke* heads turn round' (242; 169; 1.30).

In reality Julien shatters his dream of belonging to the nobility when he shoots Mme de Rênal. Nevertheless, the ideal of the dukedom lives on, not only in Julien's supposition that Mathilde will eventually marry the duc de Croisenois but also in the nostalgia of the marquis de La Mole. In this way the ultimate rank of French aristocracy passes from the attainable and the actualized to the virtual and the historical. Stendhal's oversight reveals a profound social change in the making.

The common thread that runs through these disparate presentations of three minor characters is the analysis of power relations, a fundamental aspect of the novel. This approach can easily be complemented with other foci and approaches. These three examples show that one can devise ways to break down the novel into more manageable parts, to focus the students' reading more closely, to introduce them to important theoretical writings, and to get both majors and nonmajors to understand the richness of *The Red and the Black*.

QUESTIONS OF GENDER AND CLASS IDENTITY IN *THE RED AND THE BLACK*

Contextualizing the Canon: New Perspectives on *The Red and the Black*

Doris Y. Kadish

Reading canonical works such as *The Red and the Black* can and perhaps should be a different enterprise for today's students than for those of earlier generations, for two main reasons. First, we now live in an increasingly complex and diverse society that requires a heightened consciousness of and sensitivity to issues of race, class, and gender. And second, persons who want jobs outside academia expect our courses to supply more of the kind of cultural information and contextualization of literature that may be useful to them in a variety of professional fields, including secondary education. Skills in analyzing literature still need to remain a predominant component of a literary education. But it is not enough to confine oneself to admiring the canonical author's creative genius and understanding the workings of his or her style, as one often does in the French tradition of close, formalistic readings of literary works. Students also need to acquire skills in analyzing culture, including ways to deal intelligently with the traces of classism, Eurocentrism, and masculinism that arise in many texts, including canonical works. Instead of cultivating those skills only in separate culture and civilization or women's studies courses, I would urge, it is beneficial to integrate them into literature courses by contextualizing the canon: that is, combining canonical works with other, related texts that, together, provide an enhanced cultural and historical understanding of the past.

I propose here a way of reading that can actually help with what I see as the major problems in teaching *The Red and the Black*, namely, its length and its complexity. Students find reading Stendhal, especially in French, to be a very long and demanding process, requiring several weeks or a month. When those weeks of reading are squeezed into a busy survey or nineteenth-century novel course, students may become impatient. One solution, the approach I describe below, consists of using *The Red and the Black* as the high point of a cultural studies type of course in which, instead of trying to get through a progression of works related primarily by genre or period, one strives to present a complex web of canonical, less canonical, or noncanonical treatments of race, class, and gender that overlap and intersect. Instead of just moving from text to text, students can focus on a common set of issues throughout the course and work consistently on developing comparisons and contrasts among the works. The unifying component in the course I propose is the period surrounding 1830 in France. Although I can envision various approaches to structuring the course assignments, I would recommend beginning with the noncanonical or less canonical works because they are typically easier, shorter, or more direct and then devoting the second half or final third of the course to *The Red and the Black*. In the evaluations I received for a version of the course, one student summed up the advantage of such an approach, stating that one of the less canonical texts "really got me to think about the society and helped me to know what I should be looking for while reading *Le rouge et le noir*."

The choice of less canonical texts naturally depends on the particular themes one wishes to highlight. Two such themes I discuss here are literacy and oppression. Although issues of class, race, or gender might dominate discussions of one or another theme, all three sets of issues would ultimately overlap: in the unit on literacy, for example, one would come to see that literacy was an important issue not only for peasants and workers but also for women and persons of color as well. What texts can one use to bring out the intricately imbricated workings of class, race, and gender in the nineteenth century? Works by George Sand, notably *Indiana*, provide a rich source of material. In addition to being easy to obtain both in English and French, *Indiana* dates from the same time as *The Red and the Black* and presents a related but, in my opinion, more woman-centered perspective. Another work from around the same time is the text edited by Michel Foucault *I, Pierre Rivière, Having Slaughtered My Mother, My Sister, and My Brother* . . . , a first-person account by a peasant subject, which is also available in both English and French. Moreover, there is a film version in French that provides a wealth of cultural and linguistic material. Placing a presumably authentic subaltern example such as *Pierre Rivière* alongside *The Red and the Black* invites a host of observations and insights regarding the class issues that play a crucial role in Stendhal's novel.

A good place to begin to contextualize *The Red and the Black* is with Julien Sorel's ability to read, which is revealed near the beginning of the novel in the often-quoted passage in which Julien's father finds Julien reading a book instead of tending to the machinery at the family sawmill: "Il l'aperçut à cinq ou six pieds plus haut, à cheval sur l'une des pièces de la toiture" 'At last he saw him, five or six feet higher, astraddle one of the roof beams.' Having drawn attention to Julien's intellectual superiority through his elevated physical position, the text then stresses his exceptionality: his ability to read, in contrast with his father's illiteracy; his romantic appearance ("sa taille mince, peu propre aux travaux de la force, et si différente de celle de ses aînés" 'his slender figure, unsuited to hard labor and unlike his elder brothers' '); his sensitivity and passion for literature ("Il avait les larmes aux yeux, moins à cause de la douleur physique, que pour la perte de son livre qu'il adorait" 'His eyes were full of tears, less from physical pain than for the loss of his book, which he worshipped') (38; 13; 1.4). In addition to illustrating Stendhal's use of the Romantic theme of exceptional characters, this celebrated passage can lead to a discussion of the Christian symbolism that pervades the novel (Talbot 66–67) and is apparent here in such details as Julien's carpenter-related activities, his suffering at the hands of his father, his transcendent pose, and so on.

Students also need, however, to place Julien's exceptionality in its proper cultural context. To pursue the issue of reading, it is worth noting that other figures, such as Pierre Rivière—and François in Sand's *François le champi*—also read; all three, what is more, are endowed with the same exceptional memory and suffer from a similar sense of social alienation because of their ability to read as Julien. The similarities involving Pierre are especially striking. Like Julien, he reads about Napoleon, who inspires in him dreams of glory and upward mobility:

> je travaillai a la terre avec mon pére; mais ce n'etait pas là bien mon penchant, j'avais des idées de gloire, je me plaisais beaucoup à lire. [. . .] j'étois devoré des idées de grandeur et d immortalité, je m'estimai bien plus que les autres, et j'ai eu honte de le dire jusque ici, je pensais que je me eleverais au dessus de mon etat. (124–25)
>
> I worked the land with my father; but that did not suit my inclination at all, I had ideas of glory, I took great pleasure in reading. [. . .] I was consumed by ideas of greatness and immortality, I esteemed myself far better than others, and I have been ashamed to say so until now, I thought I would raise myself above my condition. (101–02)

Noting such similarities between Julien and Pierre enables students to question Julien's personal superiority and the uniqueness of his intellectual ability, which a canonical reading of Stendhal's novel would lead one to accept, and to view him in relation to predictable patterns of class mobility at the time. They can also observe the extent to which history and literature overlap and intersect. Julien and Pierre read texts to discover models of class ascent, and they in turn become literary and historical models for a Romantic culture that was fascinated with exceptional, aberrant figures on the margins of society.

One can also discover insights into the nature of subaltern language in the nineteenth century by reading *The Red and the Black* in relation to Pierre Rivière. Consider for example such small details as Mme de Rênal's letter written "sans la moindre orthographe" 'full of misspellings' (146; 95; 1.20) or Julien's misspelling of *cela* as "cella" when he begins to work for M. de La Mole (278; 195; 2.2). Having had the opportunity in studying the textual and filmic versions of Pierre's story to see his limited mastery of standard French, students can see these details from *The Red and the Black* in the context of the varying degrees of literacy that women, workers, slaves, and other subaltern groups at that time could acquire. Mme de Rênal thus ceases to be viewed only as a privileged member of the provincial upper class and comes also to exemplify the limitations of women's education in the nineteenth century. We learn, for example, that having forgotten all the ridiculous things she learned in the convent, Mme de Rênal "finit par ne rien savoir" 'ended by knowing nothing' (59; 29; 1.7); that, married at sixteen, she is "une femme extrêmement ignorante" 'an extremely ignorant woman' (118; 75; 1.17); and that, not surprisingly in the light of this ignorance, if her husband were to stop giving her money, she like other women of her class would fall into "l'état d'ouvrière à quinze sols par journée" 'the condition of a workingwoman at fifteen sous a day' (154; 106; 1.21).

The Red and the Black can thus enable the class to study both literature and literacy in the early nineteenth century and thereby to combine an emphasis on the individual, psychological plane with an emphasis on the collective, social features of the text. To serve this purpose I would recommend incorporating material from works such as Roger Chartier's *L'éducation en France*, in which we learn, for example, that reading represented a lower level of literacy than writing, which was taught separately, and that some historians believe reading was considered inferior at the time to signing one's name, the standard measure of literacy in historical records of the past (Chartier 88–91). That there were negative social implications of writing that did not apply to reading is apparent in the scene from *The Red and the Black* in which the abbé Pirard warns Julien

> Le marquis n'aime pas les écrivailleurs, je vous en avertis; c'est sa seule antipathie. Sachez le latin, le grec si vous pouvez, l'histoire des Égyptiens, des Perses, etc., il vous honorera et vous protégera comme un savant. Mais n'allez pas écrire une page en français, et surtout sur des matières graves et au-dessus de votre position dans le monde. [. . .] (296)
>
> The marquis doesn't like scribblers, let me warn you; it is his only antipathy. Know Latin and Greek if you can, the history of the Egyptians, the Persians, and so on, he will honor you and protect you as a man of learning. But don't venture to write a single page in French, and above all on serious matters above your station in life. [. . .] (209; 2.4)

Chartier's work also contextualizes literacy with respect to geographic location, enabling us to situate Julien and Pierre within the higher pattern of literacy among men in the north of France at the time (Chartier 107–08). This kind of information will enrich students' understanding of the past and will encourage them to see literature as a rich repository of historical and cultural as well as aesthetic material.

Turning now to the theme of oppression, I begin with Julien's presentation in Stendhal's novel as a representative of the lower classes and a victim of social and economic persecution, for example, in the celebrated passage at the end of the novel in which Julien addresses the jury that will condemn him: "Messieurs, je n'ai point l'honneur d'appartenir à votre classe, vous voyez en moi un paysan qui s'est révolté contre la bassesse de sa fortune" 'Gentlemen, I have not the honor to belong to your social class, you see in me a peasant in open revolt against his humble station' (530; 387; 2.41). Admitting that he attempted to kill a woman who was like a mother to him, Julien claims nonetheless to be the victim of a society that seeks to punish and discourage "cette classe de jeunes gens qui, nés dans un ordre inférieur, et en quelque sorte opprimés par la pauvreté, ont le bonheur de se procurer une bonne éducation, et l'audace de se mêler à ce que l'orgueil des gens riches appelle la société" 'a certain class of young men—those who, born to a lower social order, and buried by poverty, are lucky enough to get a good education and bold enough to mingle with what the arrogant rich call good society' (530; 387–88; 2.41). In point of fact, the text makes clear that Julien's father is the wealthy owner of a sawmill and thus that Julien is hardly a member of a "lower social order [. . .] buried by poverty." Indeed, he is acutely aware of the difference between himself and the true members of the lower class, for example, the young men in the seminary, accustomed to living on curdled milk and black bread, eating meat only five or six times a year, and lacking adequate food and clothing in the winter. Yet Julien seems to relish opportunities to call attention to his social inferiority through references to himself as a peasant, worker, subordinate, plebeian, and so on. What is at issue, clearly, is his sensitivity to the issue of equality and to his social status. The speech to the jury and the references to social oppression elsewhere in the novel serve to express the psychology of oppression—the feeling of being an outsider and an inferior—rather than any genuine material, economic deprivation.

Thus although students can learn much about oppression, inequality, and alienation by analyzing those themes in *The Red and the Black*, they ultimately learn more about the provincial and Parisian elites who inspire Julien's feelings of inferiority than about the precise conditions of the downtrodden or about subalternity in early nineteenth-century France. Pierre Rivière's account, in contrast, shows us the actual material features of daily life at the time. As Pierre dwells on the sordid succession of quarrels between his parents, we come to comprehend the importance both for the lower classes and for women of such actions as signing contracts, acquiring property, exercising conjugal rights, ploughing a field, buying a mattress, incurring debts, passing on property, signing contracts, and hundreds of other aspects of everyday life. Clothes, furniture, animals, food, illness, taxes, conscription, religion, education, and the workings of the judicial system all figure prominently, as do the ways in which peasant women like Victoire Rivière, Pierre's mother, actively resisted patriarchal society: for example, refusing to sleep or live with her husband, denying him control of her property, insisting on her legal rights, and involving herself in all financial matters. This historical description of resistance provides an enlightening backdrop against which we can measure and assess the description of resistance in *The Red and the Black*, notably Mathilde's recourse to such measures as controlling her love affair with Julien, defying her father's social expectations, manipulating male figures of power, and so on. Although I do not mean to imply that Pierre is more interesting or important than Julien, or that Victoire is necessarily more emancipated than Mathilde, I would argue that comparing the forms of oppression of these historical and literary figures enriches our understanding of the culture and the literature of the nineteenth century.

Comparing *The Red and the Black* and *Indiana* is especially enlightening because it expands the issue of oppression to include class, gender, and race. Consider the use of animal imagery at the beginning of the two works. Stendhal's novel starts with Julien's father calling him a "chien de lisard" 'you little hound' (40; 14; 1.5) and referring to him on a number of other occasions as an animal. Indeed, the brutality with which the father brings his son down from the roof beam on which he was reading seems more like the way a master would treat a rebellious slave than the way a father would treat his son: "Descends, animal. [. . .] Son père [. . .] alla chercher une longue perche pour abattre des noix, et l'en frappa sur l'épaule" '—Get down from there, animal. [. . .] His father [. . .] took a long pole used for knocking down nuts and struck him across the shoulder with it' (38–39; 13; 1.4). Not surprisingly, Julien is especially sensitive to being treated like a dog by the Rênal children: "Ces enfants me caressent comme ils caresseraient le jeune chien de chasse que l'on a acheté hier" 'These children are fond of me just as they're fond of that new puppy who was bought yesterday' (83; 48; 1.9). For Julien, treatment by a master is tantamount to oppression and brutality. Indiana similarly experiences a sense of oppression in the opening scene that is related to the treatment of a dog, by her brutal husband, "devant qui tout tremblait, femme, serviteurs, chevaux et chiens" 'who made everyone tremble, wife, servants, horses, and dogs' (49; 15; 1.5). Common to the two novels, then, are the role of the master under a patriarchal, inegalitarian system of family and society and the oppression endured under this system by animals, women, slaves, and members of the lower classes. By focusing on animal images and the role of the master, one can emphasize, as Stendhal appears to want to do, other elements in *The Red and the Black* that call attention to inequality between classes or sexes. We learn, for example, that on the night before she was married Mme de Rênal was warned by her aunt against confiding in a husband, "qui après tout est un maître" 'who after all is a master' (92; 53; 1.11); and repeatedly, in Mathilde's references to Julien as her master and herself as his slave, Stendhal foregrounds the issues of oppression and submission, perhaps calling our attention, ironically, to Mathilde's less than thoroughly feminist grasp of those issues.

Raising the topic of oppression in *The Red and the Black* can lead to fascinating class discussions in which students adopt markedly different positions and offer varied and interesting interpretations. For example, one of my students argued that Mathilde was the least feminist of all the women we studied because she is confined in her movements, condemned to repeating the past of her ancestors, a victim of obsessive love, and predictably the bearer of a masculine child to carry on male, patriarchal values. In contrast, others saw her in a very positive light, stressing that she undertook the forms of resistance noted earlier, proved herself a strong and educated woman, and participated in the chiefly feminine opposition to Julien's execution at the hands of male authoritarian figures. Still others were ambivalent, seeing her emancipation from her father in choosing Julien as positive but her desire that Julien be integrated into a patriarchal, aristocratic system as negative. To further spark the fire of debate, I recommend assigning or referring to Simone de Beauvoir's analysis of Stendhal, which supports a positive interpretation of Mathilde: "Et ces femmes qui ont su préserver à vide leur liberté, dès qu'elles rencontreront un objet digne d'elles s'élèveront par la passion jusqu'à l'héroïsme" 'And these women who have been able to maintain their liberty—empty as it has been—will rise through passion to heroism once they find an objective worthy of them' (380–81; 54–55). Whereas some students will agree with Beauvoir that Stendhal's women characters acquire heroic stature, others may consider that despite her feminist credentials Beauvoir unwittingly endorses women's subordination to men through love. Regardless of the final outcome of the discussion, its very existence helps make the point that ideological limitations affect male and female writers and that critical reading is as appropriate for canonical feminist works as for other canonical works of literature.

A discussion of the different ways in which Mathilde and Indiana compare themselves to slaves is especially enlightening. In *The Red and the Black* the comparison is expressed in ambiguous terms that raise questions about Stendhal's ironic relation to his characters: "Punis-moi de mon orgueil atroce, lui disait-elle [. . .] tu es mon maître, je suis ton esclave, il faut que je demande pardon à genoux d'avoir voulu me révolter. [. . .] [R]ègne à jamais sur moi, punis sévèrement ton esclave quand elle voudra se révolter" 'Punish me for my atrocious pride, she told him [. . .] you are my master, I am your slave, I must beg your pardon on bended knees for having tried to revolt. [. . .] [R]eign forever over me, punish savagely your slave whenever she tries to rebel' (400–01; 291; 2.19). In contrast, in *Indiana*, the comparison between women and slaves is direct and carries a tone of strong recrimination: "Je sais que je suis l'esclave et vous le seigneur. La loi de ce pays vous a fait mon maître. Vous pouvez lier mon corps, garrotter mes mains, gouverner mes actions. Vous avez le droit du plus fort, et la société vous le confirme; mais sur ma volonté, monsieur, vous ne pouvez rien, Dieu seul peut la courber et la réduire" 'I know I'm the slave and you're the lord. The law of the land has made you my master. You can tie up my body, bind my hands, control my actions. You have the right of the stronger, and society confirms you in it. But over my will, Monsieur, you have no power. God alone can bend and subdue it' (232; 176). Whereas Stendhal's more ambiguous comparison between women and slaves lends itself to literary discussions of character and style, Sand's more direct comparison lends itself to theoretical discussions of the implications of comparisons of women and slaves, often drawn by writers and critics then and today. Both kinds of discussions are fruitful and enlightening for undergraduate students, and both are easier to develop by drawing comparisons among several novels.

Comparing Stendhal's and Sand's novels also has the advantage of bringing out issues related to race that might otherwise remain invisible in *The Red and the Black*, and if there is one important thing that literary theory has taught us and that we need to pass on to our students it is that the "non-dit" 'unsaid' of a text often points to its most telling and significant subtexts. I would argue that for both novels, and for early nineteenth-century literature generally, that subtext is the violent events of the 1790s in Saint Domingue (now Haiti), which haunted the political unconscious of Europeans and Americans well beyond the abolition of slavery in the French colonies in 1848. Now, we only hear about Saint Domingue directly in Stendhal's novel when mention is made of a maid from that island, a mention that coincides, interestingly, with Julien's facetious description in pseudo-Creole of his plans to escape at night from Mathilde's room like a runaway slave: "Et comment moi m'en aller? dit Julien d'un ton plaisant, et en affectant le langage créole" 'And how me gwine get way? said Julien, speaking playfully and assuming a Creole dialect' (379; 275; 2.16). In Sand's work race is more consistently significant. The very fact of setting the novel in the West Indies and giving its ostensibly pure white heroine a name connoting the nonwhite race of Indians is significant, as is the focus on Noun as a person of color whose fate in many way mirrors Indiana's and therefore points up the association between the oppression of women and of persons of color (Kadish 22–30). But whether more explicit in *Indiana* or almost silent in *The Red and the Black*, I would urge that race is relevant to the study of both works and that it adds meaning to the theme of Julien's class inferiority. Repeatedly the novel calls attention to the obsessive fear among the upper classes of an uprising by the people: "nous payons vingt francs par domestique afin qu'un jour ils ne nous égorgent pas" 'We pay twenty francs for every servant, to prevent them from cutting our throats some day' (119; 76; 1.17); "S'il y a une nouvelle révolution, tous les nobles seront égorgés" 'If there's a new revolution, the aristocrats will all have their throats cut' (176; 126; 1.23). Now, it was in Saint Domingue, not France, that an uprising resulted in servants' cutting their masters' throats; and it was the image of violence in Saint Domingue that came to the minds of many when social stability seemed threatened, as it did with Julien's crime. It is apt therefore, I would argue, to see Julien as an embodiment not only of the lower classes but also more generally of the uprising masses, including slaves, and thereby to make race issues an integral part of a discussion of the culture of revolution in nineteenth-century France.

The type of course I propose here has several advantages over more traditional approaches to teaching *The Red and the Black*: it provides a great deal of detail about daily life and culture in the nineteenth century; it raises controversial issues that lead to lively class discussions; it deals directly with issues of class, race, and gender; it brings students into current theoretical debates without actually requiring them to study theory as such; and it teaches students how to approach canonical works critically. Student evaluations revealed that all the students were enthusiastic about the focus on daily life and culture and the animated discussions that resulted from the choice of texts. Some students appreciated the other, more theoretical or critical features of the course, while others expressed no opinion on them. Now, I recognize that some of my colleagues may object that the course I describe does not pay enough attention to the aesthetic features of Stendhal's novel; I would respond that for many of us that part comes so naturally that we perhaps need to work against our own tendencies and training as formalistic readers. Indeed, my efforts to emphasize the cultural, linguistic, and theoretical side of *The Red and the Black* did not keep me from weaving into my teaching the full range of its distinctive literary features, including irony, symbolism, description, focalization, and the modalities of narrative voice. But unlike other times I taught it in the past, those were not the only matters that concerned me. Nor, lest we forget, are they the only matters that concern students today.

Julienned Identities

Sandy Petrey

My goal in teaching *The Red and the Black* is for students to share the heady delight the novel gives me. I therefore see one of my principal pedagogical tasks as simply staying out of the way. Stendhal's narrator and characters possess a remarkable seductive power that works very well on its own.

Another task, however, is removing obstacles that can reduce the novel's appeal, particularly historical estrangement. *The Red and the Black*, deeply embedded in an age that contemporary students rarely know or care about, assumes social and political information they seldom have. Before getting out of the way, therefore, I try to make sure that the blanks in students' background will not make their reading of Stendhal too grueling to be gratifying.

One deterrent to gratification, however, arises not because students' training has been deficient but because it has been rich, because they have assimilated a critical discourse that roundly abuses realist fiction as unworthy and unappealing. Given that *The Red and the Black* is among realism's consecrated masterpieces, some of our liveliest students approach it with formidable suspicion. They have been taught that realism is outmoded and oppressive. If the lesson got through, they must consider taking delight in a realist novel to be the equivalent of fraternizing with the enemy.

"The realist illusion" has recently become a stock phrase with an impact comparable to what "the realist achievement" used to bear. Purportedly the aesthetic form assumed by the belief that individual and social identities are set and inflexible, realism has been taken as grounding its representation of the world in objective facts that brook no dissent. For students committed to the belief that categories of identity are human constructs that vary with human action, a realist text can appear rigidly authoritarian, unrelievedly glum. How can a novel delight students who believe it exemplifies a dead genre that doesn't deserve resuscitation?

It can't, which means that the teacher's obstacle clearing has to include demonstrating that realism has little to do with the definition of it circulating in certain critical circles with resonant influence. *The Red and the Black* is a glorious text for making this demonstration. Rather than depict identity as the ineluctable result of objective facts, rather than derive characters from an innate core they are powerless to change, Stendhal makes identity an exuberantly creative process.

Realism is accused of reproducing foundationalist concepts by representing race, class, and gender as if they were more physiological than sociological. Unlike realism, the argument goes, progressive literature sees those categories as not foundationalist but performative. Never given in advance, race, class, and gender appear as the by-products of role-playing undertaken in conjunction with ongoing collective rituals. From a performative perspective, the male body does not manifest itself in masculine behavior. Instead, masculine behavior is a set of learned patterns whose coalescence establishes a mystified idea of maleness. The same reversal holds with femininity and femaleness, with racial characteristics and race, and with other identifying features mistakenly considered to be bred in the bone. Performative identity repudiates the idea that we are what nature makes us, an idea that, according to one view, realism endorses through its depiction of characters.

In fact, however, if we establish an axis that runs from foundationalism (identity as inherent being) to performativity (identity as role playing), *The Red and the Black* sets itself squarely on the side of performativity. Julien Sorel plays roles skillfully, successfully, and in efficacious conformity to the expectations of his society. Foundationalist thought is physiological; it takes the body to be ground, source, and origin, understands race and gender as bodily attributes that pattern bodily actions. For Julien, though, the body is not an origin but an instrument. With it he makes himself into a perfect future priest whose gestures, eye movements, gait, and stance loudly proclaim his holy calling. On it he inflicts punishment when the proclamation is unpersuasive, as when he binds his arm against his chest and keeps it there for two months to remind his mouth to stay in line. Rather than a ground and a source, Julien's body is a costume and a tool.

The costume is painstakingly tailored, the tool impeccably maintained, as is clearest during Julien's months in the Besançon seminary. "Les habiles au séminaire ne regardent qu'aux détails" 'In the seminary clever fellows pay attention only to the details' (209; 143; 1.26); when Julien goes to the seminary, therefore, he tries mightily to make his body attend to details with enough care to ensure they say all the right things. "Au séminaire, il est une façon de manger un œuf à la coque qui annonce les progrès faits dans la vie dévote" 'in the seminary there's a way of eating a boiled egg which declares how far one has progressed down the saintly path' (211; 145; 1.26). As Julien and Stendhal's narrator understand thoroughly, however, what egg eating declares hasn't the slightest connection to what the egg eater believes. Like every other "*significant* action" (145; 1.26; emphasis in the orig.) that supposedly communicates what a person is, one's way of breaking an eggshell and spooning out a yolk is pure performance. Julien the atheist can project saintly beatitude no less successfully than a beatified saint, for in *The Red and the Black* a performance's underside has no effect on what it expresses.

In a foundationalist definition of faith and its manifestations, faith comes first, manifestations follow. In Julien's manifestations of it, faith doesn't come at all. This neophyte priest memorizes the Latin New Testament as an actor memorizes lines. Also like an actor, Julien understands perfectly that learning lines has the sole purpose of impressing an audience. In his case, the impression is gratifyingly intense, for each time he says what he has learned he inspires in the citizens of Verrières an admiration destined to last a hundred years (102; 61; 1.13). The effects of performance are durable as well as dramatic.

Yet they reveal nothing about performers other than their level of skill. The inhabitants of Verrières, rapt with admiration, are comically misguided in their assurance that Julien's mastery of pious language comes from his own piety. They continually adhere to the foundationalist myth that what people do expresses what they are.

M. de Rênal, for instance, unhesitatingly infers from Julien's interest in the church that everything else Julien feels must be in harmony with his "faith." "Ce Sorel étudie la théologie depuis trois ans, avec le projet d'entrer au séminaire; il n'est donc pas libéral" 'young Sorel has been studying theology for the last three years, hoping to enter the seminary; so he isn't a liberal' (34; 9–10; 1.3). M. de Rênal's "donc," 'so,' perfectly at home in a foundationalist universe, is grotesque and farcical when performativity is at issue. In *The Red and the Black*, it is grotesque and farcical.

One reason for realist fiction's frequent association with foundationalism is the number of positivist philosophies that circulated during its heyday. For instance, Johann Lavater's pseudoscience of physiognomy, a sterling instance of foundationalist thought, was at its peak when Stendhal was writing his best-known works. For Lavater the body does indeed manifest an inner core, one initiates can read because bodily features visibly express the invisible self. Throughout *The Red and the Black*, however, the organization of outer features is no more reliable a guide to inner states than ways of eating soft-boiled eggs are. That is why Mathilde de la Mole can use the Lavaterian fetish word, *physionomie*, in a way that knocks all Lavaterian ideas into a cocked hat. In Mathilde's usage the face is as meaningless as the color of one's clothes because it too is something you put on and take off as circumstances require. While thinking of Julien, Mathilde regrets "les désavantages de son éternel habit noir et de cette physionomie de prêtre, qu'il lui faut bien avoir, le pauvre garçon, sous peine de mourir de faim" 'the disadvantages of his perpetual black coat and that priestly face he has to put on, poor boy, if he is not to die of hunger' (352; 253; 2.12). Like a priest's knowledge, a priest's face is not a revelation but a prop. When Julien exults in his ability to choose the "uniform of my century" (262; 2.13), he means the features of his face as well as the clothes on his back. Mathilde sets clothes and face in apposition because both are costumes dissociated from the person wearing them, because both are tools of a trade instead of doors to a truth.

What he wears, how he looks, what he says, where he goes, how he eats, when he sleeps—every aspect of Julien's life as an aspirant to the priesthood constructs a role whose purpose is to mystify and deceive. Almost nothing he does conveys the slightest information about his inner being. Like the Bishop of Agde practicing how to look older in front of a mirror, Julien transforms himself. He acts with consummate skill and achieves grand results. In that sense, *performative* is absolutely the right word to describe Julien's churchly identity.

Within the terms of performativity as defined by Judith Butler's influential work *Gender Trouble*, however, it's absolutely the wrong word. Butler insists that our performances create what we are for ourselves as well as for others. Nothing comes before the performance, no one stands outside it as producer-observer. As a result, hypocrisy cannot be performative in Butler's sense. No matter how effectively it manipulates others, hypocritical role-playing never takes in the hypocrite. Because Julien remains perfectly conscious of his atheism, his priestly skills stop well short of being performative as Butler defines the term. Julien does at times take himself in—"En cet instant il se fût battu pour l'Inquisition, et de bonne foi" 'At that moment he would have fought for the Inquisition, and with full conviction' (134; 86; 1.18)—but only rarely and briefly. His dominant trait is not "full conviction" but no conviction at all. Because his imitation of a priest creates the illusion of a subjectivity but not a subjectivity, his behavior is performative only in the theatrical sense. It does not meet Butler's criteria for a performative identity.

But Julien's priestly role is not his only performance in *The Red and the Black*. He also learns to play the part of a man of far higher birth than his own, and here performativity does indeed work both ways, on performer as well as audience. In Paris Julien gives himself aristocratic appearances and accomplishments the same way he gave himself Christian piety in Verrières, through observation and imitation of the best models available. But this time he is very far from retaining the inner distance that defines a hypocrite. In performing nobility, Julien convinces even himself that he is authentically noble.

Although I discuss the performativity of class only in relation to Julien, it holds for other characters in *The Red and the Black* as well. Given the ideological configuration of Restoration France, this vision of class's performative constitution has clear affinities with recent analyses of the remaining members of the modern triad of identity, race and gender. The Restoration view was that class—along with sex and race—was given at conception to last unchanged until death. It is crucial to distinguish this essentialist view of class from the vaguely financial view held by most American students who think about class at all. Julien's rise from peasantry to aristocracy differs massively from class mobility in a market economy, from the perennial rags-to-riches story of Western literature's Horatio Algers. An order of the world based on money is strengthened rather than roiled when a person without money changes status by acquiring it. But class mobility is radically disruptive to an order based on birth: When social position is based primarily on net worth, it's logical for an increase in assets to enhance position. But when position comes with birth, such a change implies that birth means nothing when it ought to mean everything.

On shifting its scene from the provinces to Paris, *The Red and the Black* goes to some lengths to emphasize that here status is indeed based on birth. "L'argent ne vient que longtemps après" 'Money comes far behind' (271; 189; 2.1), the abbé Pirard explains to Julien at the very beginning of the Parisian episode. It is not wealth but parentage that gives kings "des droits imprescriptibles aux respects de tous et surtout aux respects d'êtres sans naissance" 'unquestionable right to respect from everyone, particularly creatures of no birth' (271; 190; 2.1), Pirard continues, and what holds for kings holds for everyone else born to authority. Like whites in a racist society, like men in patriarchy, nobles in an aristocracy hold superior positions by innate, inherent right.

Yet Julien Sorel, inherently and innately a nobody, the very model of a "creature of no birth," acquires a position far above anything an ideologically congruent biography could have furnished. He rises so far he literally becomes someone else, an aristocrat named the chevalier de La Vernaye, with elevated tastes, talents, prospects, revenues—and parentage. For an aristocratic worldview this play with the mutability of identity carries the same threat as cross-dressing for sexists, as passing for racists. It means that the barriers organizing the world are porous, that society has an illusion at its base. Julien's adventures among the aristocrats demolish all the certainties necessary to any hierarchy based on birth.

Once more, these adventures engage the body—how best to train it to perform effectively. Immediately after meeting him, the marquis de La Mole decides Julien needs dance lessons to smooth provincial awkwardness out of his carriage. Later, the marquis also advises that Julien make regular visits to the opera and carefully watch the audiences coming out, to learn how to move like a Parisian. This peasant learns to look like an aristocrat the same way aristocrats do, by watching people who have already completed the course he is just starting.

Imagine a foundationalist comment about the aristocratic body on display, something like "You could tell at a glance X was born to rank." Or take this thought of the newly smitten Julien: "En apercevant Mlle de La Mole à trente pas de distance, un homme de goût devinerait le rang qu'elle occupe dans la société" 'Looking at Mlle. de La Mole from a distance of thirty feet, a man of taste would be able to recognize at a glance her social rank' (371; 268–69; 2.14). The message of Julien's initiation into aristocratic appearance is that how people look reveals nothing more than what they have learned. Whether from thirty feet or thirty millimeters, what the body shows is its training rather than its bloodlines.

That again makes it an instrument rather than the vehicle of an epiphany. It does indeed speak, but only to say what it's been taught. An aristocratic demeanor is learned behavior, like reciting the New Testament in Latin. As a consequence, aristocrats are "tous copies les uns des autres" 'each copied from the other' (396; 288; 2.19), which means the peasant Julien can copy their model as well.

In the world in which it took place, dueling was an essentially aristocratic activity, something that happened only when both parties were of unquestionably noble birth. When Julien—not a nobleman but a secretary—duels with the chevalier de Beauvoisis, therefore, the chevalier has to do something fast to keep his own aristocratic credentials intact.

What he does provides a broadly comic take on the foundationalist-performative twist characterizing aristocracy in *The Red and the Black*. After dueling with a commoner, the chevalier de Beauvoisis simply announces to the world that he did no such thing. His status requires that the blood he spilled be as blue as his, so that's what he says it is. "Le soir même, le chevalier de Beauvoisis et son ami dirent partout que ce M. Sorel, d'ailleurs un jeune homme parfait, était fils naturel d'un ami intime du marquis de La Mole. Ce fait passa sans difficulté" 'That evening the chevalier de Beauvoisis and his second spread everywhere the story that this M. Sorel, a most agreeable young man for that matter, was the illegitimate son of one of the Marquis de La Mole's intimate friends. This tale passed easily' (307–08; 218; 2.6). The foundationalist view: duels take place between men who come to the dueling ground as nobles. The performative view: when men meet on the dueling ground, discourse represents them as noble because ideology requires that they be so. *The Red and the Black* incorporates the performative view with such mock earnestness that it joins Beauvoisis in calling a fantasy a fact. The narrator, not the chevalier, tells the reader that Julien's noble birth is a "fait" 'fact' that passed easily; one measure of the outrageous unconventionality of such a view of facts is the translator's decision to say that what passed was not a fact but a "tale," presumably to keep things in their foundationalist mold. In Stendhal's text that mold has no purchase.

The novel's penchant for performativity receives another comic overlay when the marquis de La Mole decides to give Julien two identities during their dealings with each other. One makes the commoner into a nobleman, a shift achieved by a change of clothes. In black, Julien works steadily as a secretary; in blue, he chats wittily as an aristocrat. Here is the marquis's announcement of the parameters that will effect the metamorphosis: "Permettez, mon cher Sorel, que je vous fasse cadeau d'un habit bleu; quand il vous conviendra de le prendre et de venir chez moi, vous serez, à mes yeux, le frère cadet du comte de Chaulnes, c'est-à-dire le fils de mon ami le vieux duc" 'Allow me, my dear Sorel, to make you a present of a blue suit; when you feel disposed to put it on and pay me a call, you will be, in my eyes, the younger brother of the Comte de Retz, that is to say the son of my friend the old duke' (309–10; 219; 2.7). Go to the opera and learn to move like an aristocrat, the marquis tells Julien. He also tells Julien to change his suit and be one. It just doesn't get any more performative than this.

Especially if we contemplate the particulars of Julien's new identity. The duc de Chaulnes is famous for holding aristocratic prejudices (250; 189; 2.1), prejudices that entail unwavering belief in the foundationalist tenet that birth determines identity absolutely. By pretending that the duc de Chaulnes is the father of a son whose birth he doesn't know a thing about, the marquis de La Mole makes fun of everything underpinning aristocracy and everyone who believes its underpinning is solid. And there's more: the duc de Chaulnes is also the father of the marquise de La Mole, which means that Julien's blue-suit identity obliterates the aristocratic integrity of the de La Moles as well as the Chaulnes. A change of clothes allows Julien to pass as the marquis de La Mole's brother-in-law and Mathilde's uncle. (Again the performative thrust of Stendhal's text is too much for the translation, which makes Julien the son of the "duc de Retz" instead of the duc de Chaulnes. The French version shreds the family, the bedrock of aristocratic ideology; the English version leaves it intact.) Julien's performative aristocracy climaxes when his prospective marriage to Mathilde leads the marquis de La Mole to remake him into "M. le chevalier Julien Sorel de La Vernaye" (441; 358; 2.34). Other characters (Mathilde, the abbé Pirard), instantly begin to speak and think of him under this new name, and so does Julien himself. Commissioned into the army, he quickly instills in his fellow officers the respect his new name deserves through noble accoutrements maintained "avec une correction qui aurait fait honneur à la ponctualité d'un grand seigneur anglais" 'with a smartness that would have done credit to the style of an English gentleman' (494; 360; 2.35—here too the translation wimps out; Stendhal's outrageous "punctiliousness of a great English lord" becomes the tame "style of an English gentleman"). It wasn't only at the opera that Julien was observing closely so as to perform successfully. He can be a great English lord as persuasively as a budding French priest.

But there is the capital difference that Julien's performance of aristocratic birth, unlike his imitation of Christian faith, defines what he is for himself as well as for the rest of the world. The man who learned to walk the walk and talk the talk of an aristocrat finally comes to think like one too, putting his faith in the foundationalist credo that identity comes only from birth. "Serait-il bien possible, se disait-il, que je fusse le fils naturel de quelque grand seigneur, exilé dans nos montagnes par le grand Napoléon? A chaque instant cette idée lui semblait moins impossible. Ma haine pour mon père serait une preuve. Je ne serais plus un monstre!" 'Is it actually possible, he asked himself, that I might be the natural son of some aristocrat exiled among our mountains by the terrible Napoleon? At every instant this idea appeared less improbable to him. My hate for my father would be a proof. I would no longer be a monster!' (493; 360; 2.35). Julien Sorel, who has gone through all the steps that make an aristocrat and therefore knows perfectly well that aristocrats are made, not born, nevertheless comes to believe that they are born, not made. I am as punctilious as a great English lord, Julien seems to have said to himself, as self-possessed as the comte de Chaulnes, as dashing on the field of honor as the chevalier de Beauvoisis. If I'm not of noble birth, how could I possibly possess so many noble virtues? The narrative of Julien's life in Paris, a long exploration of rank's artificiality, concludes with the protagonist deciding rank must be natural—inherent, innate, foundationalist.

Julien's speculation on his noble father comes just after the abbé Pirard has informed "M. de La Vernaye" that there is no need to consider "M. Sorel, a carpenter at Verrières" as anything other than the man hired to care for M. de La Vernaye during his childhood (492; 359; 2.35). Julien's response is ecstatic and hallucinatory: "Julien ne fut plus maître de son transport, il embrassa l'abbé, il se voyait reconnu" 'Julien could no longer master his transports; he embraced the abbé; he saw himself recognized' (492; 360; 2.35).

When does Julien feel recognized? During a series of measures taken to prevent anyone from recognizing that he's Julien. Recognition comes in two forms, perceptual and legal. The sham of Julien's legal recognition by a noble father—the abbé Pirard claims to bring M. de La Vernaye money sent by "son père, qu'il est inutile de désigner autrement" 'his father, whom it is useless to identify in any other way' (492; 359; 2.35)—takes unquestioned priority over the perceptually recognizable fact that he remains who he was. Julien Sorel goes into ecstasy because he gets the loopy idea that he's not Julien Sorel.

Louis Althusser, in his broadly influential essay on ideology and ideological state apparatuses, examines ideology's capacity for massive distortion of perception. What we call recognition is in fact miscognition (*reconnaissance* is *méconnaissance*); it cannot produce reliable knowledge (*connaissance*). On seeing himself recognized, Julien becomes a textbook illustration of Althusser's point. Ideology defines aristocracy as an effect of birth, and Julien moves into the aristocracy; therefore, his birth must be noble.

He even takes his loathing for his father as "proof" that he must be somebody else's son: "My hate for my father would be a proof." That M. Sorel treated Julien with savage brutality and sneering contempt isn't enough to explain the hatred. In aristocratic circles blood counts more than behavior, so Julien is quite consistent in believing that blood rather than behavior explains why he can't stand his father. Intensive and extensive participation in the generative rites that construct identity finally leads Julien to "recognize" that identity is inherited. The final step in his display of performativity at work is his orthodox foundationalism.

I say above that Julien's creation of a subjectivity for the subject as well as for others clearly demarcates his role as M. de La Vernaye from his role as an aspirant to the priesthood. These two forms of imitation—conscious hypocrisy and performative self-patterning—are themselves demarcated from Julien's final identity, which he discovers in prison after repudiating and destroying his aristocratic ambitions. On his joyous reunion with Mme de Rênal, Julien stops performing and starts living.

When he does, the reproach that realism recirculates the naive concept of identity as direct experience of an integral self seems justified. To read, for instance, that in prison "Julien se sentait fort et résolu comme l'homme qui voit clair dans son âme" 'Julien felt himself strong and resolute, like a man who has seen clearly into his own soul' (550; 403; 2.44) is to encounter a person whose identity doesn't need to be performed. It simply is. At the end of his life, Julien learns to recognize himself in a sense diametrically opposed to Althusser's. Instead of needing others to mediate his identity—real people like the audience leaving the opera, fictitious people like M. de La Vernaye's aristocratic father—Julien now needs only to look into his soul to understand what and who he is.

For readers convinced that the idea of such reliable insight into selfhood is a mystification, therefore, the conclusion of *The Red and the Black* might legitimately provoke a reaction congruent with realism's recent bad press. But the novel's conclusion does not undo its previous representation of identity as performance. It simply takes its heroes out of the setting that must always empower performativity, society with its ritualized conventions. Julien and Mme de Rênal deliberately shut themselves off from the rest of the world, and it is the rest of the world that makes performance work. *The Red and the Black*'s insights into what we are among our fellows remain valid despite Stendhal's decision to give two of its characters a magical idyll in which their fellows just don't matter. Despite the novel's final representation of identity as a fortress against society, its earlier vision of how identity is constituted within society remains breathtakingly modern.

The Quest for the Mother: A Psychoanalytic Feminist Reading of *The Red and the Black*

Lisa G. Algazi

Whatever happened to Julien's mother? This question, long pondered by readers and students of Stendhal, lies at the heart of Julien's quest for acceptance and, finally, love in the arms of the two mother-mistresses in *The Red and the Black*, Mme de Rênal and Mathilde. Only Julien's social ambition rivals his unconscious longing for maternal affection as his prime motivation, and in the end, in the sanctuary of his prison cell, it is the latter that triumphs. In this essay I propose a psychoanalytic feminist approach to understanding the role of the mother in *The Red and the Black* and its relevance to a critical analysis of the text as a whole. To this end I examine Stendhal's ambiguous portrayal of the maternal figure and its implications both for Julien and for future generations of French women.

The Representation of Mothers: From Christian Tradition to Psychoanalysis

Traditional maternal imagery in the Western Christian tradition tends to revolve around the sacred figure of the Virgin Mary, the mother of Christ whose example all women should follow. In keeping with this image the ideal mother has traditionally been represented as a chaste and selfless extension of her (mostly male) offspring, dedicated solely to their care and nurturing, to the total exclusion of her own needs and desires. In maternal representations in French literature from Rabelais to Rousseau, women who become mothers are automatically excluded from the realms of sexuality and active selfhood of any kind, leaving only their capacity to mother as the central expression of their identities as women. Most often, they become accessories to the hero, mere props that help to explain the personality and character of the protagonist.

With the rise of psychoanalytic theory came a new understanding of this traditional vision of motherhood and its underlying symbolic mechanisms, starting with Freud's theories on the preœdipal stage of child development and the sexual nature of the relationship between the (male) infant and the mother. Later theorists have modified Freud's concepts to create an image of the mother as a refuge from the patriarchal world, representing a state of being that both precedes and supercedes patriarchal society. According to the French psychoanalyst Jacques Lacan, the symbolic, or the realm of language, is essentially patriarchal,because of the privileged position of the phallus as transcendental signifier. The law of the father represents the law of a phallic society where no thought can exist outside language and no language can exist without assuming the preexistence of the phallus. As a complementary realm to the symbolic in Lacan's theory of child development, the imaginary represents the early infant period when there is no distinction between subject and object, self and other, and the child experiences a symbiotic relationship with the mother's body; its identity and its mother's merge and become inseparable.

This blissful period, when the child's world seems free of contradictions or uncertainties, ends when the child becomes aware of the father and the outside world represented by the father: the preestablished structure of social and sexual roles that make up the family and society and that Lacan calls the symbolic order. When the child enters the symbolic order, learning language and differentiating the self, it becomes a part of a world radically different from that in which it had existed with its mother. The blurry boundaries of the Imaginary and the womblike peace of life before language fade as the child begins its new life in the public realm controlled by the father and those like him. French feminist and psychoanalytic theorist Julia Kristeva (*Soleil*) sees the period of child development before the interference of the father as a possible source of prelinguistic communication. The sensual, wordless language between mother and child becomes *le sémiotique,* drawing on the rhythms of the merging bodies and the strength of the instinctive drives expressed between mother and infant. For Kristeva this special time before patriarchal intervention allows both mother and child to experience a world free from the strictures of patriarchal law, of the law of language, of the symbolic. It is such a world to which Julien wishes to return, and his quest will lead him from the provinces to Paris to a provincial prison, where he finally finds his *sémiotique* with his quintessential woman, Mme de Rênal.

Mme de Rênal, Mother and Savior

The Red and the Black revolves around a motherless hero, leaving the maternal role in Julien's development conveniently open. From the moment he arrives at the Rênal's home to take up his tutoring duties, we find an abundance of metaphors for birth, or rebirth: Julien's symbolic bath in the fountain, his wet hair, and his unsure manner all lead Mme de Rênal to treat him like a lost child and take him under her maternal wing. Her first words to him, "Que voulez-vous ici, mon enfant?" 'What do you want here, my child?' (48; 21; 1.6) begin their relationship on a more intimate footing than the reserved Mme de Rênal would normally tolerate with a stranger, particularly a man. Neither her convent education, which the narrator describes as worthless, nor her experience with loud and abrupt men such as her husband and his friends has prepared her for this encounter with a sensitive, effeminate young peasant who seems to her more like a shy young girl than the authoritarian, mean-tempered brute she had expected. Overwhelmed with relief, she welcomes Julien as an addition to her family, thinking that he will be a friend to her eldest son, who is not much younger than Julien.

As Julien settles into the routine of educating the young sons of this aristocratic family, his privileged relationship with the mistress of the house becomes ever more intimate, as she takes charge of his social education much as he teaches her sons their Latin. For Mme de Rênal, this tender interest in someone other than her children is a new and strange experience; her emotional universe had previously been confined to maternal love, as befitted a good Catholic wife and mother. Her innocence in affairs of the heart and her tendency to treat Julien like a son blinds her to the enormity of her transgression, allowing her to step outside the traditional limits of motherhood to feel and act on her own desires. In contrast to earlier literary portrayals of mothers who strayed from the chaste ideal, however, the author does not censure Mme de Rênal for neglecting her children as she slowly evolves from Julien's surrogate mother to his passionate mistress. On the contrary, her transformation provides Julien with both his missing mother figure and a means of escape into the imaginary world of the prison. As Mme de Rênal becomes more active in protecting and nurturing her lover-son, Julien slowly realizes that the key to his happiness lies in her love, not in social recognition or power; the return to the presymbolic maternal space gives him more pleasure than any of the worldly gifts that his other mistress, Mathilde, can offer.

After Julien tries to kill her, Mme de Rênal defies patriarchal religion and propriety by defending her attacker, using all her newfound self-assurance in her efforts to bring about his pardon. However, these efforts are and must be in vain: as a woman and mother, she has no power over the symbolic order. Only in the maternal space of the prison can she control the life of her lover-son, just as she brought him food and water when he was temporarily imprisoned in her bedroom. Her appearance in his cell, and the contrast between her un-self-conscious devotion and Mathilde's ostentatious displays, renew Julien's will to live:

> [I]l fut éveillé par des larmes qu'il sentait couler sur sa main. Ah! c'est encore Mathilde, pensa-t-il à demi éveillé. [. . .] Ennuyé de la perspective de cette nouvelle scène dans le genre pathétique, il n'ouvrit pas les yeux. [. . .] Il entendit un soupir singulier; il ouvrit les yeux, c'était Mme de Rênal.
>
> —Ah! je te revois avant que de mourir, est-ce une illusion? s'écria-t-il en se jetant à ses pieds. [. . .] Sache que je t'ai toujours aimée, que je n'ai jamais aimé que toi. (537–38)

> [H]e was awakened by tears which he felt trickling on his hand.
>
> Ah! it's Mathilde again, he thought, still half asleep. [. . .] Bored by the prospect of another scene in the pathetic vein, he did not open his eyes. [. . .] He heard an unusual sob; he opened his eyes, it was Mme. de Rênal.
>
> —Ah! So I can see you again before I die, or is it an illusion? [. . .] You must know that I've always loved you, I never loved anyone but you.
>
> (393–94; 2.43)

His claim that he never loved anyone but her is an indication of his redefinition of love since the time of his imprisonment: Julien finally understands the value of maternal passion and the futility of *l'amour-vanité*, as Stendhal calls the vainglorious, self-conscious infatuation that he distinguishes from sincere and natural passion (*l'amour-passion*). Only in prison does Julien recognize that his infatuation with Mathilde had more to do with vanity and ambition than with his own emotions; belatedly, he grasps the full extent of Mme de Rênal's maternal devotion, entrusting his fate and that of his unborn son to her care. In the midst of their lovemaking Julien tells her: "songe [. . .] qu'il faut que tu vives pour mon fils, que Mathilde abandonnera à des laquais [. . .]" 'You must suppose [. . .] that you are required to live for my son, whom Mathilde will abandon to the care of lackeys [. . .]' (440; 395; 2.43). His perception of Mathilde's inability to mother becomes the determining factor in his preference for the englobing efficacy of his surrogate mother, Mme de Rênal.

Sacrificing her reputation and her religion to her desire, Mme de Rênal achieves total separation from the authority of the father, returning to the prison against both her confessor's wishes and her husband's explicit orders. Exceeding even the efforts of the wealthy and aggressive Mathilde, Mme de Rênal obtains permission to see Julien twice a day, and the two lovers treasure their last moments together in his little cell, finally isolated from the petty interferences of the symbolic by the walls of the patriarchal prison. Within this protected maternal space, Mme de Rênal becomes Julien's mother once more, protecting him from his jailers and living from day to day in a blissfully symbiotic harmony that not even their time in the woods of Vergy had granted them. United at last with his adored mother-mistress, free of the distractions of the symbolic order, Julien finally finds the happiness that had eluded him in his frantic pursuit of masculine ambitions:

> [I]l vivait d'amour et sans presque songer à l'avenir. Par un étrange effet de cette passion, quand elle est extrême et sans feinte aucune, Mme de Rênal partageait presque son insouciance et sa douce gaieté.
>
> —Autrefois, lui disait Julien, quand j'aurais pu être si heureux pendant nos promenades dans les bois de Vergy, une ambition fougueuse entraînait mon âme dans les pays imaginaires. [. . .] Non, je serais mort sans connaître le bonheur, si vous n'étiez venue me voir dans cette prison. (552–53)

> [H]e was living on love and almost without a thought for the future. By a strange effect of this passion when it is at its height and perfectly sincere, Mme. de Rênal almost shared in his indifference and gentle gaiety.
>
> —In the old days, Julien told her, when I could have been so happy during our walks through the forest at Vergy, smoldering ambition dragged my soul way into imaginary lands. [. . .] No, I should have died without ever knowing happiness if you had not come to see me in this prison. (405; 2.45)

Living in such complete harmony that they share the same feelings and thoughts, the two lovers spend their precious last days together in a presymbolic paradise, interrupted only by periodic unwelcome visits of the rejected mistress, Mathilde. After Julien's execution, while Mathilde is occupied with the disposition of his mortal remains, Mme de Rênal continues her pattern of maternal devotion to her lover at the expense of her own children: in spite of her promise to live for the sake of Julien's son, three days after his death, "elle mourut en embrassant ses enfants" 'she died in the act of embracing her children' (556; 408; 2.45).

Mathilde de La Mole, or the Maternal Failure

Julien's preference for Mme de Rênal's real maternal passion over Mathilde's self-conscious infatuation demonstrates his willingness to sacrifice all the things he had once thought important—career, wealth, social status—for the pleasure of a nostalgic return to the original mother-child realm of blissful unity, beyond the reach of the patriarchal structures that have continually oppressed and excluded him. His nostalgia for such an extrasymbolic bond cannot be satisfied by the cold Mathilde, even though she is carrying his child. While her actions demonstrate her untiring devotion to her lover, she ultimately cannot fulfill Julien's emotional and psychological needs, because of an essential lack. What is this lack that defines, by opposition, the ideal Stendhalian woman? Both Mme de Rênal and Mathilde are mothers, at least in the physiological sense. Both use every means available to help Julien in his struggle against patriarchal society. Finally, both women sacrifice the most precious possession of any respectable nineteenth-century Frenchwoman, their reputations, to their love for Julien, defying their families and their social peers to help him.

The real difference lies in Julien's perception of the maternal role and of Mathilde's inability to fulfill that role. For Julien, the moment when he discovers the sublime nature of unconditional love comes when Mme de Rênal's youngest son, Stanislas, falls ill. Mme de Rênal's conviction that she will be damned for all eternity because of her adultery, as well as her continuing love for Julien in spite of this conviction, melts the core of Julien's skeptical heart:

> La méfiance et l'orgueil de Julien, qui avait surtout besoin d'un amour à sacrifices, ne tinrent pas devant la vue d'un sacrifice si grand, si indubitable et fait à chaque instant. Il adorait Mme de Rênal. [. . .] Leur bonheur était désormais d'une nature bien supérieure, la flamme qui les dévorait fut plus intense. (137)

> Julien's suspicion and anxious pride, which required above all a love built on sacrifice, could not hold out against a sacrifice so vast, so unquestionable, so continual. He adored Mme. de Rênal. [. . .] Henceforth their

> happiness was of a finer grain; the passion that devoured them was more intense. (93; 1.19)

Julien's first meeting with Mathilde gives a very different picture. Although Mathilde is described as weak and pale, the narrator notes that her voice "n'a rien de féminin" '[is] short, sharp, completely unfeminine' (291; 220; 2.7). Despite the feminine frailty of her body, her spirit is masculine. When Julien first sees her, he compares the haughty Mathilde with his image of womanhood based on his experience with Mme de Rênal and subsequently denies her womanhood, faithful to the ideal created by the maternal devotion of the only woman he has ever known. On his next encounter with Mathilde, he repeats his disapproval of Mathilde's lack of femininity: "Julien lui trouva [. . .] l'air dur, hautain et presque masculin" 'Julien [. . .] decided she looked hard, arrogant, almost masculine' (283; 198; 2.3). His instinctive revulsion for this hybrid of masculine and feminine traits will be temporarily overcome by a surge of vanity, only to resurface at the end of the novel in his rejection of Mathilde's unwelcome attentions.

Where Mathilde shows enthusiasm only for intellectual pleasures, Mme de Rênal overflows with "natural" passions, as Julien reflects when he first encounters Mathilde: "Quand les yeux de Mme de Rênal s'animaient, c'était du feu des passions [. . .]" 'When Mme. de Rênal's eyes grew animated, it was with the fire of passion. [. . .]' (280; 196; 2.2). Mathilde seems vain and artificial in comparison, causing Julien to regret the loss of his beloved surrogate mother:

> Quelle différence avec ce que j'ai perdu! quel naturel charmant! quelle naïveté! Je savais ses pensées avant elle, je les voyais naître, je n'avais pour antagoniste, dans son cœur, que la peur de la mort des ses enfants; c'était une affection raisonnable et naturelle, aimable même pour moi qui en souffrais. J'ai été un sot. Les idées que je me faisais de Paris m'ont empêché d'apprécier cette femme sublime.
>
> Quelle différence, grand Dieu! et qu'est-ce que je trouve ici? de la vanité sèche et hautaine, toutes les nuances de l'amour-propre et rien de plus. (338)

> What a difference from the woman I have lost! what natural charm there! What simplicity! I knew her thoughts before she did herself; I saw them forming in her mind; within her heart my only opponent was her fear that her children might die; it was a sensible and natural affection, such that even I, who suffered from it, found it admirable. I've been a fool. My imaginings about Paris prevented me from appreciating that glorious woman.
>
> What a difference, good God! And what do I find here? Vanity, dry and arrogant, every conceivable variety of self-approval, and nothing else. (242; 2.10)

Where Mme de Rênal possesses all the qualities of Julien's ideal woman, including the maternal passions that he calls "raisonnable et naturelle [et] aimable," Mathilde has nothing but vanity and pride. This assessment of his preference for the sincere woman with the capacity for maternal affection explains his eventual rejection of Mathilde and his return to the security of Mme de Rênal's arms and the charms of the imaginary.

In the midst of their stormy relationship Mathilde suddenly discovers that she is expecting a child. From the first she treats her pregnancy as a tool, to expedite her ambition of marrying Julien. She joyously informs her lover of her condition, adding: "N'est-ce pas une garantie? Je suis votre épouse à jamais" 'Isn't this a guarantee? I am your wife forever' (475; 347; 2.32). In her coldly calculating manner, she views the unborn child dispassionately, determined to use her pregnancy to manipulate her father. Seeing a chance for her own advancement in the potential glory of her lover, Mathilde will stop at nothing to satisfy their mutual ambition; her pregnancy fills her with joy, not for sentimental reasons, but because it gives her the opportunity to sacrifice her reputation to her lover and at the same time to bind Julien to her forever. This strategy, although reminiscent of Julie's premarital pregnancy and miscarriage in Rousseau's *La Nouvelle Héloïse*, meets with greater success: M. de La Mole, after his initial outrage and much deliberation, actually gives Julien both a noble title and a commission as lieutenant in the army. Just as his daughter had hoped, M. de La Mole prefers to safeguard the family honor by elevating Julien, since the pregnancy makes their marriage unavoidable.

While Mathilde uses her pregnancy as a bargaining tool in the negotiations with her father, however, Julien thinks only of the welfare of his future son. Never doubting that the child will be a boy, he dreams of his future nurturing role as a father, which suddenly gives purpose to his life and his ambitions. When he offers his life to the marquis de La Mole as just retribution for his daughter's dishonor, he does so reluctantly, thinking, "J'aime la vie. [. . .] Je me dois à mon fils" 'I am fond of life. [. . .] I have a duty to my son' (481; 351; 2.33). His earlier ambitions take on a more generous air as his thoughts dwell on the future of his son: "Lorsqu'elle apprit à Julien qu'il était lieutenant de hussards, sa joie fut sans bornes. On peut se la figurer par l'ambition de toute sa vie, et par la passion qu'il avait maintenant pour son fils" 'When she told Julien he was a lieutenant of hussars, his joy knew no bounds. It can be estimated from the ambition of his whole life, and from the passion that he was now feeling for his new son' (491; 359; 2.34). In the dynamics of the couple the traditional roles are now completely reversed: Mathilde tends to the business of social and financial success, leaving Julien to dream about the future of their child in an effort to compensate for Mathilde's obvious lack of interest in mothering. To Mathilde, motherhood becomes a means of coercion, which she employs most effectively against the prejudices and plans of her aristocratic father. Indeed, Mathilde as future mother would have accomplished her goal of union with an ennobled Julien, if not for the fatal intervention of Mme de Rênal's letter and its reminder of the attraction of the maternal bond.

After his imprisonment, Julien longs for "une tendresse simple, naïve et presque timide," 'a simple, a naive and almost timid approach' (516; 378; 2.39), adjectives that remind him of Mme de Rênal and that indicate the essential qualities lacking in the hypocritical, glory-seeking, and aggressive Mathilde. Julien's infatuation with Mathilde was a child of his vanity, a product of mimetic desire that overcame his initial resolution that she would never be a woman in his eyes. When Mathilde bravely attempts to intervene on his behalf during his imprisonment, Julien seems more shocked than grateful, preoccupied with his thoughts of Mme de Rênal. His love for Mathilde begins and ends with his worldly ambition; once he is liberated from that driving ambition by the prospect of death, his love for her (*l'amour-vanité*) fades overnight, replaced by an all-consuming passion for his ideal woman, Mme de Rênal.

Mathilde fails to measure up to Julien's standards of femininity in part because of her numerous "masculine" traits. In many respects Mathilde is androgynous; she is denied Julien's moment of glory not because of her gender, which the narrator repeatedly describes as masculine, but because of her sex. In fact Mathilde seems even more aggressive and ambitious than Julien, seeing her motherhood, that much-praised sacred female occupation, only as a tool with which to manipulate her father, while her lover thinks of the welfare of the unborn child. Afraid for the safety of his only offspring, Julien expresses his lack of confidence in its mother's feminine and maternal capacities, saying to Mathilde even before his reunion with his first mistress:

> J'ai une grâce à vous demander [. . .] mettez votre enfant en nourrice à Verrières, madame de Rênal surveillera la nourrice. [. . .] La mort de mon fils serait au fond un bonheur pour l'orgueil de votre famille, c'est ce que devineront les subalternes. La négligence sera le lot de cet enfant du malheur et de la honte. [. . .]
>
> Il se trouvait de nouveau vis-à-vis cette idée si choquante pour Mathilde: Dans quinze ans madame de Rênal adorera mon fils, et vous l'aurez oublié. (518–20)

> I have a favor to ask of you [. . .] put your child out to nurse at Verrières; Mme. de Rênal will keep an eye on the nurse. [. . .] The death of my son would gratify the pride of your family, and that's what the flunkies will guess about it. Neglect will be the lot of this child of misery and shame. [. . .]
>
> He found himself once more face to face with this idea which so distressed Mathilde: in fifteen years, Mme. de Rênal will adore my son, and you will have forgotten him. (379–80; 2.39)

Concerned about the child's welfare, Julien entrusts his son's care to Mme de Rênal, having no doubt of *her* capacity to mother. During his long hours of self-examination in the lonely prison cell, Julien passes judgment on Mathilde, thinking: "On peut devenir savant, adroit, mais le cœur! . . . Le cœur ne s'apprend pas" 'You may become learned, you may become shrewd, but the heart! . . . the heart can't be trained' (535; 391; 2.42). In spite of Mathilde's accomplishments, Julien implies that she lacks some instinctive quality that cannot be taught. His repeated references to Mathilde's indifference to their child, coupled with his total rejection of her attentions, suggest the importance of maternal instinct for the motherless Julien and thus the reason for his rejection of Mathilde in favor of the essential mother figure, Mme de Rênal. A failure as a mother, Mathilde must also be a failure as Julien's mistress and protector; only a maternal figure can re-create the peace and harmony of the imaginary for a weary Julien searching for a respite from the harsh symbolic order that has condemned him.

Julien's quest for the mother, then, ends in prison, where he finds at long last the symbiotic unity of unconditional maternal love with Mme de Rênal. Julien's own mother, perhaps dead as a result of his birth (a common occurrence in early-nineteenth-century France), haunts him, yet her absence leaves him conveniently free to play the son of a wealthy and beautiful surrogate mother with whom he is free to act out his incestuous filial desire in the privileged space of the imaginary. In this Romantic passion play Mme de Rênal becomes both more aware of her own selfhood through her desire for her lover and more selflessly devoted to him, opening the door to a new version of the traditional maternal image, one in which the mother and the woman are allowed to coexist, defying the tradition of maternal purity in favor of a new maternal ideal.

In *The Red and the Black* Stendhal creates a space in which women who mother can exist as free individuals, not only as mothers. Although the author dooms Mathilde's attempts at selfhood to failure because they stray completely from the feminine roles of mistress and mother, Mme de Rênal's discovery of maternal self-determination provides a new and attractive option to women who wish to combine traditional and nontraditional gender roles. By studying this space and recognizing it for the unique, however ephemeral, innovation it is, readers of Stendhal can better understand the attitudes and ideals that influence Western culture's definition of womanhood and can begin to explore possible avenues of escape from the strictures of traditional gender identity.

Sacred Hearts and Stolen Smarts: Rewriting French Noblewomen in *The Red and the Black*

Cheryl A. Morgan

By the time my students read *The Red and the Black* they are familiar with narratives of the *mal du siècle* and the *nègre romantique*. They therefore perceive in Stendhal's novel the motifs of paternal authority, filial revolt, and illegitimacy identified by Peter Brooks and Janet Beizer. Surprisingly though, my twenty-something, mostly female students empathize with Julien despite their irritation with his bursts of sensibility and his calculated battles, amatory and otherwise. Their un-"resisting" readings (Fetterley) privilege Julien's revolt and the class conflict it codes over what they take to be the "other" plot, the sentimental one, in which Mme de Rênal and Mathilde de La Mole function predominantly as competing objects of Julien's desire. Thus, while it may be clear to students that Julien Sorel's peasant origins and male hero worship drive his erotic and ambitious urges, they usually overlook how class and gender intersect in the stories of the noblewomen Mme de Rênal and Mathilde de La Mole, members of Julien's enemy class.

Drawing on recent sociohistorical and cultural scholarship, my approach to Stendhal's "chronique du XIXe siècle" 'chronicle of the XIXth century' seeks to integrate its sexual politics with the foregrounded Restoration "politics." Mme de Rênal and Mathilde de La Mole are as entangled in postrevolutionary society as Julien is, and the novel's myriad literary and historical references engage, in true Stendhalian oblique fashion, the vexed question of the place of upper-class women in the social, political, and literary imagination of the "new" France. The novel's explicit contrast of Mme de Rênal, the naive, provincial mother, with Mathilde de La Mole, the overread, single Parisienne who becomes pregnant, explores the issue of female "nobility." These opposing characters are first made to attract (both Julien and one another) only to assume hierarchical positions along the lines of an unconventional domestic and spiritual arrangement. Mme de Rênal, the "good mother," triumphs even if she is "bad," and Mathilde de La Mole, the "bad girl," loses no matter how much she wishes to be "good." The peasant usurper of Stendhal's novel may move up the Restoration social order, but the noblewomen figure a *déclassement*. Their intersecting trajectories suggest the particular workings of bourgeois domestic ideology with revitalized Catholic dogma in which old female aristocratic alliances and practices yield to newly ennobled forms of motherhood and "natural" feminine moral intuition. During the Revolutionary period and its aftermath, Republicans, Napoleon, conservative thinkers, and a growing print culture for women appropriated a Rousseauist model of the simple and natural mother to articulate and promote a new kind of female "nobility" acquired through reverent devotion to husband, children, and home and open to all women, regardless of class.

Appreciation of father-son motifs in *The Red and the Black* should be predicated on a sociohistorical understanding of the importance of gender and motherhood as organizational and symbolic categories in postrevolutionary France (Darrow; Pope; Reid). Students can then examine the ways many of the historical and literary referents in *The Red and the Black* place women in society and print culture. One of Julien's favorite authors, Rousseau, clearly sets the virtuous, silent, and ignorant mother against the promiscuous aristocrat who flaunts herself: "la véritable mère de famille, loin d'être une femme du monde, n'est guère plus recluse dans sa maison que la religieuse dans son cloître" 'the true family mother, far from being a worldly woman, is scarcely more cloistered in her home than the nun in her cloister' (*Emile* 508; my trans.). Rousseau's ideal woman is not educated in the convent, which he blames for repressing girls' desires and training them in trivial social graces. Instead, like Sophie, Emile's mate, or Rousseau's Julie in *Julie ou la Nouvelle Héloïse* (1761), she is permanent pupil to but a male tutor or two: a lover, a husband, or preferably both in the same person. The unworthy model is the female aristocrat who makes a spectacle of herself, portrayed in Rousseau's *Lettre à M. d'Alembert* (1758) as opinionated, loud, too visible, and holding sway over a salon of enthralled, obsequious men (115).

Julien's other idol, Napoleon, also sought to protect the family from the presumed dangers of aristocratic sociability, and he is known for his intolerance of intellectual women, notably Germaine de Staël, whom he exiled and whose books he censored. The Civil Code of 1804, to which M. de Rênal refers in the novel (146; 99; 1.21), made women, especially married ones, legal minors. It thus furthered the work begun by the First Republic, which had denied women citizenship in 1793. Echoing Pierre Chaumette's cry in 1793 that "natural" women should labor for the "sweet anxieties of maternity" and seek their reward as "the divinity of the domestic sanctuary" (qtd. in Levy 119–20), Napoleon's comments to the Council of State belie similar anxiety about women's unruliness outside the domestic safehold: "The husband must possess the absolute power and right to say to his wife: 'Madam, you shall not go out, you shall not go to the theater, you shall not receive such and such a person; for the children you will bear me shall be mine'" (qtd. in Herrold 136). In the nascent, de-Christianized postrevolutionary order in which God was distant and the king was no more, patriarchy rewrote itself in the Civil Code, the 1802 concordat with the Catholic Church, and the newly organized educational system. While Napoleon's reforms were designed to certify and mobilize French (male) talent, women's minds were left to the church and private efforts for much of the nineteenth century. State neglect unwittingly strengthened the church's role in women's social formation.

Stendhal introduces his first heroine as a "bonne mère de famille" 'good mother of a family' (71; 38; 1.8) and ideal spouse in an imperfect marriage.

Whether in the house with its carceral “grille de fer” ‘iron grating’ (25; 3; 1.1) or strolling on the arm of her husband along the ironically named “Cours de la Fidélité” ‘Loyalty Square’ (28; 6; 1.2), Mme de Rênal is first identified through husband, children, and the household space that protects her from the “gens à argent” ‘money men’ (60; 30; 1.7) in Verrières. When readers first encounter her, she is a vigilant, maternal “œil” ‘eye’ and a disembodied “voix douce” ‘gentle voice’ before actually materializing as “une femme de trente ans, mais encore assez jolie” ‘a woman in her thirties, but still quite handsome’ (29; 6; 1.2). While this section of the novel explicitly ironizes her marriage to the boorish mayor with a “volonté [. . .] despotique” ‘supreme will’ (28; 5; 1.2), Mme de Rênal remains remarkably unknowable and unself-conscious until the passion awakened by Julien triggers revelations about her character and her past.

Mme de Rênal’s class origins, unlike Mathilde’s, are unclear and contribute to her vague social grounding. While she married young into a family with aristocratic pretensions and presides over a household full of servants, which is more characteristic of noble households than bourgeois ones, the narrator says next to nothing about her family history. All we know of her family is that she stands to inherit a lot of money from her aunt and maintains a friendship with a distant relative, Mme Derville, who also attended the convent school with her. What else we learn about Mme de Rênal blocks reading her either as a *grande bourgeoise* or as an aristocrat, for while she avoids society, she is equally unconcerned with money matters. Her dislike of “ce qu’à Verrières on appelle de la joie, lui avait valu la réputation d’être très fière de sa naissance” ‘everything that in Verrières is considered fun caused her to be thought a snob’ (35; 10; 1.3). She is most lively and graceful when “loin des regards des hommes” ‘unconstrained by the sight of men’ (48; 21; 1.6), and she prefers solitary walks in her garden. Her reclusive existence and calm subordination to her husband are interpreted differently by both sexes of the decidedly bourgeois Verrières community. The husbands view her self-sacrificing manner as exemplary, while their wives find her “sotte” ‘a fool’ (35; 10; 1.3) because she is “sans nulle politique à l’égard de son mari” ‘[without any] policy of behavior concerning her husband’ (35; 1.3; no trans.).

However, the narrator only partially corrects the unreliable public readings of Mme de Rênal, confirming her noble bearing without attributing it to culture or family ties: “la conduite habituelle de son âme était en effet le résultat de l’humeur la plus altière” ‘she still managed her existence on the principle of the most lofty distance’ (59; 29; 1.7). He further clouds the issue of her social rank by declaring that Mme de Rênal’s indifference to her husband is greater than that shown to her servants by any “princesse, citée à cause de son orgueil” ‘princess distinguished for her pride’ (59; 29; 1.7). Indeed, the only significant details with which to make any sense of Mme de Rênal’s nobility are her convent education and a “penchant décidé à la dévotion passionnée” ‘distinct leaning toward passionate devotion’ (59; 29; 1.7). The obvious anticlericalism of the passage describing how Mme de Rênal had “assez de sens” ‘enough sense’ to forget the "absurde" 'ridiculous' convent lessons does not, however, negate her marked piety and love of God. Although the narrator raises the subject of women's tutelage in a specific ecclesiastical teaching order, he also denies its influence in shaping Mme de Rênal's enigmatic "manière de vivre tout intérieure" 'whole inner life of her own' (59; 29; 1.7). The reader is left to ponder Mme de Rênal's unexplained and unadulterated adoration of God the Father.

The blank in Mme de Rênal's education facilitates her complete absorption in her sons and her love for Julien, both states of being tinged with unparalleled "passionate devotion." Whether she has read no novels or a few, Mme de Rênal remains natural in her unnatural world. Her lack of "expérience de la vie" 'experience in life' (59; 29; 1.7) and "instinct de femme" 'woman's instinct' (65; 34; 1.7) combine to give her an "angélique douceur" 'angelic temper' (67; 36; 1.8). Such devotional capacity nonetheless affiliates her with the "religieuses adoratrices passionnées du *Sacré-Cœur de Jésus*" 'devotional nuns with a passion for the *Sacred Heart of Jesus*.' She, who "de la vie, n'avait adoré que Dieu [. . .] au *Sacré-Cœur* de Besançon" 'in her whole life had never adored anyone but God [. . .] in the *Sacred Heart* of Besançon' (59; 29; 1.7), easily transfers her worship to Julien.

Students may not notice that both Mme de Rênal and Mathilde de La Mole issue from the Convent of the Sacred Heart, the name of which is underscored more than once in the text. The double stress introduces a difference, however, opening the question of the Catholic Church's role in the social and intellectual, if not spiritual, life of upper-class women during the Restoration. Invigorated by its ties to the restored Bourbon monarchy and seeking to regain its hold, the church found in women an instrument for the exercise of its moral and social will, demonstrated clearly by Mme de Rênal's temporary submission to her confessor. However, as historian Edward Berenson notes, a variety of reformers "all adopted a vocabulary and overall frame of reference remarkable for their Christian content" (36), which suggests the particularly strong expressive value of religious rhetoric in an increasingly secular and hypocritical French society. As the concept of women could be tied to socialist utopian notions of social progress, so too was she a gauge for conservative assessments of the past, present, and future state of French society. Some twenty years before the church declared the Virgin Mary immaculate in 1852, Alfred Nettement coded his social vision for Christian progress in the following succinct terms: "c'est par Eve que les sociétés tombent, c'est par Marie qu'elles se relèvent" 'societies fall because of Eve; they rise again because of Mary' (360; my trans.).

While *The Red and the Black* does not specifically refer to Mme de Rênal as the Virgin Mary, she possesses qualities of the Madonna that distinguish her from both the hypocritically devout and the converted. Yet her love for God the Father and, by extension, for her sons on earth, is rooted in the *Société des religieuses du Sacré Cœur*. Otherwise known as "les Dames du Sacré Cœur," 'Ladies of the Sacred Heart' this convent order was founded in 1800 and grew to forty establishments by the late 1830s. Devoted primarily to the education of girls from both the aristocracy and the upstart bourgeoisie, its cult of Christ's sacred heart was successfully expanded by the religious reaction of the Restoration.

During Mme de Rênal's evolution from a "femme simple et timide" 'simple, timid woman' to one who is "éclairée" 'enlightened' by her "fatale passion" 'fatal passion' (185; 125; 1.23), the behaviors and desires she exhibits undermine her saintly maternity and align her with the "unnatural" aristocratic mother. She acquires a taste for fashion and the canniness to deceive her husband. Although she still prefers a cloistered love, Mme de Rênal's fantasies also belie a conflicted subjective process. On learning that her chambermaid Elisa wishes to marry Julien, a troubled Mme de Rênal imagines their conjugal happiness: "[l]a pauvreté de cette petite maison [. . .] se peignait à elle sous des couleurs ravissantes" '[t]hat meager little house [. . .] seemed altogether heavenly to her' (69–70; 37; 1.8). This first subversive image of Julien's humble, domestic bliss with, of all people, a chambermaid is later replaced by grander delusions of Julien as Mme de Rênal's "maître" 'master' when she sees in him a "grand homme futur" 'future great man,' "pape" 'the pope,' or even "premier ministre comme Richelieu" 'a great minister, like Richelieu' (122; 77; 1.17). Mme de Rênal becomes more and more like Mathilde as her wilder, gothic side reveals itself notably in church. The arrival of the accusatory anonymous letter triggers Mme de Rênal's obsession with a Vergy legend, leading her to a more macabre cult of Julien's heart: she "se figurait sans cesse son mari tuant Julien à la chasse [. . .] et ensuite le soir lui faisant manger son coeur" 'continually imagined her husband killing Julien while out hunting [. . .] and then that evening forcing her to eat his heart' (154; 101; 1.21). Ultimately though, she reaches a compromise fantasy in which M. de Rênal is dead and she has married Julien. The new family sets up house surprisingly in Paris, where mother, father, and children "tous étaient parfaitement heureux" 'all would be perfectly happy' (184; 124; 1.23).

Julien's departure for the seminary makes this fantasy move impossible and eclipses Mme de Rênal, but she continues to haunt the rest of the novel. In Paris Julien frequently compares her with Mathilde. Before Julien's departure though, the curious, brief appearance of the young girl poet Delphine Gay at the bishop's dinner directs Mme de Rênal's adulterous misstep into a stride toward sainthood. Gay's recital of the poem "La Madeleine" introduces a new performance of pious female passion right into the conniving world of the male-dominated seminary (237; 165; 1.29). Appearing at this important transitional moment in the novel, before Mme de Rênal's "fatale rechute" 'fatal relapse' (253; 178; 1.30) and Julien's rise to the top, the figure of Mary Magdalene better suits Mme de Rênal than the Virgin Mary does precisely because of her carnal sin and penitence. Marina Warner tells us that this "prototype of the penitent whore" (232) "has absorbed to some extent the role of classical goddesses of love" (235). The novel's oblique reference to Mary Magdalene, I would argue further, adjusts Mme de Rênal's earlier role as a kind of Virgin of Sorrows in preparation for the final chapters in which she comforts a Christ-like Julien. Mary Magdalene's remorse, like Mme de Rênal's, occasions a purifying and enlightening love. And just as Mary Magdalene's "regenerate sexuality" makes her an ideal image of penance (Warner 235), Mme de Rênal's adultery becomes the means by which she achieves grace.

The potential for Mme de Rênal's transcendence is actualized only after Julien's encounter with the bookish, aggressive, and very public aristocrat Mathilde de La Mole. She embodies in the extreme the qualities that "denaturalized" women in the eyes of postrevolutionary culture: she is smart, independent, and ambitious. Flanked by a group of young men in her parents' salon, Mathilde puts Julien off even though he is dazzled by her "port de reine" 'queenly bearing' (335; 2.9; my trans.). Her look is "dur, hautain, et presque masculin" 'hard, arrogant, and almost masculine' (283; 198; 2.3), and her voice "n'a rien de féminin qu'emploient les jeunes femmes de la haute classe" '[is] completely unfeminine [. . .] which is customary among young women of the upper class' (318; 226; 2.8). Mathilde "outre toutes les modes" 'exaggerates all the styles' (319; 227; 2.8) and her speech has "quelque chose d'un peu coloré pour la délicatesse féminine" 'something a little too highly colored for feminine delicacy' (347; 250; 2.11). Her sharp intelligence and biting wit set her apart in the "asphyxie morale" 'moral asphyxiation' of Paris salons (288; 203; 2.4). In short, she is the Restoration avatar of Rousseau's dreaded female aristocrat and Chaumette's "impudent woman who wants to become a man" (qtd. in Levy 220).

There is no question of Mathilde's family roots and the legacy of her high birth. Her education, summed up as "éminement religieuse et monarchique, chef d'œuvre du Sacré-Cœur" 'eminently monarchical and religious [. . .] masterpiece of the Sacred Heart' (283; 198; 2.3), hints at the social function of convent education for elite women of the Restoration. It was about not only creating brides for Christ but also preparing well-to-do young women for earthly marriage and politically important social alliances. Mathilde's convent experience quite possibly resembles that of the countess Marie d'Agoult, who abandoned husband and children for Franz Liszt. Not only did she bear Liszt's children, but she also became a writer of fiction and history under the name Daniel Stern. Marie d'Agoult describes the education she received from the Convent of the Sacred Heart in 1821 Paris as a waste of young women's intellectual potential. The curricular focus on "talens dits 'd'agrément'" 'so-called social graces' sought to help women procure the "mari conjectural" 'conjectural husband' and marked even "la femme la plus sérieuse" 'the most serious woman' for life (Stern 1: 151–53; my trans.). Mathilde is unwillingly headed for the "conjectural husband" and a place at the royal court. Unwilling because she rejects the conventional script for noble young women, wanting no part of a marriage that would be a "nouvelle édition du bonheur des [ses] cousines" 'new version of [her] cousins' happiness' (349; 251; 2.11). Unwilling too because Mathilde seeks and nowhere finds what Mme de Rênal encountered unwittingly; the unexpected

("Tout était imprévu pour elle" 'everything for her was unexpected' [90; 52; 1.11]). Unwilling finally because she knows the unexpected does not occur in gilded Restoration salons. While both women reject their given dreary worlds, Mathilde's principal failing is that she is aware of her dissatisfaction before Julien ever appears. Her "esprit supérieur" 'superior mind' (408; 297; 2.20) distinguishes her most from Mme de Rênal.

Mathilde is most "at home," then, looking for the unknown in the books she purloins from her father's library. She determinedly revises the Sacré-Cœur curriculum by turning to history, fiction, and legends for models of passion. In an early scene Mathilde searches the library for the second volume of Voltaire's *Princesse de Babylone* (1768), a tale of a beautiful princess's love for a lowly shepherd's son. When, after accomplishing great feats in a contest for her hand, this humble suitor leaves the country to tend his ill father, the princess embarks on a quest to find "le plus grand des hommes" 'the greatest of men' (Voltaire 352; my trans.). Like her, Mathilde seeks someone unlike the "patron commun" 'common run' (367; 266; 2.14), but she does not leave the "nouvelle Babylone" 'new Babylon' (276; 193; 2.2). Unlike the traveling princess, Mathilde does not find her man on her imaginary journeys.

Her ramblings do, however, produce a number of noble, if not always regal, aberrant female figures. Her ancestor, Marguerite de Valois, stands out among these models for her intelligence, culture, and passion; but significantly she bore no children. When Mathilde, writing to Julien, fears his power as "master," the murderous mother-lover of Greek legend comes first to her mind: "Quelles ne sont pas ses prétentions, si jamais il peut tout sur moi? Eh bien! je me dirai comme Médée: *Au milieu de tant de périls, il me reste MOI*" 'What won't he pretend to, if ever he is in a position of power over me? No matter! I can say like Medea: *Amid so many perils, still I have MYSELF*' (368; 267; 2.14).

Although Julien delights in seeing Mathilde as Catherine de' Medici (358; 258; 2.13), the most unusual starring "rôle" Mathilde imagines for herself comes not from the period of Henri III but from the French Revolution (395–96; 287; 2.19). Imagining a future revolution, Mathilde sees herself as Manon Roland and Julien in the role of the husband who committed suicide after his wife's execution in 1793. Ironically, Mathilde prefers Manon Roland to the more spectacular female performer, Mme de Staël because "l'immoralité de la conduite sera un obstacle dans notre siècle" 'immoral behavior is going to be a great impediment in our century' (396; 287; 2.19). This identification is unusual for a number of reasons, not the least of which is Roland's membership in Stendhal's group of elite, ideal readers (*Œuvres intimes* 2: 429, 536, 834; *Correspondance* 1: 175, 214). But Mme Roland stands out particularly in Mathilde's story because she was not an aristocrat and was reputed to be a loyal wife and loving mother. A self-educated daughter who married above her station, Manon Roland presided over a salon that was the heart of the Girondin movement, and she was condemned for conspiring against the republic. She was imprisoned and executed within weeks of Marie-Antoinette and Olympe de Gouges, two other women decried by the press as "denatured" mothers. The *Moniteur universel* overlooked the differences in their crimes and social ranks to make a single example of them: Marie-Anoinette was unquestionably a "debauched mother" while Mme Roland was a "mother [who] sacrificed nature to rise above it, her choice to be an intellectual led her to forget the virtues of her sex" (qtd. in Kelly 125–26).

Mathilde's admiration of Mme Roland is in part explained by Mathilde's loathing of her unheroic peers and those descendants who let themselves be executed like "moutons" 'sheep' in 1793 (367; 266; 2.14). But the example of Mme Roland also suggests a possible and alluring compromise between private, domestic virtue and public acts and recognition. She even seems to authorize Mathilde's attraction to motherhood as an heroic act. Queenly models give way to Mathilde's view of herself as Julien's wife, slave, and servant. Mathilde even renounces "l'exercice de [s]a raison" 'the right to exercise [her] own reason' (402; 292; 2.19). Once her pregnancy supplies the irrefutable "garantie" 'guarantee' and proof of her true wifeliness (466, 471; 340, 344; 2.30, 2.31), she readily claims that she will follow her duty, become "Mme Sorel," and live "pauvrement avec son mari en Suisse, ou chez son père à Paris" 'in poverty with her husband in Switzerland, or with her father in Paris' (483; 353; 2.33). In effect, Mathilde's willingness to give Julien what he wants, "un amour à sacrifices" 'a love built on sacrifice' (142; 92; 1.19) signals her retreat from the salon and the library.

Before Julien's pistol shot in the church, Mme de Rênal's and Mathilde de La Mole's fantasies affiliate the two women in a chiasmatic figuration of passionate maternity that temporarily breaches the boundaries of their social and narrative locations. Each woman dreams of a narrative different from her own in which self-sacrifice and devotion acquire "heroic," domestic dimensions. In the final section of the novel, however, the play of their own desires submits to the Christlike condemned man who fixes Mme de Rênal and Mathilde's final positions.

Julien's newly discovered need for solitude and intimacy shall be fulfilled by Mme de Rênal's presence and absolution of his crime. Having braved public opinion, Mme de Rênal becomes both "une héroïne d'anecdotes" 'the subject of stories' (540; 395; 2.43) and Julien's "chimère d'une maîtresse tendre et qui ne songe plus à sa propre existence du moment qu'elle a fait le bonheur de son amant" 'phantom of a mistress who should be naturally tender and give not a thought to her own existence as soon as she has made her lover happy' (385; 279; 2.17). She makes a spiritual declaration of total self-sacrifice: "je ne suis plus qu'amour pour toi. Je sens pour toi ce que je ne devrais sentir uniquement pour Dieu: un mélange de respect, d'amour, d'obéissance" 'I feel nothing but love for you, or rather the word "love" is too feeble. I feel for you what I should feel only for God: a mixture of respect, love, devotion' (539; 395; 2.43). By leaving Verrières Mme de Rênal plays out a scenario she contemplated earlier in the novel. During her son's illness Mme de Rênal had momentarily considered avowing her adultery in the hope that her public penance might save her son. In the novel's close she is able to proclaim herself "une femme perdue d'honneur" 'a woman of lost honor' (540; 395; 2.43) and, like Mathilde, is willing to "se donner en spectacle" 'mak[e] a public spectacle of herself.' Protecting his new intimacy with Mme de Rênal, Julien forbids her to make them a "spectacle au public" 'public spectacle' (554; 406; 2.45) and persuades her to remain with him in his decidedly domestic cell.

Mathilde, try as she might to make herself inconspicuous disguised as Mme Michelet, a peasant, inevitably attracts undue public attention in Besançon. However, the "sacrifice de sa réputation" 'sacrific[e] of her reputation' (516; 378; 2.39) and the public disclosure of her condition do not qualify as signs of the authentic sacrificial love sought by Julien. Mathilde's "imagination exaltée et courageuse" 'exalted and courageous imagination' can only be a self-indulgent masquerade now that Julien is "fatigué d'héroïsme" 'tired of heroism' (516; 378; 2.39). Julien's last wish, to strip Mathilde of her maternal duties by giving their "fils" 'son' (520; 380; 2.39) to Mme de Rênal, harshly proscribes any compromise between sociability and domesticity that Mathilde may have been inclined to make. The narrative condemns the overeducated Mathilde as an unfit mother who should have been born a man ("Le ciel devait à la gloire de ta race de te faire naître homme" 'For the honor of your family, providence should have formed you a man' [536; 392; 2.42]), and bestows on the adulterous heroine a halo of "regenerate sexuality" coded as private and expiatory maternal devotion. Mathilde's predicament arises from her "unnatural" imagination and brains; having stolen her learning from her father, she is indeed, as the narrator claims, an "exception" (346; 249; 2.11). Heavy with child but caught up in her spectacular cult, Mathilde spins out of the control of the narrative and reminds the reader that "denatured women"—those who want history to acknowledge them—cannot become "good mothers" just by getting pregnant.

Mme de Rênal's fatal maternal embrace, which ends the novel, leaves us with a haunting disembodiment representing French early nineteenth-century bourgeois domestic ideology that would have women's knowledge (carnal and otherwise) derive not from novels, history, or salon society but from God, the father, and children. In this respect Mme de Rênal, virginal in sorrow and penitent in adultery, calls to mind both the Madonna and Mary Magdalene as the "divinity of the domestic sanctuary."

The Red and the Black: Transforming the Maternal Myth

Maryline Lukacher

> Mme de Rênal had been like a mother to me. My crime is atrocious, and it was *premeditated*.
>
> —Stendhal, *The Red and the Black*
>
> There are mothers . . . and then there are mothers.
>
> —Marguerite Yourcenar, *Oriental Tales*

Stendhal's representation of nontraditional or atypical mothers in *The Red and the Black* (1830) is at odds with the representation of mothers in the nineteenth-century French novel. For instance, Victor Hugo's moving description of La Sachette's discovery of her missing daughter, Esmeralda, at the end of *Notre-Dame de Paris* (1831) and their subsequent death together offers a more traditional approach to motherhood. In Gustave Flaubert's *L'éducation sentimentale* (1869), Mme Arnoux misses her rendezvous with her would-be lover, Frédéric, in the superstitious belief that sacrificing her adulterous liaison will save her ailing son's life. But the decision costs her her last chance at happiness. Her imaginary bargain with God indicates the priority of her affections. Unlike these depictions of motherhood, *The Red and the Black* ironically examines what happens when mothers step off the traditional path. I propose to read *The Red and the Black* in a new light; not to oppose Mme de Rênal and Mathilde de La Mole as is traditional, but to examine how Stendhal's two heroines each subvert the concept of traditional motherhood by offering versions of rebellious and nontraditional mothers. As an example of intertextuality, I also examine the influence of Stendhal's atypical mothers on Marguerite Yourcenar's "Aphrodissia, the Widow." Students learn that Yourcenar's tale is an intricate rearticulation of the underlying secret of the maternal figures in *The Red and the Black*.

In his *Life of Henry Brulard* (1836) Stendhal imagines that readers will still be interested in his work fifty or a hundred years later. Marguerite Yourcenar was perhaps one of those readers. She begins her tale "Aphrodissia, the Widow" at the point where Stendhal ended *The Red and the Black*. Yourcenar's story is particularly striking in its elevation of the colors red and black to mythic proportions. The widow Aphrodissia is not only a passionate, sensual woman but also a murderess. She is first seen in the aftermath of the death of her lover Kostis the Red, who has been killed by the village peasants: "Her muffled sobs shook her breast underneath the thick folds of her black worsted dress" (104). For six years she has publicly been the old priest's widow while carrying on an affair with Kostis, her husband's murderer. Now that he is dead, Aphrodissia recalls the details of their love affair and criminal deeds. She was once pregnant with Kostis's child and was forced to smother the child since she was a widow: "And it was there that the child was born, and there that it had been necessary to stifle him between two mattresses, weak and naked like a newborn kitten" (109). The villagers do not know of Aphrodissia's remorseless passion for Kostis, and it is only at his death that she thinks back on the details of their secret life. Aphrodissia has to act quickly if she wants to save her lover's decapitated body from being further desecrated. Once she has put the headless body into her dead husband's tomb, she takes Kostis's bloody head to bury it in a secret place that she can visit. Accused of having stolen a watermelon because of the head's shape under her apron, she begins running along a precipice and finally falls into it at sunset.

In *Entretiens radiophoniques avec Marguerite Yourcenar* (1972), Patrick de Rosbo stressed the relation of Aphrodissia's death to its mythological roots. Yourcenar herself said about Aphrodissia's story: "The narrative originates from a real event that someone recently told me, the story of a peasant woman who fled with her lover's head, who was a bandit executed by the gendarmes, somewhat like Mlle de La Mole who fled with Julien Sorel's head at the end of Stendhal's novel" (153). However, one still can wonder why Yourcenar integrated the Stendhalian red/black opposition within Aphrodite's myth. The more traditional interpretations of red/black as army/priesthood, love/death, or the chance game roulette are here eclipsed by Yourcenar's decision to return to the mythical source.

"Aphrodissia, the Widow," one of the stories in Yourcenar's *Oriental Tales*, was originally entitled "Le chef rouge" (1938) but was renamed in the 1963 Gallimard edition "La veuve Aphrodissia." Frederick Farrell and Edith Farrell have already marked the transformation of *rouge* in "Le chef rouge" into *noir* in "La veuve Aphrodissia." While their main concern was to examine how the *rouge* and *noir* images "are used at structurally significant points" (233), I show below how "Aphrodissia, the Widow" repeats Julien's and Mathilde's story while offering another ending. This shift in focus has the pedagogical advantage of acquainting students with the influential position of Stendhal's novel in particular and with the phenomenon of intertextuality or reinscription in general.

Yourcenar's reading of *The Red and the Black* focuses on its romantic and cruel ending. Her gruesome tale of love and vengeance reinvents a story around the vision of Mathilde taking her lover's head to be buried at the place he chose: "Mathilde suivit son amant jusqu'au tombeau qu'il s'était choisi [. . .] à l'insu de tous, seule dans sa voiture drapée, elle porta sur ses genoux la tête de l'homme qu'elle avait tant aimé" 'Mathilde followed her lover to the tomb he had selected [. . .] unknown to all, alone in her draped carriage, she carried on her knees the head of the man she loved so much.' Mathilde's heroic gesture is modeled after Queen Marguerite de Navarre's action: "Le souvenir de Boniface de la Mole et de Marguerite de Navarre lui donna sans doute un courage inhumain" 'The memory of Boniface de La Mole and Marguerite de Navarre no doubt gave her superhuman courage' (556; 408; 2.45). Stendhal stresses the identification between Mathilde de La Mole and Queen Marguerite several times, and it informs his presentation of Mathilde as a widow, although she has never been married: "Julien fut distrait de son humeur par le grand deuil de Mlle de La Mole, qui le frappa d'autant plus qu'aucune autre personne de la famille n'était en noir" 'Julien was distracted from his broody thoughts by the deep mourning worn by Mlle. de La Mole; it was the more striking since no other member of the family was in black' (337; 241; 2.10). As Julien is told, Queen Marguerite was in love with Boniface de La Mole, Mathilde's ancestor, and could not save him from being executed on 30 April 1574. In asking for her lover's head, Queen Marguerite establishes a historical paradigm that Mathilde wants to repeat. The burial scene is the model Mathilde will imitate: "Et la nuit suivante [. . .] à minuit, elle [la reine] prit cette tête dans sa voiture, et alla l'enterrer elle-même dans une chapelle" 'And the following night, at the stroke of twelve, she [the queen] took that head in her carriage and went to bury it with her own hands in a chapel' (340; 244; 2.10). Both Queen Marguerite and Mathilde are cast as tragic "widows" who insist on burying their lovers properly. While Mme de Rênal quietly dies soon after Julien, Queen Marguerite and Mathilde survive their lovers' death.

In "Aphrodissia, the Widow" Aphrodissia is falsely accused by her uncle Basil of having stolen a watermelon, but to save Kostis's head she does not deny the accusation. Instead, she runs away from her accuser: "I am poor, Uncle Basil, all I have taken is a red, red watermelon. A red watermelon with black seeds" (115). While Yourcenar insists on the red and black coloring of the head and its eyes, here assimilated to the watermelon, one must recall her other source of inspiration. In John Keats's poem "Isabella; or, The Pot of Basil" (1820) Isabella buries her lover's head in a basil pot, and the plant grows, fed by her daily tears. Yourcenar read Keats when she was young and refers directly to this gruesome poem through the name Basil. The passage from the common herb basil to the proper name Basil in "Aphrodissia, the Widow" is an interesting analogue of the shift from the head to the basil pot. Yourcenar's focus, however, is on Kostis's severed head, which she implicitly compares to the red and black watermelon, making the final shift from basil to watermelon. Aphrodissia's accidental death occurs at sunset. The name Aphrodissia is derived from Aphrodite, the goddess of love, which aptly defines Yourcenar's heroine. Her tragic end can still be seen as a condensation of the Greek myth of death and regeneration and *The Red and the Black*: "At last, a stone gave way under her foot, fell to the bottom of the precipice as if to show the way, and Aphrodissia the widow plunged into the abyss and the evening, taking with her the head all smeared with blood" (115). The meditation on the fate of the lover's head belongs to a long literary tradition; Keats himself refers to Boccaccio as the source of his poem. In Yourcenar's version both lovers perish together.

As we noticed earlier, Mathilde's story is already inscribed within Queen Marguerite's fate. The execution of Boniface de La Mole foreshadows the death of Julien on the guillotine. In Yourcenar's tale Kostis is beheaded during the night of Saint George, who was himself decapitated on 23 April in the fourth century. The doubling of executions of Boniface and Julien and of Saint

George and Kostis suggests that they are already part of another discursive, historical space. But while Marguerite and Mathilde survive their unfortunate lovers, Aphrodissia is engulfed in the abyss at sunset. The terrifying vision of the "head all smeared with blood" and the sunset recalls the myth according to which Aphrodite is also the goddess of rebirth. In *Greek Mythology and Poetics* Gregory Nagy argues that the association of Phaeton—a son of Helios, the sun—and Aphrodite is especially significant: "It arises from a sexual theme implicit in a solar transition from death to rebirth. In the logic of the myth, it appears that the setting sun mates with the goddess of regeneration so that the rising sun may be reborn. If the setting sun is the same as the rising sun, then the goddess of regeneration may be viewed as both mate and mother" (246). Aphrodissia's fatal plunge into the abyss and the evening echoes the myth of death and regeneration. However, Yourcenar does not deal with the theme of incest, nor does she deal with infanticide. What is troubling in Yourcenar's fiction is that procreation is meaningless: "And when they [the village matrons] saw her [Aphrodissia] again a few weeks later, belly flat underneath the large skirts, they all wondered what Aphrodissia had done to get rid of her load so easily" (108). Aphrodissia's resolution of her pregnancy is described so crudely that one wonders what is behind her infanticide.

We should also recall that Stendhal and Yourcenar lost their mothers in childbirth. Stendhal's confesses his oedipal love for his mother in *The Life of Henry Brulard* when he declares, "My mother, Mme Henriette Gagnon, was a charming woman and I was in love with my mother. Please be kind enough to remember that I lost her in childbed when I was barely seven" (21–22). The mother's untimely death comes to mark the moment in his memoirs when Stendhal's separation anxiety is replayed. In *The Red and the Black* Mme de Rênal dies kissing her children, a scenario that is another staging of Stendhal's maternal separation anxiety. In *Souvenirs pieux* Yourcenar describes succinctly her mother's death, which occured when she was only one week old (39, 42). The trauma of losing one's mother in childbirth becomes the secret of both Stendhal and Yourcenar. Procreation is always uncertain, and the death of the mother or of the child stresses the risks of birth. In *The Red and the Black* Mathilde proposes killing herself and her child without a second thought. In ruthlessly killing her child, Aphrodissia goes one step further. For Stendhal and Yourcenar a way to circumvent the mother's death, at least momentarily, is to kill off the children. But no matter what, fate cannot be changed, and the mother is doomed sooner or later.

Mathilde's absorption in the fate of her lover, Julien, is complete by the end of the novel: "Elle lui proposa sérieusement de se tuer avec lui" 'She seriously proposed to kill herself with him' (510; 373; 2.38), and in the next chapter she says, "S'il meurt, je meurs après lui" 'If he dies, I shall die after him' (518; 379; 2.39). Mathilde's death wish suggests that she has already forgotten her child, since her suicide will necessarily kill it. However, Mathilde's "infanticide" is not seriously considered in the novel since she will not, after all, kill herself. The child's disappearance is echoed earlier in *The Red and the Black* by Stendhal's own textual forgetfulness. Stendhal describes Mme de Rênal's three children: "l'œil de Mme de Rênal suivait avec inquiétude les mouvements de trois petits garçons" 'Mme de Rênal was watching anxiously the gyrations of three little boys' (29; 6; 1.2). The description parallels that of père Sorel's family: "M. de Rênal vit de loin le vieux Sorel, entouré de ses trois fils" 'he saw in the distance old Sorel, surrounded by his three sons' (26; 4; 1.1). Curiously, Mme de Rênal's three children have quietly been reduced to two, Adolphe and Stanislas-Xavier, when they are first introduced to their tutor Julien Sorel in book 1, chapter 6. Stendhal's "error" might also suggest that Sorel's third son, Julien, will disappear just as quietly from the novel. In *The Red and the Black* Julien's death upsets the natural order of inheritance since he leaves his estate to his father, Sorel. Julien's execution itself puts paternal authority into question since his child will be born without a father.

Ironically, Mathilde's pregnancy only serves to make Julien call into question the possibility of her being a good mother. Aware that he will soon die, Julien recognizes the need to make provisions for his child's future. Julien is several times confronted with the idea that Mathilde's son must be placed in Mme de Rênal's care: "Il se trouvait de nouveau vis-à-vis de cette idée si choquante pour Mathilde: dans quinze ans Mme de Rênal adorera mon fils, et vous l'aurez oublié" 'He found himself once more face to face with that idea which so distressed Mathilde: in fifteen years, Mme. de Rênal will adore my son, and you will have forgotten him' (520; 380; 2.39). But Julien fails to make Mme de Rênal the surrogate mother, since she dies shortly after him. Mme de Rênal's early promise not to kill herself is fulfilled at the end of *The Red and the Black*: "Mme de Rênal fut fidèle à sa promesse. Mais trois jours après Julien, elle mourut en embrassant ses enfants" 'Mme. de Rênal was true to her word. [. . .] [B]ut three days after Julien, she died in the act of embracing her children' (556; 408; 2.45). Mme de Rênal's inability to live without Julien stresses that her passion is stronger than her love for her children. Her leaving her children without a mother parallels Julien's leaving his child fatherless. Julien's and Mme de Rênal's demises are already orchestrated by Mme de Rênal's judgment when she writes to Julien: "Quoi qu'il puisse arriver, sois sûr d'une chose: je ne survivrai pas d'un jour à notre séparation définitive. Ah! mauvaise mère!" 'Whatever happens, you may be sure of one thing: I shall never survive our final separation, not for a day. Ah, what a wicked mother!' (148–49; 97; 1.20). In *Maternal Fictions* I argue that Mme de Rênal registers the difference between the "good mother" and the "bad mother." She points out what separates her from women whose only concern is motherhood. In momentarily forsaking her children for Julien, Mme de Rênal marks the difference. Mme de Rênal is also an exception since she is financially independent and can choose to leave her husband to live with her rich aunt. Mme de Rênal thus escapes the traditional gender definition of the female as the subordinate helpmate of the male.

In *Reading the Romantic Heroine* Leslie Rabine has also underlined how Mme de Rênal is a mother conflicted between her love for her children and her love for Julien. She demonstrates that while Mme de Rênal transforms the historical image of women by momentarily directing the plot of *The Red and the Black*, she returns soon afterward to "good motherhood." I contend that Mme de Rênal transgresses the frontier of traditional motherhood even in her death. Her concern for Julien surpasses everything else, and even when she is defending herself against the accusation of adultery, she cannot help writing to Julien: "Grand Dieu! je sens que j'aime mieux mes enfants parce qu'ils t'aiment" 'My God, it seems to me I love my children more because they love you' (147; 96; 1.20). Mme de Rênal constantly reroutes her maternal attention to her children toward Julien. Stendhal thus shows how Mme de Rênal is "guilty" toward her children since her fate is linked not to them but to Julien. While Stendhal questions good motherhood in both Mathilde and Mme de Rênal, Yourcenar goes a step further in having Aphrodissia murder her child. Yourcenar presents a violence that is inseparable from procreation. The child is not only irrelevant (père Sorel is delighted by the idea of inheriting from his son Julien) but cumbersome (Yourcenar refers to Aphrodissia's "load" when speaking of her pregnancy). In the death and life of the mother and child, Stendhal and Yourcenar symbolically relive the mother's demise in childbirth. While Mme de Rênal and Mathilde offer deviations from the conventional nineteenth-century French mother that make the future of motherhood questionable (what will happen to the children if their mothers die with their lovers?), Yourcenar succeeds in showing that once mothers have stepped out of the path of traditional motherhood, there is no end to it. Of course, "there are mothers . . . and then there are mothers," as the male narrator declares at the end of another of the *Oriental Tales*, "The Milk of Death" (51). While Stendhal constantly reworks his presentation of motherhood within his personal Oedipal desire, Yourcenar's mothers challenge the occidental description of the maternal.

Yourcenar's fascination for oriental myths allows her to imagine mothers who go further in their sacrifice or their monstrosity than their nineteenth-century French counterparts. And yet, as Julia Kristeva has argued in *Tales of Love*, Stendhalian heroines "have the strength of destiny, the power of ancient divinities. Through their secular side, they secure or destroy the social power of their lovers, while through their nocturnal side they bring about the madness and death of their Werthers" (362–63). The fatal force of Stendhalian heroines is replayed by Yourcenar's mythical women. One understands why the integration of *The Red and the Black* is as natural as it is in "Aphrodissia, the Widow" and how the representation of "bad mothers" is essential in the revision of the tradition. In attributing "the power of ancient divinities" to Stendhalian heroines, one understands Yourcenar's fascination for them. The historical and geographical displacement of Marguerite/Mathilde into Aphrodite/Aphrodissia is particularly significant. Mothers have become ambivalent because they are no longer reduced to a family function. Unlike Hugo's La Sachette and Flaubert's

Mme Arnoux, who are sacrificed to patriarchal values, Mathilde and Aphrodissia take upon themselves their destiny. The literary transformation of Mathilde into Aphrodissia finalizes the trajectory of these rebellious mothers.

Students can clearly see how this rebellion can also be read as an attempt to subvert the social order. Mme de Rênal's and Mathilde de La Mole's contempt for their social class is clear from their choice of a lover below their status, and it indicates a malaise that did not escape Yourcenar's attentive eye. Aphrodissia's secret love for the outlaw Kostis is scandalous: "Since her widowhood, no one suspected the dangerous meeting with Kostis on moonless nights" (108), and it is influenced by Stendhal's heroines. Stendhal shows that he is quite aware of this social disruption when Julien addresses the jury: "Messieurs, je n'ai point l'honneur d'appartenir à votre classe, vous voyez en moi un paysan qui s'est révolté contre la bassesse de sa fortune" 'Gentlemen, I have not the honor to belong to your social class, you see in me a peasant in open revolt against his humble station' (530; 387; 2.41). Julien's statement of course results in his being sentenced to death. But this scene is not the only occasion on which Stendhal shows the division of social classes. In his final novel, *Lamiel,* which was posthumously published in 1889, Lamiel has always been fascinated by bandit stories such as those of Mandrin and Cartouche. At the end of a series of love affairs, she finally falls in love with the outlaw Valbeyre, who declares: "I make war on society, which makes war on me" (189). Women are in effect the ones to question social order since their choice of lovers determines the limits of men's power. Stendhal's irony in *The Red and the Black* signals the possible fall of a society based on rank and privileges: "Mlle de La Mole apprit la mort du marquis de Croisenois. M. de Thaler, cet homme si riche, s'était permis des propos désagréables sur la disparition de Mathilde; M. de Croisenois alla le prier de les démentir. [. . .] La sottise triompha; et l'un des hommes de Paris les plus dignes d'être aimés, trouva la mort à moins de 24 ans" 'Mlle. de La Mole learned that the marquis de Croisenois was dead. M. de Thaler, that man who was so rich, had indulged himself in various disagreeable remarks on the disappearance of Mathilde; M. de Croisenois paid a call to ask him to withdraw them. [. . .] Stupidity was triumphant; and one of the men most deserving of love in all Paris was dead at the age of 24" (551; 404; 2.45). Undoubtedly, a man's death is the price for a woman's independence in the Paris of 1830. Stendhal's ironic account of de Croisenois's demise ensures Mathilde's decision to remain Julien's widow. In retelling *The Red and the Black* in the guise of "Aphrodissia, the Widow," Yourcenar gave Stendhal a future for his rebellious mothers.

Stendhal in Cyberspace: Virtual Reading as Oppositional Practice

Anthony Purdy

In the late 1960s, at the height of the vogue for French literary structuralism, Gérard Genette published a remarkable essay on Stendhal that draws some inspiration from the methodology of the day but respects few of its strictures and happily transcends its limitations. In the essay he argues for a paradigmatic reading of Stendhal in which plot and narrative sequence would be less important than relations of homology. Such a reading would be harmonic, or vertical, rather than following the linear development of melody and would play on several registers, constantly exceeding the bounds of any individual text to reveal the presence of intertextual networks of interference, a multidimensional space of writing (or inscription) in which a relatively small number of themes recur in endless variation ("Stendhal," *Figures II*: 179–80).

In another justly famous essay, specifically on *The Red and the Black* and published in the mid-1980s, Peter Brooks goes against the dominant deconstructive grain of American criticism of the time by reading for the plot and suggesting that Julien Sorel's capacity for self-invention is typical of the highly metonymic character of the Stendhalian hero in general. He even goes so far as to maintain that "the entire narrative mode of Stendhal's novels is in fact markedly metonymic, indeed virtually serial, giving the impression of a perpetual flight forward, a constant self-invention at the moment and of the moment. [. . .] The astonishing sense of rapidity given by these novels was matched in fact by rapidity of invention, a refusal of revision and the return backward: they are the least palimpsestic texts imaginable" ("Novel" 76–77).

The conflation of the activities of reading and writing in this passage seems to do two things: first, it suggests, perhaps unintentionally, that Stendhal's novels not only were written quickly but also are a quick read; second, in the larger context of Brooks's essay, it engages us in a series of binaries in each of which Stendhal's writing practice and the kind of reading that practice elicits are identified with the first term—metonymic as opposed to metaphoric, syntagmatic as opposed to paradigmatic, linear (or serial) as opposed to palimpsestic (or layered), and so on. In some senses, though not all, these oppositions might seem to authorize a return to a well-established way of thinking about Stendhal's novels as being somehow straightforward, not "written" in the strong, Barthesian sense of the term, less tightly textual (in the etymological sense of "woven") than transparently referential. And as any reader of Stendhal will know, there is more than a grain of truth to this impression.

The distance between Genette and Brooks is probably not as great as my presentation might imply. I have deliberately isolated particular aspects of the two essays to obtain the maximum effect from juxtaposing them. This is, I believe, a legitimate pedagogical strategy insofar as my object is neither to provide a history of the reception of Stendhal's novels nor to do justice to the full complexity of the approaches taken by two of his finer readers. Starkly separating the axes of Stendhal's narrative prose, associating its theoretically constructed binaries with the names of two critics, will, I hope, allow me (and, more important, my students) to think more clearly about the relation between those axes and the implications of privileging one over the other. In particular, this gesture might help us understand what I consider to be one of the characteristic features of *The Red and the Black*, the novel's ability to weave an intricate fabric (or spin a web or create a network) of political allusion without ever slowing down our reading of the plot with the weight of historical detail. At the same time, it might encourage us to retain a sense of what Genette called the "enigmatic transparency" of Stendhal's narrative discourse ("Stendhal," *Figures II* 192), a phenomenon I attempt to explain in terms of a process of textual refraction, of displaced and deviant reading trajectories that exist alongside or behind or beneath (choose your metaphor—the space they conjure up is purely virtual) the story of Julien Sorel.

The pedagogical analogy I evoke here in exploring the textual topography of *The Red and the Black* is with hypertext. I have chosen the metaphor for three main reasons: first, because today's students, even those who are less computer literate, are thoroughly familiar, from a variety of everyday experiences, with the basic hypertext technique of clicking on links to progress through sequences of screens; second, because hypertext (or hypermedia) applications are now becoming sophisticated enough to be very practical interactive learning tools in the electronic language and literature classroom; and third, because hypertext encourages, even demands, multilinear reading strategies that can only make students more aware of levels of complexity in the textual organization of an apparently "straightforward" narrative like *The Red and the Black*. I start with a brief overview of actual hypertext, then return to its potential use as a metaphor for a specific kind of literary textuality that can be seen at play in Stendhal's novel.

Hypertext

Hypertext, as conceptualized in the 1960s by Theodor H. Nelson and more recently explored by literary theorists like George P. Landow and critic-practitioners like Stuart Moulthrop (the author of the hypertext novel *Victory Garden*, as well as a hypertext version of Borges's "The Garden of Forking Paths"), is text composed of blocks of text linked electronically by multiple paths or chains (Landow 3–4). Nelson describes it as "*nonsequential writing*—text that branches and allows choices to the reader, best read at an interactive screen" (Nelson)—and Landow invests this description with poststructuralist implications, drawing parallels with Derrida and Foucault and borrowing from Barthes's *S/Z* the term *lexia* to denote any text block linked to others in a virtual network. While some of the parallels with poststructuralist theory are striking and suggestive, the more immediate applications of hypertext to literary studies have been in the supposedly more conservative domain of textual scholarship, in which recent developments in hypermedia (hypertext with sound, images, and animation) have opened up many new possibilities for the production of critical editions.

Hypermedia editions of literary works are seductive because they afford almost instant access to a potentially vast storehouse of electronically linked information. An annotated hypertext edition might, for example, embed the literary work in a rich electronic environment of dictionaries, reference works, manuscript variants, critical studies, biographies, and chronologies, which would allow readers to retrieve relevant information from the virtual archive and bring it up on the screen, alongside the text, simply by clicking on a link (usually a word or group of words) or by pulling down a menu. A hypermedia presentation of *Ulysses* being prepared by the Joyce scholar Michael Groden goes even further to include, as well as a much expanded version of the traditional textual apparatus of a critical edition, a wide range of texts, sounds, and visuals—source works such as *The Odyssey* and *Hamlet*, specially commissioned critical readings of the novel, maps of Dublin, spoken pronunciation guides, photographs, songs, film clips, and so on—which bring the text to life in surprising ways.

Of course, the skeptic might say, it is one thing to produce a hypermedia version of a novel like *Ulysses* that is already, in the words of one critic, a hypertext reformatted to accommodate the print medium (Bolter), but quite another to inflict such treatment on Stendhal's novels, which, according to Brooks, are not only "markedly metonymic, indeed virtually serial" but also "the least palimpsestic texts imaginable." Why, then, go to a great deal of trouble and expense to produce something that might seem to promise little in return? Two answers come immediately to mind. First, as I suggest above, Brooks's characterization tells only half the story. For the other half, we need to turn again to Genette, who reminds us that, while Stendhal may indeed have revised relatively little in his manuscripts, his texts are most certainly palimpsestic in other senses of the word. Thus, when we take into consideration the extensive marginalia; the plagiarisms; the proliferation of pseudonyms, secret codes, and foreign languages; the anagrams and inscriptions; the initials traced in the dust with a cane; and the comments scribbled on Brulard's suspenders, it is difficult not to concur with Genette's argument that the Stendhalian text is *one* and that it makes no sense to try to establish—through more or less arbitrary exclusion, as successive editors have—a definitive supertext that would be Stendhal's œuvre. As Genette concludes, everything that Beyle wrote is Stendhal, without distinction or hierarchy ("Stendhal," *Figures II* 169).

Such language is, of course, extremely suggestive in the context of a discussion of hypertext, which, as Landow observes, calls on us to "abandon conceptual systems founded upon ideas of center, margin, hierarchy, and linearity and replace them with ones of multilinearity, nodes, links, and networks" (2). One of the more interesting features of hypermedia critical editions is their curious blurring of the boundaries between text and margin and, since both annotations and critical readings are linked not only to the text itself but also to one another, between primary and secondary literature. (It is only now, in checking a page reference, that I realize that Brooks has a footnote reference number immediately after the sentence that ends "the least palimpsestic texts imaginable." When I turn to the back of the book, I am surprised and delighted to find that the note refers me to . . . Genette's essay. In a hypertext edition of Stendhal, Brooks's article could be included in its entirety and his note would provide an electronic link to the full text of Genette's piece. Similarly, and again to my enormous surprise—and now I am using my computer's modest word-processing capacity to layer my own text, inserting this observation several days later in the wake of a subsequent discovery—I find George Landow quoting from the same essay by Genette, in the 1982 English translation, *Figures of Literary Discourse*, to suggest that what is being described there is the way a reader encounters the web of hypertextual narrative [113–14]. Clearly, our own web is starting to tighten as cross-references multiply. Open link, close parenthesis.)

The point I am trying to make about hypertext editions is that they not only make a huge amount of information available to the scholar and the student but also encourage the reader to explore multiple reading trajectories while navigating from lexia to lexia in pursuit of an interesting chain of ideas or associations. And this point brings me to my second reason for believing that a hypertext or hypermedia edition of Stendhal would be a useful project. Hypertext is, by virtue of its multiple internal and external links, multilinear or multisequential. As such, it has the built-in ability to disrupt the reading habits associated with the linearity of the print medium. Similarly, since it tends to blur the boundaries between center and margin, since it imposes no hierarchy and allows no last word, hypertext has the potential to open the individual work up to forms of Bakhtinian polyphony and dialogism, not only by linking it to very different and conflicting critical readings but also by using intratextual (as well as intertextual) links that would encourage the student, especially on a second reading, to resist the linear pull of Stendhal's storytelling and explore some of the byways of the text, which often lead us to unsuspected sites of (virtual) opposition. Hypertext, if used creatively, should help students engage more actively with the oppositional potential of Stendhal's narrative by inviting them to test the "room for maneuver" (Chambers) that the text allows them. (Although Stendhal is not one of the authors Ross Chambers writes about, he makes an excellent case study of what the critic calls the politics of oppositionality, by which Chambers means "the form of resistance available to the relatively disempowered" [xi]. Indeed, it would be difficult to think of another novelist who so consistently tries to seduce his readers—the proverbial "happy few"—into reading, and therefore desiring, differently, against the grain of the text, so to speak.) Ideally, of course, a hypertext edition should be fully interactive; that is, students should not only be able to navigate from lexia to lexia according to trajectories of their own selection but also be able to create links, thereby blurring even further the distinction between reading and writing.

Virtual Reading as Oppositional Practice

For the time being, a hypermedia edition of Stendhal—or even a hypertext *The Red and the Black*—remains an unrealized project, something we can certainly conceive but that would be enormously time-consuming and expensive to produce. But we can at least ask our students to imagine what reading *The Red and the Black* in this medium would be like. (The imaginative approach has the advantage of allowing the students right from the start to propose their own links.) Clearly, such a tactic might take many forms depending on the level and orientation of the course, and I invite others to let me know what works for them. Given space constraints, I confine myself here to a brief account of an exercise that I have used with graduate students and upper-level undergraduates and that I consider particularly successful.

I begin with the hypothesis that one can locate in *The Red and the Black* a certain number of narrative crossroads that are marked in various ways by what I call inscriptions and that serve as centers of textual energy or intense textual activity. These inscriptions can be thought of as functioning much like the electronic links in the hypertext novels of our own time, in which (w)readers (interactive reader-writers) navigate from node to node or from lexia to lexia following unpredictable itineraries. One possible illustration of this principle would be *The Red and the Black*'s epigraphs, which often make little sense when read linearly in relation to the chapters they introduce but suddenly come to semiotic life when juxtaposed with other epigraphs or inscriptions, often in the preceding or following chapter but sometimes considerably distant or in another text altogether (Hamm, "*Rouge*"). The kind of (w)reading practice solicited by such a textual topography bears a strong resemblance, in its use of multilinear, discontinuous jumps, to that of hypertext.

To ensure that our textual travels do not degenerate into instances of ludic postmodernism imposed willy-nilly on the architecture of the long-suffering nineteenth-century novel, I take great pains to anchor our navigations in the social discourse of the period. (Doing so also counters the impression, fostered by the proliferation of spatial metaphors, that hypertext has no time for history, no time for time.) A favorite tactic of mine is to take up a small number of quasi-proverbial political statements circulating widely in the social discourse of the late 1820s and show how *The Red and the Black* dissolves them into their constituent parts, which are then redistributed (or recycled) through the novel, inscribed (literally) in a textual residue of anagrams, false titles, true and false signatures, epigraphs, epitaphs, patronyms, hoardings, and nameplates. My object is to show how such inscriptions function as privileged sites of textual and intertextual activity—overdetermined textual crossroads at which multiple discourses and thematic networks intersect and energize one another. Such inscriptions do not slow down a linear reading (for the plot); indeed, in many instances the borrowed words act as textual generators or signposts that hasten the story toward its destination. But at the same time they point to different textual routes, to alternative metonymic chains that traverse the text in other directions, joining inscription to inscription in a palimpsestic web firmly anchored in the political and social discourse of the period.

The Red and the Black is an ideal text for this kind of study, for as Michel Crouzet has recently argued, history, in the shape of contemporary political discourse and anecdote, is present on every page of the novel, but in curiously displaced and fragmented forms (*Rouge* 21–35). The thread of history is woven throughout, informing every scene, character, and episode, but Stendhal never directly presents history itself in any kind of fullness: it is manifest obliquely and allusively; it exists as the dust of a pulverized actuality that penetrates everything and obscures its own origins. Julien Gracq once observed that, in a novel subtitled *Chronicle of 1830* and published in the same year, the name of the reigning monarch is not mentioned once (25). (In fact the king's name is mentioned [554; 406; 2.45].) And yet, like history itself, Charles X is omnipresent in *The Red and the Black*, his words woven into the text of the novel like flecks of color in a fabric. The challenge for the reader is to locate and decipher this fragmented discourse of the (political) Other, to reconstitute its syntax and interpret its presence. I limit myself here to two sayings of Charles X that, I would argue, form part of the novel's genotext. The text never quotes them in their entirety, but the deployment of their scattered fragments is suggested by two symmetrically positioned markers or inscriptions in the first chapter of each of the novel's two books. (Classroom analysis of these two chapters begins after the students have read the novel and have an overall idea, established through discussion, of how its broader themes are developed and how they relate to the political context of Restoration France.)

The first inscription comes in book 1, chapter 1, immediately after the narrator's presentation of M. de Rênal and the potted history of his growing prosperity through the transition from Napoleon to the Restoration and the expansion of his property holdings under Louis XVIII and Charles X (who of course remains nameless):

> Les jardins de M. de Rênal, remplis de murs, sont encore admirés parce qu'il a acheté, au poids de l'or, certains petits morceaux de terrain qu'ils occupent. Par exemple, cette scie à bois, dont la position singulière sur la rive du Doubs vous a frappé en entrant à Verrières, et où vous avez remarqué le nom de SOREL, écrit en caractères gigantesques sur une planche qui domine le toit, elle occupait, il y a six ans, l'espace sur lequel on élève en ce moment le mur de la quatrième terrasse des jardins de M. de Rênal. (25)

> M. de Rênal's gardens, encumbered with walls, are still admired because he purchased, for their weight in gold, certain minute scraps of land which they cover. For example, that sawmill, so singularly situated on the bank of the Doubs, which struck you as you entered Verrières, and on which you read the name SOREL, written in gigantic letters on a board nailed to the rooftree—six years ago, it stood precisely where the wall for the fourth terrace of M. de Rênal's gardens is going up. (3)

Right from the very start of the novel, we are plunged into what was probably the central debate of the Restoration, turning around the crucial question (mediated, of course, by money) of legitimacy and usurpation. The name of the father ("SOREL"), closely associated throughout with money—"le père Sorel, comme on l'appelle depuis qu'il est riche" 'old Papa Sorel (as they call him since he has been rich)' (26; 4; 1.1)—has been literally displaced (though at a price) by the gardens of the usurper, by the symbolic capital (or signature) of a newly enriched and empowered industrial nobility whose politics will depend, in the long term, on its own economic self-interest.

But how might we explain the choice of a sawmill, so prominently situated and advertised that it is bound to attract the attention not only of the traveler entering Verrières but also of the reader opening the pages of Stendhal's novel? Most commentators offer either a biographical explanation (usually to do with Beyle's travels in the area in 1811) or a thematic reading as one of several prefigurations of the guillotine. (To return to our pedagogical analogy, the Louis Jenrel episode in book 1, chapter 5, another anticipation of Julien Sorel's fate, would constitute a hypertext lexia linked to the "SOREL" marker by the anagrammatic inscription on the scrap of paper: for *Louis Jenrel*, read *Julien*

Sorel.) If we follow the thematic path, we will jump (hypertextually) to a second inscription in the next chapter:

> Je ne trouve, quant à moi, qu'une chose à reprendre au COURS DE LA FIDÉLITÉ: on lit ce nom officiel en quinze ou vingt endroits, sur des plaques de marbre qui ont valu une croix de plus à M. de Rênal; ce que je reprocherais au Cours de la Fidélité, c'est la manière barbare dont l'autorité fait tailler et tondre jusqu'au vif ces vigoureux platanes. Au lieu de ressembler par leurs têtes basses, rondes et aplaties, à la plus vulgaire des plantes potagères, ils ne demanderaient pas mieux que d'avoir ces formes magnifiques qu'on leur voit en Angleterre. Mais la volonté de M. le maire est despotique, et deux fois par an tous les arbres appartenant à la commune sont impitoyablement amputés. (28)

> For my part, I can find only one thing to criticize on LOYALTY SQUARE; this official name is to be seen in fifteen or twenty places on marble plaques which earned an extra cross for M. de Rênal. What I would criticize on Loyalty Square is the barbaric way the administration clips and snips these vigorous plane trees back to the very quick. They stand there, with heads held low, shaved and flattened like the most vulgar of domestic vegetables, when they would like nothing better than to assume those splendid shapes they are free to take in England. But the mayor's will is supreme, and twice a year all the trees belonging to the town are pitilessly pruned back. (5; 1.2)

From this "amputation"—the French is more explicit than Robert Adams's translation—to the politics of the guillotine is a short step: Julien, we recall, will be described as "une belle plante" 'a fine plant' (507; 371; 2.37) and he too will feel the heavy hand of the authorities.

The most intriguing detail, however, lies in the explicit contrast between the humiliated heads of the French trees and the magnificent growth of their English counterparts. Here again, commentators evoke biographical explanations (Beyle's travels in England), but the point is surely more important (or less anecdotal) than that. In fact, political comparisons with England were common throughout the Restoration, often taking the form of a parallel between the anticipated fate of the Bourbons and that of the Stuarts in the Glorious Revolution of 1688. The conversation between the Bonapartist Falcoz and the philosopher Giraud early in book 2 and Mathilde's subsequent comments about Julien's conversation (2.19) allow us to reconstruct the homology that likens the death of Louis XVI to that of Charles I and predicts for Charles X the same fate as that met by James II, chased from the throne by his son-in-law William of Orange and the promise of a constitutional monarchy (Purdy). Again we find ourselves at the heart of the conjectures of the Restoration concerning the all-important question of legitimacy and usurpation.

Our hypertextual link from inscription to inscription has led us to a meditation on a common theme of the social and political discourse of the day. But has it answered our question about the sawmill? Certainly, by suggesting an analogy with the guillotine, the link has engaged us in a vitally important thematic of violent revolution, regicide, and constitutional reform through a comparison with the political history of England. But we can take our analysis even further. A perusal of histories of the Restoration turns up several variants of an utterance attributed to Charles X—"J'aimerais mieux scier du bois que de régner à la manière du roi d'Angleterre" 'I would rather saw wood than reign like the King of England'—by which the constitutional monarch with absolutist ambitions meant that he wanted no constitution at all (Bertier de Sauvigny, *La restoration* 363; my trans.).

In class I would invite students to flesh out this branching network of associations by following a number of similarly linked pathways. Since I have insufficient space to do that here, let me move straight on to the second of my two networks, which, as I suggest above, might be seen as linked to the first by the symmetrical positioning of an inscription in book 2, chapter 1. Julien has just arrived in Paris with abbé Pirard:

> Le fiacre s'arrêta; le cocher souleva le grand marteau de bronze d'une porte immense: c'était l'HOTEL DE LA MOLE; et, pour que les passants ne pussent en douter, ces mots se lisaient sur un marbre noir au-dessus de la porte.
>
> Cette affectation déplut à Julien. Ils ont tant de peur des jacobins! Ils voient un Robespierre et sa charrette derrière chaque haie; ils en ont souvent à mourir de rire, et ils affichent ainsi leur maison pour que la canaille la reconnaisse en cas d'émeute, et la pille. (273)
>
> The cab stopped; the driver raised a bronze knocker on an immense door: it was the Hôtel DE LA MOLE; and, lest the passersby remain in any doubt, the same words were to be seen on a black marble slab over the door.
>
> This affectation displeased Julien. They are so fearful of the Jacobins! They see a Robespierre and his cart behind every hedge; they're so worked up, it would make you die laughing, and they placard their house like this so the rabble will recognize it in a riot and be sure to sack it. (191)

Our link brings us to the threshold of the faubourg Saint-Germain, a world and a way of life that will not survive the July Revolution of 1830 and the coming to power of Louis-Philippe, the bourgeois king and the king of all the French. The mention of Robespierre and his cart conjures up once again the events of 1793, in particular the execution of Louis XVI. From one inscription, one name of the father, to another—from "SOREL" to "LA MOLE"—Julien's path is traced: it is the path of his "novel," the path of his self-invention, marked by a series of transfers of paternity (Brooks, "Novel").

Again, in class we would elaborate a whole network around this second lexia by linking a series of discontinuous text-blocks. Here, I simply indicate a minimalist routing that takes us from "le premier pas" 'the first step' in book 1, chapter 5 (in which Julien leaves his father's house for that of M. de Rênal and sees his name anagrammatically dissolved and reconstructed: Julien Sorel → Louis Jenrel) to "les premiers pas" '[the] first steps' of book 2, chapter 3, which Julien takes on horseback (282; 198). A reading of the latter chapter establishes a link between the juxtaposition of sawing and riding here and in book 1, chapter 4. Furthermore, Julien's second outing on horseback, after a first fall, takes him to the place Louis XVI. Here students need to be reminded—a hypertext edition would certainly do so—that the place de la Concorde had reverted, during the Restoration, to its former name of place Louis XV. On 3 May 1826 Charles X erected an expiatory monument on the site of Louis XVI's execution. According to Charles X's biographers, the king was in the habit of pointing at the monument from his palace on the other side of the Tuileries to reinforce his refusal to make concessions. Once again we encounter one of his famous pronouncements, which had already entered the social discourse of the late 1820s: "Les concessions ont perdu Louis XVI, j'aime mieux monter à cheval qu'en charrette" 'Concessions were the downfall of Louis XVI; I prefer to ride on a horse than in a cart' (Beach 314).

It is in this recycling of the discourse of the Other, this process of decomposition and redistribution of the king's words, that we see a striking example of the oppositional at play in Stendhal's novel. As we have observed, in this chronicle of 1830 not only does Stendhal choose not to represent the events leading up to the July Revolution, he only once mentions the name of the reigning monarch. Therefore, *The Red and the Black* does not explicitly contest the legitimacy of Charles X's rule. Moreover, the novel's "big" metaphors—the ones most often singled out for comment by the critics, like the saw as metaphor for the guillotine—have little oppositional value in themselves. To become fully operational they have to be narrativized—unpacked or unfolded as metonymies that not only serve as signposts pointing the story of Julien Sorel forward to its destination but also set up lateral or multilinear networks of signifiers (saw → trees → England | cart → horse → Place Louis XVI) that disrupt and subvert the silences of that story by allowing us to read, in palimpsest, the shadowy syntax of another, different narrative, that of history itself.

O Twenty-First Century!
Using Technology to Teach *The Red and the Black*

Carol de Dobay Rifelj

For reading a novel like *The Red and the Black*, there is a wonderful technology: the book. It is inexpensive, user-friendly, portable, and compatible across platforms (and sofas, airplanes, beaches). If you want to get to Robert M. Adams's note explaining an allusion to the battle of Arcola, no need to click—just look at the bottom of the page (187). And the ease of navigation! But other kinds of technology provide historical background to the novel, help instructors elicit discussion about it, and help students write about it. They range from more traditional media like slides and films to the new multimedia environments of CD-ROMs and the World Wide Web. Although no one would want to use them all for presenting *The Red and the Black*, a judicious choice of materials that are available at one's institution can enrich students' appreciation of this eminently forward-looking book.

Placing The Red and the Black *in Its Cultural and Historical Context*

Erich Auerbach famously calls Stendhal the founder of the serious realism of modern times, and he claims that the scene from *The Red and the Black* he discusses "would be almost incomprehensible without a most accurate and detailed knowledge of the political situation, the social stratification, and the economic circumstances of a perfectly definite historical moment, namely, that in which France found itself just before the July Revolution" (463, 455). We may debate just how accurate and detailed this knowledge must be, but our students certainly need some sense of the historical moment in which the novel is set. In particular they must understand something of Napoleon, the Restoration, and social classes in early-nineteenth-century France. One way to accomplish this objective is to send students to printed sources like Gordon Wright's *France in Modern Times*. Another is through a combination of texts and visual sources. Images make the cultural context more present; whether presented through slides, films, CD-ROMs, or Web sites, they help students literally see what was going on in this period.

Nineteenth-century paintings are a rich store of information. They are especially useful in presenting the cult of Napoleon. We find in them Napoleonic emblems like the bee and the eagle and the various aspects of the cult: Bonaparte the young military hero; Napoleon the great emperor; and Napoleon the champion of possibilities for the young, whose slogan was "careers open to talent." For example, David's *Napoleon Crossing the Alps* [*La montagne Saint-Bernard*] has many elements familiar to readers of *The Red and the Black*. It represents and glorifies the crossing of the Alps in Lombardy in 1800. We see Napoleon on a rearing horse whose antique pose recalls equestrian statues. The horse is skittish, but Napoleon is calm, pointing forward, or rather, upward. In the rocks beneath his horse's feet are inscribed the names of previous conquerors whose footsteps he is following: Hannibal, Charlemagne. He is in a blue uniform, but a huge red cloth swirls about him, its color picked up by other red highlights on his uniform, scabbard, and saddle. The echoes of this painting in *The Red and the Black* are obvious: the heights (especially the rocky promontory Julien scales on his way to see Fouquet; in this passage Julien is compared to a "oiseau de proie" 'bird of prey' [96; 57; 1.12]); the color red; the parade at Verrières, where, dressed in a blue uniform with spurs, he feels a hero when his horse shies and he does not fall: "Il se sentit un héros. Il était officier d'ordonnance de Napoléon et chargeait une batterie" 'He was one of Napoleon's orderlies in the act of charging a battery' (127; 81; 1.18). Julien wishes to follow Napoleon's traces as Napoleon followed his illustrious predecessors':

> Julien, debout, sur son grand rocher, regardait le ciel. [. . .] Il voyait à ses pieds vingt lieues de pays. Quelque épervier parti des grandes roches au-dessus de sa tête était aperçu par lui, de temps à autre, décrivant en silence ses cercles immenses. L'œil de Julien suivait machinalement l'oiseau de proie. Ses mouvements tranquilles et puissants le frappaient, il enviait cette force, il enviait cet isolement.
>
> C'était la destinée de Napoléon, serait-ce un jour la sienne? (87)

> Julien, standing atop his great rock, looked up into the sky. [. . .] At his feet lay twenty leagues of countryside. A solitary eagle, risen from the rocks over his head, appeared from time to time, cutting immense silent circles in the sky. Julien's eye followed mechanically the bird of prey. Its calm, powerful movements struck him; he envied this power, he envied this isolation.
>
> Such had been the destiny of Napoleon; would it some day be his? (50–51; 1.10)

Other pictures show different aspects of Napoleon's career and influence. Gros's *Napoleon at Arcola* presents him as a slim young man bound for glory; his *Battle of Eylau* depicts the triumphant but humane conqueror; Debret's *The Legion of Honor* and David's *Distribution of Eagles at the Champ de Mars* show the new honors and social hierarchy Napoleon instituted, based on military or civil service; Ingres's *Napoleon on the Imperial Throne* represents him as a great emperor, surrounded by icons of power and Napoleonic emblems, including the eagle woven into the rug at his feet.

The cult of Napoleon did not end with the First Empire. It was revived under Louis-Philippe, when Napoleon's ashes were brought back in great ceremony and installed in Les Invalides. It continues to this day. A striking manifestation earlier this century is Abel Gance's film *Napoléon*. Even a short sequence from the film helps students get a sense of the mythic hero who so captivates Julien. For example, the scenes of the boy Napoleon at school show how his fellow students mock and reject him. He proves his bravery and his leadership in a snowball battle (complete with forts, flags, and officers); yet his only companion is an eagle, which flies into his solitary room. The film is available on both videocassette and laser disc. The latter makes it easy to use not just one sequence but a series of passages to illustrate elements of the myth that resonate in *The Red and the Black*.

Other aspects of the period lend themselves to visual presentation, including the Restoration, social classes, the revolution of 1830, and Romanticism. What media can one use to present this material? For paintings, art historians still prefer slides, which give the best resolution and color. Electronic images are rapidly improving, however, and they present the advantage of accessibility outside class. They also include much besides artworks. Students can find visual, textual, and aural information about the period on CD-ROM reference works like *Larousse multimédia encyclopédique* and *Dictionnaire Hachette multimédia*. They may search the works for historical topics, for Stendhal, and for paintings by artists like Gros and David. Gros's *Battle of Eylau* is also featured on the widely distributed Louvre CD-ROM (Brisson), with background material and an analysis of the painting. Students can find more detailed information about the period on CD-ROMs like *2000 ans d'histoire de France*, *Le romantisme*, *Napoléon, l'Europe et l'Empire*, and *Stendhal: Œuvre romanesque*. By the time this essay appears, there will no doubt be other relevant CD-ROMs available.

CD-ROMs present both advantages and problems. They incorporate various media; for instance, the Romanticism CD features four hours of music, as well as literature, painting, sculpture, and architecture. CD-ROMs also provide individualized instruction: students can follow the links that interest them at their own pace; and each student can have a different assignment or choose a different subject to explore. The disadvantage of the format is that, like a videodisc, a CD-ROM is a single copy: only one person can use it at a time. For a small class, however, an instructor may put one or two copies on reserve. CD reference works are no doubt already on permanent reserve in the library. One may ask students to prepare an aspect of the period for class presentation and discussion. The instructor may use CDs in class, selecting images and sound from them to illustrate a background lecture. They may also provide images for a World Wide Web page, if the page is password-protected.

A Web page on Stendhal, as a linked page within an electronic course syllabus or on its own, solves the problem of simultaneous access; it allows for an even greater range of information; and it permits the instructor to include whatever he or she wishes. Visual material might include paintings, drawings, photos of the Franche-Comté and Besançon, and documents like bulletins of the Grande Armée. Texts of all kinds are possible (although I recommend short selections to minimize reading online, which many people find tiring): an annotated bibliography, a list of regimes in nineteenth-century France, relevant passages from *Racine et Shakespeare*, quotations from Vigny and Musset about young men coming of age under the Restoration, Romantic poetry, perhaps a selection of passages from critics. If the Web page is restricted to members of the class, like a sort of multimedia handout, one can avoid many problems of copyright. If the site is open, it may be necessary to obtain permission for images (they are complete works) and for texts under copyright, including translations of Stendhal. Once online video is fast enough and of good enough quality, it may be worth including excerpts from, for example, the Gance film, the Autant-Lara film version of the novel, or the scene after Boniface de La Mole's execution in *La reine Margot*. To project images in class instructors may use Powerpoint slide shows, the slide-show functions of various graphics programs, or the Web site itself.

Another advantage of a Web page is that it affords access to relevant existing Web sites on history, art, literature, and Stendhal. Instructors need not spend hours searching and compiling materials: one can insert links to pages other professors or organizations have mounted. Current pages with relevant information include those of the French Ministère des Affaires Etrangères, one on Stendhal, several at the University of Grenoble, and many on Napoleon (the cult lives on). I will not give a list of URLs here. My hesitation to do so points to a disadvantage of links to Web sites: new sites appear every day, and they change frequently. An instructor must keep his or her references accurate and current. A further disadvantage is that students are sometimes drawn to the easy accessibility of information on the Web rather than the vastly more complete, complex, and accurate sources available to them in the library. It is part of our task as educators to teach them how to evaluate Web information and to direct them to the sources appropriate to the tasks we assign.

Discussing the Novel

An instructor may use Web sites and other media not only to provide background information but also to generate discussion of the novel, both in and out of class. An assignment to find information about Napoleon in multimedia sources might be accompanied by questions like the following: "What does Napoleon represent for Julien? Look for echoes of Napoleon's career and symbols and the related imagery of height and depth, and take them into consideration in your response." Providing a selection of critical interpretations, like the many interpretations of the motivation and meaning of Julien's crime, can help students reflect on critical issues while they read. Students should prepare discussion questions in advance, so that they will think about the novel before they arrive in class. Posting questions on a Web page also makes it possible to insert new ones at the last moment or to change them in the light of the previous class's discussion.

In courses with a writing focus, one may combine discussion questions with writing assignments. Students may prepare paragraphs to read aloud or summarize during class. Providing a choice of questions permits one to treat a number of topics in class; discussion of each can range freely, but there is an underlying structure to which it returns. For example, the assignment for the end of the novel might include a choice of questions like the following:

1. Julien thinks, "Now at last [. . .] the novel of my career is over, and the credit is all mine. I was able to make myself loved by that monster of pride, he thought, glancing at Mathilde; her father cannot live without her nor she without me" (359)
   What if the novel *were* to end at this point?
2. What changes in Julien do we see in the last section of the novel? How does the narration change? Why?
3. Umberto Eco sees the ending of *The Red and the Black* as a "problematic" one, unlike that of the popular novel:

   > After finishing the novel, the reader is confronted with a series of questions. [. . .] At the last line of the novel, the problem is still there: what perspectives does the generation coming out of the collapse of the Napoleonic world have to affirm its energy without myths and without goals? The unendurable thing the story leaves in suspense is that the reader still doesn't know whether or not to identify with Julien and whether doing it would give some satisfaction. (17; my trans.)

   Is this how you feel about the ending of the novel?

Technology can aid significantly in stimulating discussion of *The Red and the Black*: electronic bulletin boards get students to think about the novel and exchange ideas about it beyond the classroom. Instructors who have Web pages may use a Web-based conference system, so that students can respond to the posted questions directly on the Internet, but any kind of electronic conferencing can work. Students may be asked to post their comments once a week or before a certain time; they should take into account previous postings, so that they respond to one another, not to the instructor. Electronic discussions do not replace those in class; rather, they present a first look at issues, allowing in-class discussion to move farther and deeper. I have found that questions for electronic responses should be simpler than those students prepare for class; they should be designed to elicit spontaneous answers, differences of opinion, and personal reactions, so that all students feel comfortable contributing. Questions might include the following:

> Is Julien a hero? Is he a hypocrite?
>
> Why does Julien commit the crime? Revenge? Jealousy? Despair? Love? Insanity?
>
> Why is the title of the novel *Red and Black*?

In this context students feel free to express their personal reactions, including their confusion:

> I really don't know why the novel's title is *The Red and the Black*.
>
> Like Eco, at the end of this novel, I'm unsure of how to feel.
>
> So, at the end of the novel, which ends with Julien's death, it is easy to be confused with feelings. The reader can feel bad for him because his crime was an act of rage and love. He worked hard and was destroyed. Or, we can feel his death is justified because all of his motives are selfish and feel his stupidity is the cause of his death.

Students' answers are sometimes brief, but they may be more detailed and thoughtful. For instance, answering the question about the title, many of my students cited color symbolism: red for passion, red and black for death, and so on. Later postings built on these first reactions. Here is one example:

> Stendhal's novel is certainly one of passion—Romantic passion, the passion of military achievement and glory, passion for a cause. Red and black are also the traditional colors one associates with revolution; in the novel, revolutions are ocurring [*sic*] at several levels. Julien is revolting against the upper classes; Mme de Renal [*sic*] is rebelling against her husband; Matilde [*sic*] is going against the life dictated for her by her birth.

When students have begun to work through such issues beforehand, they come to class ready to probe them further. It is also easy for the instructor to copy quotations from the students' postings and bring them to class as a point of departure.

Another, older technology is also useful in eliciting class discussion: the Autant-Lara film. Students may find it dated; they tend to laugh in the wrong places. It is easy, however, to show scenes from the video to stimulate discussion of narrative voice and point of view. For example, in the scene in the garden where Julien takes Mme de Rênal's hand, Gérard Philipe delivers a long interior monologue in voiceover: "Le devoir, c'est le devoir. Je *dois* prendre cette main et la garder, un point c'est tout. Ah, tu as peur, Julien. On y va! Non, minute" 'If I must, I must. I must do it! One grasp, that's all. Afraid, Julien? Are you ready? Wait, not yet.' Autant-Lara spells out the internal conflict that his cinematography has already shown through Gérard Philipe's facial expression and close-ups of Julien's hand tentatively attempting to approach Mme de Rênal's, then pulling back. Interestingly, Autant-Lara does not use voiceover to give the view of an omniscient narrator like the one in the novel, who analyzes Julien and provides information about him that he is unable to understand himself: "bientôt la voix de Mme de Rênal devint tremblante aussi, mais Julien ne s'en aperçut point. L'affreux combat que le devoir livrait à la timidité était trop pénible pour qu'il fût en état de rien observer hors lui-même" 'soon the voice of Mme de Rênal began to tremble, too, though Julien was unable to notice it. The frightful struggle between his sense of duty and his timidity was too absorbing for him to notice anything outside himself' (76; 43; 1.9). Autant-Lara is even less able to transmit the narrator's ironic commentary on Julien's reaction: "Il avait fait *son devoir, et un devoir héroïque*" 'He had carried out his *duty, and a heroic duty*' (79; 44; 1.9; italics in the orig.). Scenes like this one show how the same words have very different effects in direct and indirect discourse.

Writing on The Red and the Black

Work on discussion questions helps students begin writing about *The Red and the Black*. In writing-intensive classes, one may ask students to respond in unified, coherent paragraphs. Students may bring in two or three copies of their responses to exchange in small groups, to work on the novel and paragraph construction at the same time. Writing about critical articles helps students come to grips with what is often difficult, unfamiliar material. Asking them to write a hundred-word abstract of Erich Auerbach or Georg Lukács makes them focus on—and understand more fully—the main points of the argument. Having students do short writing assignments while reading also stimulates them to formulate ideas they can later develop into paper topics.

Such early writing addresses one problem a long novel like *The Red and the Black* poses: especially in French, it takes students so long to read that there is not enough time afterward to prepare a carefully thought-out paper. One should not hesitate to ask them to begin writing papers, perhaps based on discussion questions, before finishing the book. Students can start work on many subjects—like the image of Napoleon, comparisons between Mathilde and Mme de Rênal, themes like colors or heights, structures like mimetic desire, stylistic features like interior monologues—halfway through the novel. As they read to the end, they will find more examples or developments of their topics. For instance, a discussion paragraph on Julien's first meeting with Mme de Rênal led one of my students to write a paper contrasting her eyes with those of Mathilde. By the time she reached the end of the novel, this student was alert to later instances of the same contrast, like Mathilde's "yeux étincelants de colère" 'eyes blazing with rage' (535; 392; 2.42), opposed to Mme de Rênal's: "La physionomie de Mme de Rênal changea tout à coup; la plus vive tendresse fit place à une rêverie profonde" 'Mme. de Rênal's features altered abruptly: passionate affection gave way to a dreamy expression' (540; 395; 2.43).

Once a student has chosen a topic, there are many ways technology can help. For example, students can find and even sometimes access critical work using technology. The *MLA International Bibliography* database is an invaluable resource for printed sources since 1963. It permits searches by, for example, work and topic. Using it, my student could find references to articles with titles like "The Eyes of Julien Sorel and Stendhal's Title *Le rouge et le noir*,"

"La perception visuelle et le regard dans *Le rouge et le noir*," and "Rires, sourires et larmes dans *Le rouge et le noir*: Un langage initiatique." Online databases provide further bibliographic material, abstracts, and the full text of some articles. For example, the Infotrac Searchbank gives many extended citations of articles that treat Stendhal, including one on representations of Napoleon and another on names in *The Red and the Black*. Two relevant articles also appear in full, a general one on Stendhal by F. W. J. Hemmings and another that appears on screen as follows:

> Stendhal's reformulation of the epic and the idyll in 'Le
> Rouge et Le Noir.' Claudia Moscovici. CLIO, Wntr 1993 v22 n2
> p145(12). Elec. Coll.: A14012101.
> Press Return for abstract and text.

A student who has found a relevant reference can consult other databases to see whether the library has the work and, if not, where the work is, and whether an article can be obtained by fax. In addition, more and more journals are being published in electronic form; students can directly access those to which their institutions subscribe. Several articles on Stendhal are already posted on the Web, and we can expect this practice to increase, though questions about peer review of materials on the Web have yet to be resolved. All these resources make it easier for students to find critical works on the topics they are writing about.

For thematic or stylistic projects by students in French courses, the *ARTFL Project* is a wonderful resource. It is a searchable database, available on the Web, of more than 2,000 French literary works. One can search the electronic text of *The Red and the Black* for all the instances of the word *Napoléon* (or *Bonaparte*), *rouge* (there are 12), or *noir* (45). Examining the instances of *tu* and *te* shows that the intimate form predominates in Julien's dialogue with Mme de Rênal, as opposed to Mathilde's self-conscious, even ostentatious use of it. Thus, when the presence of Mme de Rênal awakens Julien in his prison cell, he cries out spontaneously "Ah! je te revois avant que de mourir, est-ce une illusion?" before catching himself and addressing her as "vous" and "Madame" 'Ah! So I can see you again before I die, or is it an illusion?' (538; 393; 2.43). The ARTFL interface is particularly practical, but not all institutions subscribe to its full-search text database. However, other searchable electronic copies of *The Red and the Black* also exist on the Web.

Technology is extremely valuable to students who have begun writing papers, especially for peer criticism. Computer servers make it easy for students to work with writing partners. Students can put their drafts on a server, and their partners can comment on their work at any time of day or night. They can take their readers' comments into account as they revise their work. The instructor may monitor this peer-review process at it develops, again, at his or her convenience. It is possible for students to turn in their papers electronically to a drop box on a server. If the instructor likes to correct and grade online, no paper copy need ever be produced. One can save electronic comments and refer to them later in the semester to help gauge a student's progress in writing and literary analysis.

The more correct the student's writing is, the easier it is to grade, whether electronically or on paper. Most major word processors now have spelling checkers in French as well as English. Students in French courses may use French grammar checkers. One grammar checker that allows students to learn as they correct is *Exploratexte*. Based on sentence analysis, the program indicates the site and the nature of an error but leaves it for the student to correct. Thus, even this phase of writing has pedagogic value.

As the various forms of multimedia develop, we broaden our concept of what a paper is. Students more and more frequently incorporate images and sound into their projects. On a server or on a Web page (perhaps linked with a Web-based syllabus), their work is accessible to other students in the course or to the world at large. Widening the audience for their work gives students a new stimulus to excellence and accuracy. Such projects also lend themselves to collaborative work, either with the instructor or with other students. Many topics on *The Red and the Black*, including those on its background, described above, would benefit from multimedia presentation. One can imagine a Web page on the social classes represented in the novel. Following Wright's analysis, students could find characters from what Wright calls "old court aristocracy" (e.g., the Marquis de La Mole) or the petty bourgeoisie (e.g., Fouqué) (157). A chart listing the classes with their representatives might include illustrations of architecture and costumes of the period and links to relevant Web sites, as well as quotations from the novel that make the character's social standing clear. Another project might be annotating a chapter (with images and links as well as textual material). Whatever the topic, one should encourage students to find new ways of approaching and illuminating the text.

The wealth of resources that multimedia and computer technology provides may seem daunting in its variety, its complexity, and its fast pace of change. Yet as recently as the late 1980s papers prepared with a word processor were uncommon. In the early 1990s few literature professors used e-mail, and the World Wide Web did not exist. New technologies rapidly become part of our professional lives. True, there are caveats to bear in mind in using them: we should beware of students turning to electronic sources because they are easily accessed from their dorm rooms rather than searching the library shelves. We should make sure they are not spending more time on graphic interfaces than on analysis of *The Red and the Black*. But to understand a novel so rich in its historical setting, to think and talk about it, to find new ways to write about it, technology has much to offer us all.

NOTES ON CONTRIBUTORS

Lisa G. Algazi is assistant professor of French at Hood College. Her research and teaching interests center on maternal subjectivity in French literature, feminist psychoanalytic criticism, women's studies, and the nineteenth-century novel. She has published articles on Stendhalian mothers and has a book in progress provisionally titled *The Birth of the Modern Mother: The Story of a Stendhalian Creation.*

James Smith Allen is professor of modern European history at Southern Illinois University, Carbondale. The author of *Popular French Romanticism: Authors, Readers, and Books in the 19th Century* (1981), *In the Public Eye: A History of Reading in Modern France* (1991), and various scholarly articles, he has just completed a monograph tentatively titled *The Poignant Relations of Three Modern French Women*. His teaching responsibilities include surveys of Western civilization, contemporary historiography, and nineteenth-century Europe, in which course he assigns *The Red and the Black*.

Mary Ellen Birkett is professor of French at Smith College. She has published widely on Romanticism, and she is the author of *Lamartine and the Poetics of Landscape* (1982). She makes annual contributions on poetry to *The Romantic Movement: A Selective and Critical Bibliography* and teaches, in addition to Romanticism, courses on the Enlightenment and on classicism. Her current research interest is French diplomacy in the Pacific, particularly in the Hawaiian Islands, in the first half of the nineteenth century.

Peter Brooks is Tripp Professor of Humanities at Yale University and author of several critical studies, including *The Melodramatic Imagination* (1976), *Reading for the Plot* (1984), and *Psychoanalysis and Storytelling* (1994). He is writing a book on the problematic status of confessions in literature and the law.

Catharine Savage Brosman is professor of French emerita at Tulane University. She is the editor of five volumes in the *Dictionary of Literary Biography* series, including two on nineteenth-century French fiction, and the author of numerous books on twentieth-century novelists. Her study *Visions of War in France: Fiction, Art, Ideology* is forthcoming, as is her newest collection of verse, *Places in Mind*.

James T. Day is associate professor of French at the University of South Carolina. He is an annual contributor on Stendhal to *The Romantic Movement: A Selective and Critical Bibliography*. He is the author of *Stendhal's Paper Mirror* (1987) and articles on Stendhal, Gide, and portraits of masculinity. His research and teaching interests include gender questions, *francophonie*, nineteenth- and twentieth-century literature, and business French.

Dean de la Motte is assistant professor of French at Guilford College. He has published articles on nineteenth-century literature and culture; on Flaubert, Hugo, and Huysmans; and on bureaucracy, decadence, and utopia. He is coeditor of *Making the News: Modernity and the Mass Press in Nineteenth-Century France* (forthcoming). He is at work on *Going Nowhere Fast*, a study of narratives of progress in nineteenth-century France.

Priscilla Parkhurst Ferguson is professor of sociology at Columbia University. She has served as president of the Association for French Cultural Studies; she is the author of *Literary France: The Making of a Culture* (1987, 1991) and *Paris as Revolution: Writing the Nineteenth-Century City* (1994, 1997), a coeditor of *Literature and Social Practice* (1989), and translation editor of Pierre Bourdieu et al., *La misère du monde* (forthcoming). Her research and teaching deal with nineteenth-century literature and culture, cultural sociology, and urban culture. She is working on *Eating Orders*, a study of French culinary culture.

Michal Peled Ginsburg is professor of French and comparative literature and chair of the department of French and Italian at Northwestern University. She is the author of *Flaubert Writing: A Study in Narrative Strategies* (1986) and *Economies of Change: Form and Transformation in the Nineteenth-Century Novel* (1996), as well as articles on various British and French novelists of the nineteenth century. She teaches courses on narrative theory, the nineteenth-century novel, psychoanalysis and literature, and contemporary Israeli fiction. She is currently preparing a book on Israeli novelist David Shahar.

Stirling Haig is professor of French at the University of North Carolina, Chapel Hill. He has served as president of the AATF and editor of *The French Review* and North Carolina Studies in the Romance Languages and Literatures. He is the author of *Flaubert and the Gift of Speech* (1986), *The Madame Bovary Blues* (1987), *Stendhal:* The Red and the Black (1989) and of articles on several periods of French literature. He is editing a volume of essays on literature and the arts in nineteenth-century Europe.

Doris Y. Kadish is professor of French and women's studies and head of Romance languages at the University of Georgia. Her research and teaching interests are the late eighteenth, nineteenth, and twentieth centuries, colonialist and postcolonialist studies, literary theory, and literary translation theory. She is the author of *Practices of the New Novel in Claude Simon's* L'herbe *and* La route des Flandres (1979), *The Literature of Images: Narrative Landscape from* Julie *to* Jane Eyre (1987), and *Politicizing Gender: Narrative Strategies in the Aftermath of the French Revolution* (1991) and a coeditor of *Translating Slavery: Gender and Race in French Women's Writing, 1783–1823*. Her current project concerns slavery in the francophone world at the end of the eighteenth and the first half of the nineteenth century.

Maryline Lukacher is associate professor of French at Northern Illinois University, where she teaches courses on nineteenth- and twentieth-century women's fiction and autobiography. She is the author of *Maternal Fictions: Stendhal, Sand, Rachilde, and Bataille* (1994). She is writing a book on the relation between male and female nineteenth-century autobiography.

Juliet Flower MacCannell is professor emerita of comparative literature at the University of California, Irvine, and visiting professor of rhetoric at the University of California, Berkeley. Her articles range from studies of Rousseau and Stendhal to examinations of evil and of contemporary psychoanalytic theories of culture. She is the author of *Figuring Lacan* (1986) and *The Regime of the Brother* (1991) and the editor of *Thinking Bodies* (1994). She has served as president of the Society for the Psychoanalytic Study of Culture and Society. She has edited the *American Journal of Semiotics* and now edits *Anamorphosis* and *West Umbr(a)*. Her book *Things to Come: A Hysteric's Guide to the Future Female Subject* is forthcoming.

Cheryl A. Morgan is associate professor of French at Hamilton College. Her research and teaching interests include nineteenth-century women writers and the press, the nineteenth-century novel and gender politics, francophone women writers, and urban literature. She is coeditor of *Contre-courants: Les femmes s'écrivent à travers les siècles* (1995). She is writing a critical biography of Delphine Gay de Girardin.

Mary Anne O'Neil is professor of French at Whitman College. She has published articles on twentieth-century poets, Chateaubriand, Hugo, devotional poetry of the seventeenth and twentieth centuries, and the Spanish novel (Cervantes and Galdós). She is working on a book-length study of the poetry of Pierre Emmanuel.

Sandy Petrey is professor of French and comparative literature at the State University of New York, Stony Brook. His research and teaching focus on theory of the novel and history and literature. He is the author of *History in the Text* (1980), *Realism and Revolution* (1988), and *Speech Acts and Literary Theory* (1990). He is researching culture and society in July Monarchy France.

Gerald Prince is Lois and Jerry Magnin Family Term Professor of Romance Languages at the University of Pennsylvania. His research and teaching focus on narratology, literary theory, nineteenth- and twentieth-century literature, and film. He is the author of *Métaphysique et technique dans l'œuvre romanesque de Sartre* (1968), *A Grammar of Stories* (1973), *Narratology: The Form and Functioning of Narrative* (1982), *A Dictionary of Narratology* (1987), and *Narrative and Theme* (1992). His projects include *Le petit Prince: Guide du roman de langue française au vingtième siècle.*

Anthony Purdy is professor of French at the University of Western Ontario. His teaching and research deal with nineteenth- and twentieth-century French and Québécois literature, literature and the arts, comparative literature, and film. His most recent book, written with Bridget Elliott, is *Peter Greenaway: Architecture and Allegory* (1997). He is preparing a book on Stendhal and another titled *In Praise of Dirt: Michel Tournier and the Critique of Modernity*.

Carol de Dobay Rifelj is Fulton Professor of French at Middlebury College. She is the author of *Word and Figure: The Language of Nineteenth-Century Poetry* (1987) and *Reading the Other: Novels and the Problem of Other Minds* (1992). She works primarily on nineteenth-century literature, detective fiction, and technology in the classroom.

Pauline Wahl Willis is associate professor of French at the University of Calgary, where she teaches both language and literature courses. She is the author of several articles on Stendhal's novels and a coauthor of two French as a second language textbooks (plus ancillaries). She is doing research on gossip in Stendhal's works.

SURVEY PARTICIPANTS

In addition to the volume's contributors, the scholars and teachers listed below generously agreed to participate in the survey on approaches to teaching *The Red and the Black*. Without their assistance, this volume would not have been possible.

Victor Aboulaffia, *State University of New York, New Paltz*
Ross Chambers, *University of Michigan, Ann Arbor*
George Gibian, *Cornell University*
Warren Johnson, *Arkansas State University*
Kathryn Kinczewski, *University of Alabama, Tuscaloosa*
Ainslie A. McLees, *Governor's School for Government and International Studies*
Carol Mossman, *University of Maryland, College Park*
Catherine Nesci, *University of California, Santa Barbara*
Allan H. Pasco, *University of Kansas*
Roger Shattuck, *Boston University*
Armand E. Singer, *West Virginia University, Morgantown*
Galina Ter-Saakyanis, *Chicago, IL*

WORKS CITED

Althusser, Louis. "Idéologies et appareils idéologiques d'état." *Positions*. Paris: Sociales, 1982. 79–137.

Argyle, Michael, and Mark Cook. *Gaze and Mutual Gaze*. Cambridge: Cambridge UP, 1976.

ARTFL Project. (Project for American and French Research on the Treasury of the French Language, University of Chicago.) 8 Feb. 1997 <http://humanities.uchicago.edu/ARTFL/ARTFL.html>.

Attuel, Josiane. "L'auto-vision de Julien Sorel: 'Du paraître à l'être.'" Del Litto 131–44.

Auerbach, Erich. "In the Hôtel de la Mole." *Mimesis: The Representation of Reality in Western Literature*. Trans. Willard R. Trask. Princeton: Princeton UP, 1953. 454–92.

Autant-Lara, Claude, dir. *Le rouge et le noir.* 1957. Videocassette. Ivy Classics, 1988.

Bakhtin, Mikhail. *The Dialogic Imagination*. Trans. Caryl Emerson and Michael Holquist. Austin: U of Texas P, 1981.

Bart, Benjamin F. "Hypercreativity in Stendhal and Balzac." *Nineteenth-Century French Studies* 3 (1974–75): 18–39.

Barthes, Roland. *Mythologies*. New York: Hill, 1972.

Beach, Vincent Woodrow. *Charles X of France: His Life and Times*. Boulder: Pruett, 1971.

Beauvoir, Simone de. "Women in Stendhal." *Modern Critical Views: Stendhal*. Ed. Harold Bloom. New York: Chelsea, 1989. 51–60. Trans. of *Le deuxième sexe*. Paris: Folio (Essais), 1976. 2: 375–89.

Beizer, Janet L. *Family Plots: Balzac's Narrative Generations*. New Haven: Yale UP, 1986.

Berenson, Edward. *Populist Religion and Left-Wing Politics in France, 1830–1852*. Princeton: Princeton UP, 1984.

Bertier de Sauvigny, Guillaume de. *The Bourbon Restoration*. Trans. Lynn M. Case. Philadelphia: U of Pennsylvania P, 1966.

———. *La Restoration, 1815–1830*. Paris: Hachette, 1977.

Blin, Georges. *Stendhal et les problèmes du roman*. Paris: Corti, 1954.

Bolster, Richard. *Stendhal:* Le rouge et le noir. London: Grant, 1994.

Bolter, J. David. *Writing Space: The Computer, Hypertext, and the History of Writing*. Hillsdale: Erlbaum, 1991.

Bourdieu, Pierre. *Distinction: A Social Critique of the Judgment of Taste*. Cambridge: Harvard UP, 1984.

Brisson, Dominique. *Le Louvre: Peintures et palais*. CD-ROM. Paris: Montparnasse Multimédia (Réunion des musées nationaux), 1994.

———. *The Louvre: The Palace and Its Paintings*. CD-ROM. Paris: Montparnasse Multimédia (Réunion des musées nationaux), 1995.

Brodsky, Claudia. *The Imposition of Form: Studies in Narrative Representation and Knowledge*. Princeton: Princeton UP, 1987.

Brogan, D. W. *The French Nation from Napoléon to Pétain*. London: Hamilton, 1957.

Brombert, Victor, ed. *Stendhal: A Collection of Critical Essays*. Englewood Cliffs: Prentice, 1962.

———. *Stendhal et la voie oblique*. Paris: PUF, 1954.

———. *Stendhal: Fiction and the Themes of Freedom*. New York: Random, 1968.

———. *The Romantic Prison: The French Tradition*. Princeton: Princeton UP, 1978.

Brooks, Peter. "1830, 27–29 July—An Oedipal Crisis." Hollier 649–56.

———. "The Novel and the Guillotine; or, Fathers and Sons in *Le rouge et le noir*." Brooks, *Reading* 62–89.

———. *Reading for the Plot: Design and Intention in Narrative*. New York: Vintage, 1985. Cambridge: Harvard UP, 1992.

Butler, Judith. *Gender Trouble*. New York: Routledge, 1990.

Castex, Pierre-Georges, ed. *Le rouge et le noir*. Paris: Garnier, 1975.

———. Le rouge et le noir *de Stendhal*. Paris: SEDES, 1970.

Chambers, Ross. *Room for Maneuver: Reading (the) Oppositional (in) Narrative*. Chicago: U of Chicago P, 1991.

Chartier, Roger. *L'éducation en France au XVIe au XVIIIe siecle*. Paris: SEDES, 1976.

Chereau, Patrice, dir. *La reine Margot*. 1994. Videodisc. Miramax, 1995.

Clark, Kenneth. *The Fallacies of Hope*. Pt. 12 of *Civilisation*. 13 pts. Videocassette. Films Inc., 1970.

Cobban, Alfred. *From the First Empire to the Second Empire, 1799–1871*. Vol. 2 of *A History of Modern France*. 2nd ed. Baltimore: Penguin, 1965.

Crouzet, Michel. Le rouge et le noir*: Essai sur le romanesque stendhalien*. Paris: PUF, 1995.

———. *Stendhal et le langage*. Paris: Gallimard, 1981.

Darrow, Margaret. "French Noblewomen and the New Domesticity, 1750–1850." *Feminist Studies* 5 (1979): 41–65.

Day, James T. *Stendhal's Paper Mirror: Patterns of Self-Consciousness in His Novels*. New York: Lang, 1987.

Del Litto, Victor. *La création romanesque chez Stendhal: Actes du XIIe Congrés international stendhalien, Paris 26–29 avril 1983*. Genève: Droz, 1985.

2000 ans d'histoire de France. CD-ROM. Paris: Havas Edition Electronique, 1996.

Dictionnaire Hachette multimédia. CD-ROM. Paris: Mantra-Hachette Multimédia, 1995.

Eco, Umberto. *De superman au surhomme*. Paris: Grasset, 1993.

Exploratexte. Computer software. Québec: Machina Sapiens, 1992.

Farrell, Frederick, and Edith Farrell. "Title as Image: Marguerite Yourcenar's *Le chef rouge / La veuve Aphrodissia*." *Romanic Review* 74.2 (1983): 233–44.

Felman, Shoshana. *La folie dans l'œuvre romanesque de Stendhal*. Paris: Corti, 1971.

Fernandez, Ramon. *Messages*. Paris: Nouvelle Revue Française, 1926.

Fetterley, Judith. *The Resisting Reader: A Feminist Approach to American Fiction*. Bloomington: Indiana UP, 1978.

Foucault, Michel. *Discipline and Punish: The Birth of the Prison*. Trans. Alan Sheridan. New York: Vintage, 1979. Rpt. of *Surveiller et punir: Naissance de la prison*. Paris: Gallimard, 1975.

———, ed. *I, Pierre Rivière, Having Slaughtered My Mother, My Sister, and My Brother . . . .* Trans. Frank Jellinek. Lincoln: U of Nebraska P, 1982. Trans. of *Moi, Pierre Rivière, ayant égorgé ma mère, ma sœur et mon frère . . . .* Paris: Gallimard, 1973.

Furet, François. *Interpreting the French Revolution*. Trans. Elborg Forster. Cambridge: Cambridge UP; Paris: Sciences de l'Homme, 1981.

Gance, Abel, dir. *Napoléon*. 1927. 2 videodiscs. Images Archive, MCA Home Video, 1986.

Gazette des tribunaux. 28 and 31 Dec. 1827: n. pag.

Genette, Gérard. *Palimpsestes: La littérature au second degré.* Paris: Seuil, 1982.

———. "Stendhal." *Figures of Literary Discourse.* New York: Columbia UP, 1982. 147–82.

———. "Stendhal." *Figures II*. Paris: Seuil, 1969. 155–93.

Gide, André. *Les faux-monnayeurs*. Paris: Gallimard, 1925.

———. *Journal*. Vol. 1. Paris: Gallimard, 1951.

Girard, René. *Deceit, Desire, and the Novel.* Trans. Yvonne Freccero. Baltimore: Johns Hopkins UP, 1965. Trans. of *Mensonge romantique et vérité romanesque*. Paris: Grasset, 1961.

——— "Triangular Desire." Stendhal, *Red and Black* 503–21.

Gleize, Joelle. "Stendhal ou le miroir des livres." *Le double miroir. Le livre dans les livres de Stendhal à Proust*. Paris: Hachette, 1992. 59–96.

Godfrey, Gary M., "Julien Sorel—Soldier in Blue." *Modern Language Quarterly* 37 (1976): 339–48.

Gormley, Lane. "'Mon roman est fini': Fabricateurs de romans et fiction intratextuelle dans *Le rouge et le noir*." *Stendhal Club* 21 (1978–79): 129–38.

Gracq, Julien. *En lisant, en écrivant*. Paris: Corti, 1981.

Haig, Stirling. *Stendhal:* The Red and the Black. Landmarks of World Literature. Cambridge: Cambridge UP, 1989.

Hamm, Jean-Jacques. "Le parasite du pouvoir et le pouvoir du parasite." *Stendhal: L'écrivain, la société et le pouvoir*. Ed. Philippe Berthier. Proc. of Colloque du Bicentenaire, 24–27 Jan. 1983, Grenoble. Grenoble: PU de Grenoble, 1984. 89–98.

———. "*Le rouge et le noir* d'un lecteur d'épigraphes." *Stendhal Club* 20 (1977): 19–36.

Hemmings, F. W. J. *Culture and Society in France, 1789–1848*. Leicester: Leicester UP, 1987.

———. *Stendhal: A Study of His Novels*. Oxford: Oxford UP, 1964.

———. "To the Happy Few: Stendhal (1793–1842)." *UNESCO Courier* Oct. 1983: 11–15. Online. Information Access. Mag. Coll.: 17L6319. Elec. Coll.: A2946976.

Herrold, J. Christopher. *The Horizon Book of the Age of Napoleon*. New York: Dell, 1963.

Hollier, Denis, ed. *A New History of French Literature*. Harvard UP, 1989.

Imbert, Henri François. "Quelques réflexions sur la nature du roman stendhalien." Del Litto 21–33.

Infotrac Search Bank. Online. Information Access Company. 23 June 1998.

Jefferson, Ann. "*De l'amour* et le roman polyphonique." *Poétique* 54 (983): 149–62.

———. *Reading Realism in Stendhal*. Cambridge: Cambridge UP, 1988.

Kadish, Doris Y. "Representing Race in *Indiana*." *George Sand Studies* 11.1–2 (1992): 22–30.

Kaplan, Carol L. "*Une Extrême Energie*: Julien's Romantic Writing Project." *French Review* 59 (1985-86): 693-700.

Keats, John and Percy Shelley. *Complete Poetical Works*. New York: Random, n.d.

Kelly, Linda. *Women of the French Revolution*. London: Hamilton, 1987.

Kempf, Roger. "Les bibliothèques de Julien Sorel." *Critique* 28 (1972): 827–40.

Klein, Christine, and Paul Lidsky. Le rouge et le noir. *Stendhal. Analyse critique*. Paris: Hatier, 1971.

Kristeva, Julia. *Soleil noir: Dépression et mélancolie*. Paris: Gallimard, 1987.

———. *Tales of Love*. Trans. Leon S. Roudiez. New York: Columbia UP, 1987.

Lacan, Jacques. *Ecrits*. Paris: Seuil, 1966.

Landow, George P. *Hypertext: The Convergence of Contemporary Critical Theory and Technology*. Baltimore: Johns Hopkins UP, 1992.

Larbaud, Valery. *Ce vice impuni, la lecture*. Paris: Messein, 1925.

La Rochefoucauld, François, duc de. *Maximes*. 1665. Paris: Garnier, 1967.

Larousse multimédia encyclopédique. CD-ROM. Larousse and Liris Interactive, 1996.

Levin, Harry. *The Gates of Horn: A Study of Five French Realists*. New York: Oxford UP, 1966.

Levy, Darline Gay, et al., ed. and trans. *Women in Revolutionary Paris, 1789–1795, Selected Documents*. Urbana: U of Illinois P, 1979.

Lough, John, and Muriel Lough. *An Introduction to Nineteenth-Century France*. London: Longman, 1978.

Lukacher, Maryline. *Maternal Fictions: Stendhal, Sand, Rachilde, and Bataille*. Durham: Duke UP, 1994.

Lukács, Georg. "Balzac and Stendhal." *Studies in European Realism*. New York: Grosset, 1964. 65–84.

Marx, Karl and Friedrich Engels. *Manifesto of the Communist Party*. 1848. *The Marx-Engels Reader*. Ed. Robert C. Tucker. New York: Norton, 1978.

Mélia, Jean. *Stendhal et ses commentateurs*. 3rd ed. Paris: Mercure de France, 1911.

Miller, D. A. *Narrative and Its Discontents: Problems of Closure in the Traditional Novel*. Princeton: Princeton UP, 1981.

Molière. *Le misanthrope*. 1667. Rpt. in *Œuvres complètes de Molière*. Oxford: Oxford UP, 1900. 307–33.

Mossman, Carol A. *The Narrative Matrix: Stendhal's* Le rouge et le noir. Lexington: French Forum, 1984.

Mouillaud, Geneviève. Le rouge et le noir *de Stendhal*. Paris: Larousse, 1972.

Nagy, Gregory. *Greek Mythology and Poetics*. Ithaca: Cornell UP, 1990.

Napoléon, l'Europe et l'empire. CD-ROM. Villeurbanne: Infogrames, Perrin, Pathé, Club d'Investissement Média, Réunion des Musées Nationaux, Le Point, 1995.

Nelson, Theodor H. *Literary Machines*. Swarthmore.: n.p., 1981. N. pag.

Nettement, Alfred. "Etudes de mœurs sur la femme au XIXe siècle." *L'écho de la jeune France: Journal des progrès par le Christianisme*. 2 (1834–35): 360–67.

Pearson, Roger. "Time and Imagination in *Le rouge et le noir*." *Stendhal's Violin: A Novelist and His Reader*. Oxford: Clarendon, 1988. 67–155.

Petrey, Sandy. *Realism and Revolution: Balzac, Stendhal, Zola, and the Performances of History*. Ithaca: Cornell UP, 1988.

Pope, Barbara Corrado. "Revolution and Retreat: Upper-Class French Women after 1789." *Women, War, and Revolution*. Ed. Carol R. Berkin and Clara M. Lovett. New York: Holmes, 1980. 215–36.

Porter, Dennis. "Stendhal: Overpoliticization and the Revenge of Literature." *Rousseau's Legacy: Emergence and Eclipse of the Writer in France*. Oxford: Oxford UP, 1995. 71–105.

Poulet, Georges. "Stendhal and Time." Stendhal, *Red and Black* 470–85.

Prendergast, Christopher. *The Order of Mimesis: Balzac, Stendhal, Nerval, Flaubert*. Cambridge: Cambridge UP, 1986.

Purdy, Anthony. "Un cheval nommé Sorrel et une taupe régicide. Réflexions onomastiques sur *Le rouge et le noir*." *Stendhal Club* 22 (1980): 144–52.

Rabine, Leslie. *Reading the Romantic Heroines: Text, History, Ideology*. Ann Arbor: U of Michigan P, 1985.

Reid, Roddey. *Families in Jeopardy: Regulating the Social Body in France, 1759–1910*. Stanford: Stanford UP, 1993.

Rey, Alain, *"Revolution"—Histoire d'un mot*. Paris: Gallimard, 1989.

Le romantisme. CD-ROM. Paris: Vilo, 1996.

Rousseau, Jean-Jacques. *Emile ou de l'éducation*. Chronology and introd. Michel Launay. Paris: Garnier-Flammarion, 1966.

———. *Lettre à M. D'Alembert sur son article Genève*. Chronology and introd. Michel Launay. Paris: Garnier-Flammarion, 1967.

Sand, George. *Indiana*. Paris: Gallimard (Folio), 1984.

———. *Indiana*. Trans. Sylvia Raphael. Oxford: Oxford UP, 1994.

Sarraute, Nathalie. "Flaubert le précurseur." *Preuves* 168 (1968): 3–11.

Schehr, Lawrence. "Stendhal's Pathology of the Novel." *French Forum* 15.1 (1990): 53–72.

Serres, Michel. *The Parasite*. Trans. Lawrence R. Schehr. Baltimore: Johns Hopkins UP, 1982. Trans. of *Le parasite*. Paris: Grasset, 1980.

Spitzer, Alan. *The French Generation of 1820*. Princeton: Princeton UP, 1987. 35–70.

Starobinski, Jean. "Stendhal pseudonyme." *L'œil vivant*. Paris: Gallimard, 1961: 191–244.

Stendhal. *Armance*. Trans. C. K. Scott-Moncrieff. London: Soho, 1986.

———. *Correspondance*. Ed. Henri Martineau and V. Del Litto. Vol. 2. Paris: Gallimard, 1968.

———. *De l'amour*. Paris: Garnier, 1959.

———. *Lamiel* Trans. T. W. Earp. London: Turnstile, 1951.

———. *Life of Henry Brulard*. Trans. Jean Stewart and B. C. J. G. Knight. New York: Minerva, 1968.

———. *Lucien Leuwen*. Vol. 2. Ed. Henri Martineau. Paris: Divan, 1929.

———. *Œuvres intimes*. Ed. V. Del Litto. Paris: Gallimard, 1955.

———. *On Love*. New York: Da Capo, 1954.

———. *Red and Black*. Trans. and ed. Robert M. Adams. New York: Norton, 1969.

———. *The Red and the Black*. Trans. C. K. Scott-Moncrieff. New York: Modern Lib., 1926.

———. *The Red and the Black: A Chronicle of the Nineteenth Century*. Trans. Catherine Slater. World's Classics. Oxford: Oxford UP, 1991.

———. *Le rouge et le noir*. Ed. and introd. Michel Crouzet. 1964. Paris: Garnier-Flammarion, 1996.

———. *Le rouge et le noir*. Ed. Jules Marsan. Geneva: Cercle du Bibliophile, [1967]. Vols. 1 and 2 of *Œuvres complètes de Stendhal*. Gen. ed. Victor Del Litto an Ernest Abravanel. 1967–74. 50 vols.

———. *Souvenirs d'égotisme*. Ed. Béatrice Didier. Paris: Gallimard, 1983.

———. *La vie de Henry Brulard*. Ed. Henri Martineau. Paris: Divan, 1949.

———. *La vie de Henry Brulard*. *Œuvres intimes* 1–398.

Stendhal: Œuvre romanesque. CD-ROM. Paris: Catalogue des Lettres, 1997.

Stern, Daniel. *Mémoires, souvenirs et journaux de la comtesse d'Agoult*. Présentation et notes de Charles F. Dupêchez. 2 vols. Paris: Mercure de France, 1990.

Talbot, Emile. *Stendhal Revisited*. New York: Twayne, 1993.

Trouiller, Dominique. "Le monologue intérieur dans *Le rouge et le noir*." *Stendhal Club* 11 (1969): 245–77.

Turnell, Martin. *The Novel in France*. New York: New Directions, 1951.

Viti, Robert M. "The (Un)Re(a)d and the Black: Literary Ignorance in *Le rouge et le noir*." *Romance Quarterly* 39 (1992): 447–50.

Voltaire. *Candide*. 1759. *Romans et contes*. Paris: Garnier-Flammarion, 1966. 179–259.

———. *La Princesse de Babylone*. 1775. *Romans et contes*. Introd. and notes by Henri Bénac. Paris: Classiques Garnier, 1960.

Warner, Marina. *Alone of All Her Sex: The Myth and Cult of the Virgin Mary*. New York: Vintage, 1983.

Weber, Max. *From Max Weber: Essays in Sociology*. Trans. and ed. H. H. Gerth and C. Wright Mills. New York: Oxford UP, 1946.

White, Hayden. "The Value of Narrativity in the Representation of Reality." *On Narrative*. Ed. W. J. T. Mitchell. Chicago: Chicago UP, 1980. 1–24.

Wright, Gordon. *France in Modern Times*. 2nd ed. New York: Norton, 1995.

Yourcenar, Marguerite. "Aphrodissia, the Widow." *Oriental Tales* 103–15.

———. "The Milk of Death." *Oriental Tales* 37–51.

———. *Oriental Tales*. Trans. Alberto Manguel and Yourcenar. New York: Farrar, 1985.

———. *Souvenirs pieux*. Paris: Gallimard, 1974.

Zeldin, Theodore. *France, 1848–1945*. 2 vols. Oxford: Clarendon, 1973–77.

INDEX OF NAMES

INDEX OF WORKS

LITERATURE, PAINTING, AND MUSIC

Modern Language Association of America

Approaches to Teaching World Literature

Joseph Gibaldi, series editor

Achebe's Things Fall Apart. Ed. Bernth Lindfors. 1991.
Arthurian Tradition. Ed. Maureen Fries and Jeanie Watson. 1992.
Atwood's The Handmaid's Tale *and Other Works*. Ed. Sharon R. Wilson, Thomas B. Friedman, and Shannon Hengen. 1996.
Austen's Pride and Prejudice. Ed. Marcia McClintock Folsom. 1993.
Beckett's Waiting for Godot. Ed. June Schlueter and Enoch Brater. 1991.
Beowulf. Ed. Jess B. Bessinger, Jr., and Robert F. Yeager. 1984.
Blake's Songs of Innocence and of Experience. Ed. Robert F. Gleckner and Mark L. Greenberg. 1989.
British Women Poets of the Romantic Period. Ed. Stephen C. Behrendt and Harriet Kramer Linkin. 1997.
Brontë's Jane Eyre. Ed. Diane Long Hoeveler and Beth Lau. 1993.
Byron's Poetry. Ed. Frederick W. Shilstone. 1991.
Camus's The Plague. Ed. Steven G. Kellman. 1985.
Cather's My Ántonia. Ed. Susan J. Rosowski. 1989.
Cervantes' Don Quixote. Ed. Richard Bjornson. 1984.
Chaucer's Canterbury Tales. Ed. Joseph Gibaldi. 1980.
Chopin's The Awakening. Ed. Bernard Koloski. 1988.
Coleridge's Poetry and Prose. Ed. Richard E. Matlak. 1991.
Dante's Divine Comedy. Ed. Carole Slade. 1982.
Dickens' David Copperfield. Ed. Richard J. Dunn. 1984.
Dickinson's Poetry. Ed. Robin Riley Fast and Christine Mack Gordon. 1989.
Eliot's Middlemarch. Ed. Kathleen Blake. 1990.
Eliot's Poetry and Plays. Ed. Jewel Spears Brooker. 1988.
Ellison's Invisible Man. Ed. Susan Resneck Parr and Pancho Savery. 1989.
Faulkner's The Sound and the Fury. Ed. Stephen Hahn and Arthur F. Kinney. 1996.
Flaubert's Madame Bovary. Ed. Laurence M. Porter and Eugene F. Gray. 1995.
García Márquez's One Hundred Years of Solitude. Ed. María Elena de Valdés and Mario J. Valdés. 1990.
Goethe's Faust. Ed. Douglas J. McMillan. 1987.
Hebrew Bible as Literature in Translation. Ed. Barry N. Olshen and Yael S. Feldman. 1989.
Homer's Iliad *and* Odyssey. Ed. Kostas Myrsiades. 1987.
Ibsen's A Doll House. Ed. Yvonne Shafer. 1985.
Works of Samuel Johnson. Ed. David R. Anderson and Gwin J. Kolb. 1993.
Joyce's Ulysses. Ed. Kathleen McCormick and Erwin R. Steinberg. 1993.
Kafka's Short Fiction. Ed. Richard T. Gray. 1995.
Keats's Poetry. Ed. Walter H. Evert and Jack W. Rhodes. 1991.
Kingston's The Woman Warrior. Ed. Shirley Geok-lin Lim. 1991.
Lafayette's The Princess of Clèves. Ed. Faith E. Beasley and Katharine Ann Jensen. 1998.

Lessing's The Golden Notebook. Ed. Carey Kaplan and Ellen Cronan Rose. 1989.
Mann's Death in Venice *and Other Short Fiction*. Ed. Jeffrey B. Berlin. 1992.
Medieval English Drama. Ed. Richard K. Emmerson. 1990.
Melville's Moby-Dick. Ed. Martin Bickman. 1985.
Metaphysical Poets. Ed. Sidney Gottlieb. 1990.
Miller's Death of a Salesman. Ed. Matthew C. Roudané. 1995.
Milton's Paradise Lost. Ed. Galbraith M. Crump. 1986.
Molière's Tartuffe *and Other Plays*. Ed. James F. Gaines and Michael S. Koppisch. 1995.
Momaday's The Way to Rainy Mountain. Ed. Kenneth M. Roemer. 1988.
Montaigne's Essays. Ed. Patrick Henry. 1994.
Novels of Toni Morrison. Ed. Nellie Y. McKay and Kathryn Earle. 1997.
Murasaki Shikibu's The Tale of Genji. Ed. Edward Kamens. 1993.
Pope's Poetry. Ed. Wallace Jackson and R. Paul Yoder. 1993.
Shakespeare's King Lear. Ed. Robert H. Ray. 1986.
Shakespeare's The Tempest *and Other Late Romances*. Ed. Maurice Hunt. 1992.
Shelley's Frankenstein. Ed. Stephen C. Behrendt. 1990.
Shelley's Poetry. Ed. Spencer Hall. 1990.
Sir Gawain and the Green Knight. Ed. Miriam Youngerman Miller and Jane Chance. 1986.
Spenser's Faerie Queene. Ed. David Lee Miller and Alexander Dunlop. 1994.
Stendhal's The Red and the Black. Ed. Dean de la Motte and Stirling Haig. 1999.
Sterne's Tristram Shandy. Ed. Melvyn New. 1989.
Swift's Gulliver's Travels. Ed. Edward J. Rielly. 1988.
Thoreau's Walden *and Other Works*. Ed. Richard J. Schneider. 1996.
Voltaire's Candide. Ed. Renée Waldinger. 1987.
Whitman's Leaves of Grass. Ed. Donald D. Kummings. 1990.
Wordsworth's Poetry. Ed. Spencer Hall, with Jonathan Ramsey. 1986.
Wright's Native Son. Ed. James A. Miller. 1997.